The Birder's Guide to Oregon

Joseph E. Evanich, Jr.

D1046489

Published by
the Portland Audubon Society

In memory of

Ron Rohweder

1938-84

Non-game Biologist for

Oregon Department of Fish and Wildlife.

A rare person who treasured and

understood our natural areas and

helped countless others do the same.

© 1990 Portland Audubon Society

ISBN: 0-931686-09-1

Design and Production by Martha Gannett and Robert Goldie.

Printed in the United States of America by Graphic Arts Center.

Contents

Introduction

In 1978, the Audubon Society of Corvallis published Fred Ramsey's *Birding Oregon*, a book which finally met the needs of Oregon's birdwatchers. Unfortunately, *Birding Oregon* was only reprinted, not updated. Although the book filled a gap that no publication before or since has attempted, it has not kept up to date with new developments in the field. Oregon's birding fraternity has grown tremendously over the past dozen years, and such contest-oriented pursuits as county-listing, 'big days', and vagrant-chasing are commonplace among today's birders. Regardless of your views on these aspects of the sport (or pastime or hobby or whatever you choose to call it), one thing cannot be denied — the discovery of new birding sites has been a direct result.

This book covers these new discoveries as well as the traditional better-known sites such as Malheur and Finley National Wildlife Refuges, Tillamook Bay, the Klamath Basin, and Sauvie Island. Hopefully, the reader will be encouraged to explore some of the less-known regions of Oregon, especially those east of the Cascades. This book includes many such sites, and when visiting them, remember that new birding locations are discovered by taking that unknown dirt road or hiking that extra mile upriver from the park.

The source material for these site guides is largely the result of my fifteen years of birding throughout Oregon. Unfortunately, a number of important sites remain relatively unexplored by me; certain individuals have contributed information on these sites, either directly or indirectly, and without their help this book would not exist. Heading the list of these contributors is Harry Nehls, who has probably "discovered" more birding sites in Oregon than anyone else, and, more importantly, has shared his findings with anyone who enjoys Oregon's birds. Other important contributors include David A. Anderson, who supplied information on the northern Cascades and Portland; Alan Contreras and David Fix, who furnished information on Eugene and the southern Willamette Valley; Craig and Marion Corder, the most knowledgable birders in the Umatilla and Morrow County areas; Barb Bellin, who shared her favorite birding sites in the Salem area and has shown me around the Willamette Valley refuges; Donna Lusthoff and Verda Teale, fellow birdwatcher-explorers in the northern Willamette Valley area; Larry Thornburgh, who introduced me to the unique birding sites of Coos and Curry Counties; and the late Ron Rohweder of the Oregon Department of Fish and Wildlife, who sparked my interest in the unique birding opportunities of Northeast Oregon.

Fred Ramsey's contributions through *Birding Oregon* must also be acknowledged. Although I have had extensive birding experience in most of the areas covered in his book, much of Ramsey's information served as a foundation for numerous accounts in this book. *Birding Oregon's* coverage of such traditional sites as Malheur Refuge, Fern Ridge Reservoir, and Coos Bay simply cannot be improved upon.

Joe Evanich
Portland, Oregon
Spring, 1990

Physiography and Climate

Occupying some 96,981 square miles, Oregon ranks as the tenth largest state. It stretches approximately 350 miles from east to west, and another 300 miles north to south. Such a vast land area will undoubtedly contain a rich variety of climates and habitats, but Oregon seems unusually blessed with these features. Few other states can boast of such dramatic differences in vegetation zones, precipitation amounts, and seasonal temperatures. These are largely due to Oregon's complex physiographic make-up. Such physical features dictate the nature of the region's climate; climate, of course, is the major determining factor for the variety and distribution of vegetation. And it is necessary to understand something of these factors — physiography, climate, vegetation — to truly appreciate the richness of Oregon's birdlife.

Ultimately, most of Oregon's weather comes from the Pacific Ocean. The prevaling western winds bring warm moist air from offshore; as a result, Western Oregon receives a great amount of precipitation. Due to the lifting and cooling effect of the Coast Range, most of the moisture is deposited along the immediate coast — Tillamook County averages 90.9 inches of rain per year, making it one of the nation's wettest regions. The interior valleys of Western Oregon (the Willamette, Rogue, Umpqua, and other minor valleys) receive much less rainfall than the coast or the Coast Range. They are still wet enough to support ample woodlands, forests, and open grasslands, though. These valleys are the most important agricultural areas in Oregon with their mild summers, relatively warm winters, and moderate rainfall. After passing over these interior valleys, the moist Pacific air begins rising up the western slopes of the Cascades. These towering mountains have even more of a lifting and cooling effect on the air than do the Coast Range; as a result, nearly all the remaining moisture is deposited on the Cascades' western slopes. This precipitation supports some of the most densely vegetated lands on the entire continent. In fact, the Willamette National Forest, located on the western slopes of the Cascades, is the most heavily-timbered National Forest in the country. Due to the moderating effect of the Pacific air, Western Oregon experiences mild temperatures throughout the year.

There are seldom any lengthy sub-freezing cold spells in the areas below 4000 feet in elevation, and summer temperatures comfortably average in the high 70's and low 80's (degrees Farenheit). An exception to this is the frequently hot, dry summer weather found in the California-like zone in the lowlands of Jackson and Josephine Counties.

Paralleling the coast and stretching from the Columbia River to the California border, the Cascade Range is the most obvious physical feature of Oregon. These high mountains (including Oregon's highest point, Mt. Hood, at 11,235 feet) effectively divide the state into two distinct regions in terms of climate, biology, and even human sociology. The warm Pacific air coming from the west is mostly blocked by the Cascades, resulting in a much more continental climate in Eastern Oregon. Precipitation amounts are far less in this half of the state; in general, the farther east one goes, the drier the land becomes. Malheur County, located in extreme southeast-ern Oregon, ranks as the state's driest county with only 9.64 inches of precipitation per year! Eastern Oregon also experi-ences more pronounced seasonal differences than does the western half of the state. This is mainly due to higher average elevations, influences from interior weather systems, and an absence of the warm Pacific air. Snow is encountered throughout all of Eastern Oregon during most winters, and temperatures range from well below freezing in winter up into the 80's and 90's during summer. Oregon's highest and lowest recorded temperatures both came from the eastern half of the state: 119 degrees at the Alvord Desert (Site H-7), and - 54 degrees near Seneca in Grant County.

Rising to high elevations in Northeastern Oregon are the Blue, Ochoco, and Wallowa Mountains and their related minor ranges. These mountain systems are high enough to produce a precipitation trap much like the Cascades, but on a smaller scale. Thus, precipitation totals for the mountainous north-eastern counties are noticibly higher than those in other parts of Eastern Oregon. As an example, Union County averages around 18.79 inches of precipitation per year while most other Eastern Oregon counties receive 10 to 15 inches annually. This wetter climate results in much more timber growth in the heavily-forested mountains of this part of Oregon.

Oregon's Bird Habitats

The following 18 habitat types may be found in various parts of Oregon. The double-letter code following each habitat description corresponds to the symbols used at the beginning of each site account; the habitats at each site are listed in descending order of prevalence.

Ocean Waters (OC)
This habitat includes the open waters of bays, straits, and the open ocean up to 100 miles offshore. Most birds in this zone are strictly visitors and are more commonly encountered in other coastal habitats. Exceptions include albatrosses, shearwaters, petrels, jaegers, and many alcids.

Coastal Estuaries, Mudflats (CE)
Also included here are the extensive but frequently inaccessible salt water marshes. These sheltered habitats are often the most productive zones for birdlife. Numerous species including cormorants, ducks, geese, shorebirds, gulls, and terns use the extensive estuary mudflats and shallow waters for food and shelter.

Open Beach (OB)
Although popular with human visitors, the miles of sandy beach found on the outer coast is one of the least productive habitats in Oregon. The grass-covered dunes and their adjacent sandy flats on the open beach are important wintering grounds for raptors and such passerines as Horned Larks, pipits, longspurs, and Snow Buntings.

Rocky Shores (RS)
Included here are rocky tidal areas, jetties, breakwaters, and rugged headlands. This zone is almost entirely associated with the outer coast. Especially look for rock-loving ducks, shorebirds, and gulls in this important nesting and feeding habitat.

Farmland, Fields, Meadows (FA)
This habitat consists of large open areas of agricultural lands; as such, it is often quite devoid of birdlife. In Eastern Oregon, the extensive fields of wheat, alfalfa, and other grains often harbor little more than Horned Larks, Western Meadowlarks, and Savannah Sparrows. Along the coast, the grassy meadowlands used for grazing cattle are often utilized by wintering waterfowl, herons, gulls, and raptors.

Native Grassland (NG)

Extensive tracts of this valuable habitat are all but nonexistent in Oregon today. Most of the native grassland of Eastern Oregon has been converted to irrigated farmland or invaded by the spreading sagebrush steppe habitat. The few native bunchgrass areas found in the foothill areas of the Blue Mountains and elsewhere east of the Cascades are home to such local birds as Sharp-tailed Grouse (at least formerly), Ferruginous Hawk, and Grasshopper Sparrow.

Sagebrush Steppe (SS)

This habitat is most prevalent in the arid Great Basin region of Southeast Oregon. Although dominated by Great Basin sagebrush, this zone also consists of similar desert-tolerant plants as rabbitbrush, saltbrush, hopsage, and greasewood. The sagebrush habitat is gradually expanding to the north and west, usually at the expense of native grassland areas.

Chaparral (CH)

This is a relatively local, specialized habitat in Oregon restricted mainly to the Rogue, Umpqua, and Applegate Rivers and Bear Creek in Douglas, Jackson, and Josephine Counties. This semiarid habitat is a northern extension of such heat-tolerant and aridity-tolerant shrubby plants as manzanita, mahogany, rabbitbrush, and, especially important to the local birdlife, ceanothus. This shrubby growth is often interspersed with grassy areas and woodlots of oak or ash. The birdlife here has a distinct 'California' flavor to it: such species as Poorwill, Anna's Hummingbird, Acorn Woodpecker, Ash-throated Flycatcher, and Lesser Goldfinch are more common here than elsewhere in Oregon. Specialty birds found here and virtually nowhere else in the state include Plain Titmouse, Blue-gray Gnatcatcher, and California Towhee.

Brushy Areas, Hedgerows (BR)

Usually found on the border of woodlands, farmland, or urban areas, this 'micro-habitat' is especially important to gallinaceous birds and wintering passerines such as sparrows, finches, and warblers.

Wet Coniferous Forest (WF)

Basically, this habitat occurs throughout Western Oregon's higher areas (above 2000') and in very high (above 5000') or very wet areas of Eastern Oregon. The dominant tree is

Douglas-fir, but, west of the Cascades, such species as red cedar, grand fir, western hemlock, and Sitka spruce (coastal only) can be just as common. In Eastern Oregon, the Douglas-fir is joined by lodgepole pine, Engelmann spruce, subalpine fir, and others. This productive habitat is characterized by a multilayered canopy and an often lush undergrowth of shrubs, ferns, and other shade-tolerant plants. Birdlife is abundant during the summer, but frequently difficult to see due to the dense vegetation.

Dry Coniferous Forest (DF)

Restricted to Eastern Oregon with isolated patches west of the Cascades, this habitat is characterized by open forests of ponderosa and lodgepole pine, western larch, and other species. It is frequently interrupted with patches of aspen woodland or riparian growth in wet areas. The understory of this moderate-elevation habitat (3000-5000') is quite open, often grassy, and easy to traverse. Birding is productive and many of the summering species are easier to locate than in the previous forest type.

Juniper Woodland (JW)

The unique western juniper woodland extends as a distinct belt along the east slope of the Cascades, roughly between the ponderosa pine forest and sagebrush habitat in elevation (around 3500-4000'). This is an arid woodland, the twisted, distinct trees usually mixed with small pines or, more commonly, an open understory of sagebrush. The associated terrain is usually rocky and basaltic due to the volcanic nature of the land's past.

Broadleaf Deciduous Forest (BF)

This habitat is irregularly distributed throughout the state, both East and West, and usually at lower elevations. These forests are usually associated with water. In Western Oregon, dominant trees include big-leaf maple, red alder, Oregon ash, Oregon white oak, willows, and vine maple. Eastern Oregon's broadleaf forests are composed of black cottonwood, willows, alders, and quaking aspen. Understories are often dense with shrubs, especially in wet areas. Many birds of this habitat are distributed statewide — Downy Woodpecker, Western Wood-Pewee, Black-headed Grosbeak, etc. In the valleys of North-eastern Oregon (Grande Ronde, Wallowa, Powder, etc.) this habitat is home to a number of 'eastern' birds which reach the western limits of their ranges here in Oregon — namely the Gray Catbird, Veery, Red-eyed Vireo, and American Redstart.

Riparian Areas (RA)

This localized 'micro-habitat' is most common along water-courses in the more arid parts of Eastern Oregon. Riparian zones consist mostly of broadleaf shrubby plants that grow in dense patches within other habitats — coniferous forest, arid grasslands, juniper woodlands, etc. This is an important habitat not only to the local birdlife, but also as a system for cleansing and retaining water supplies in arid regions. Unfortunately, riparian areas in Eastern Oregon are very fragile, and many are currently under heavy pressure from uncontrolled cattle grazing. Bird species found here are very similar to those of the broadleaf forests, but riparian areas are even more attractive to 'brushy' species such as Willow Flycatcher, House Wren, Yellow-breasted Chat, and Lazuli Bunting.

Fresh-water Lakes, Ponds, Marshes, etc. (FW)

This 'micro-habitat' obviously occurs throughout Oregon within virtually any other habitat listed here. This is one of the most valuable habitats for birds anywhere in the state — the drier the surrounding lands, the more important the marsh or pond. In arid regions of Southeast and Southcentral Oregon, tremendous marshes of tule and cattail have long been popular among birds and birders — witness the excitement of the Klamath Basin marshes or Malheur NWR. Similar but much smaller wetlands occur throughout the state and are worthy of a visit by birders any time of year. Also included here are lakes, sewage treatment ponds, flooded farmfields, alkali ponds, and flats — all these habitats are important to migrating waterfowl, shorebirds, gulls, and other birds.

Alpine Areas (AL)

The truly treeless, barren alpine areas are restricted in Oregon to the very highest peaks of the Cascades, Wallowas, Strawberries, and isolated desert peaks such as Steens Mountain. Where the virtually plantless slopes give way to snowfields, look for the very local nesting birds such as American Pipits, White-crowned Sparrows, and Rosy Finches.

Rimrock Areas, Cliffs (RR)

Usually found in Eastern Oregon or high in the mountains, this 'micro-habitat' is home to such local species as Poorwill, White-throated Swift, and Rock and Canyon Wrens. Such birds as raptors, swallows, ravens, and Great Horned Owls use the rimrock cliffs for nesting and feed over a multitude of adjacent habitats.

Urban Habitats (UR)

Although highly altered by man, the habitats offered by cities and suburban sprawl can still be very productive for birds. Residential parks and gardens are often an island for birds in a sea of uninhabitable concrete. Especially good for birding are city parks, duck ponds, landfills, cemeteries, and other open areas.

A Note on Environmental Issues

The main objective of this book is to acquaint interested people with Oregon's birds and where to find them. A secondary purpose — and probably a more important one — is to introduce visitors to the rich natural environments Oregon has to offer. Hopefully, the site guides presented here will alert outdoor enthusiasts to the need for increased environmental protection. Our state has long had a reputation for pristine wilderness, but this is slowly changing as more and more of Oregon's natural areas continue to disappear. Each year, acres of wetlands are being drained and converted to farmland or prepared for development. The harvesting of Oregon's dwindling old-growth forests is currently the hottest political debate between environmentalists and the powerful timber industry. A sad result of this battle is the questionable future of the Spotted Owl, a species dependent on old-growth habitat. Most of the seemingly endless miles of desert in eastern Oregon have been grossly overgrazed by cattle or converted to irrigated farmland at the expense of native plants and animals. The loss of nearly all eastern Oregon's native grassland vegetation has virtually exterminated the Columbian Sharp-tailed Grouse from our state. These and numerous other environmental problems are beginning to form a frightening pattern in Oregon that is so evident over the rest of the country — the large-scale disappearance of original native plant and animal communities.

The key to environmental protection is public awareness. When visiting the sites in this guide, especially the wilder, more undeveloped areas, take a moment to observe what is around you. Notice how intricate the living systems are. And especially notice how man and his influences fit into these systems. The natural environment has existed and functioned perfectly well without our help for millions of years. And, left alone or with minimal disturbance, it should be here for millions of years to come.

Many natural areas, however, need more than just moral encouragement if they are to remain pristine. Sometimes only dollars can keep the bulldozers away. For this reason, such environmental organizations as the Audubon Society (both National and local chapters), the National Wildlife Federation, the Nature Conservancy, and others deserve your support.

How to Use this Guide

This book is divided into two sections: the first is used to pick good birding sites within a given region of the state, and the second is used to locate a specific species or group of birds. This second section is self-explanatory and begins on page 241.

To use the first section, the Site Guides, first determine which Region of the state you will be visiting. For convenience, Oregon has been divided into eight Regions, labelled alphabetically A through H, as shown on the map below. For the most part, borders have been drawn along the county lines. In turn, each Region contains 8 to 25 specific sites which offer the best birding opportunities; these sites are located on the reference map at the beginning of each Region's account. Preceeding the title of each site is a letter-number code as used on the maps and elsewhere in the text. Following the title are the habitats found there, the average elevation(s), and a rating system for each season (Sp=spring, S=summer, F=fall, W=winter) that indicates how productive birding can be — one star is for poor birding, two for fair, three for good, and four for excellent. Of course, there are always birds at all these sites, but the rating is based on the number and variety that can be found.

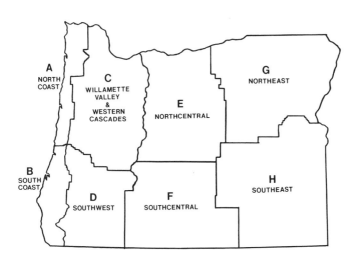

The following abbreviations are frequently used in the text: NWR, National Wildlife Refuge; WMA, Wildlife Management Area; St. Pk., State Park; Co. Pk., County Park; Nat'l. Pk., National Park; ODFW, Oregon Department of Fish and Wildlife; Co., County; CG, campground; GS, guard station; N.F. Rd., National Forest Road; US, United States Highway; OR, State Highway; I, Interstate Highway.

The maps presented in this book are designed to be used in conjunction with an Oregon Highway map, county maps, National Forest maps, U.S.G.S. topographical maps, and other official publications. It is best to consult locally published maps and brochures when birding at any of these sites. This is especially true in rural Eastern Oregon.

Readers should be aware that some of the sites in this guide may charge a user fee. This is particularly true of smaller county or city parks. Many state parks charge a fee for camping, especially the more developed ones (Cape Lookout, Wallowa Lake, Ft. Stevens, etc.) Other sites require a nominal entry fee, including Sauvie Island Wildlife Management Area, Oxbow County Park, and Scoggins Valley Park.

Region A
North Coast

Tufted Puffin

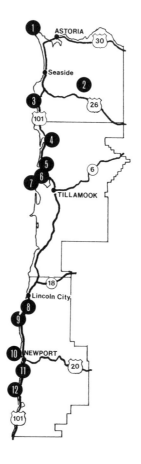

Clatsop Spit

Habitats: CE, OB, OC, RS, WF, BR, FW
Elevation: 0-20'
Seasons: Sp • • • • S • • F • • • • W • • •

Most of the birding in this area is restricted to Fort Stevens St. Pk. and its surrounding lands. To reach the Clatsop Spit part of the park, turn west off US 101 onto Ridge Rd., about 9 miles north of Seaside and 7 miles south of Astoria. Follow Ridge Rd. another 4.0 miles to the turnoff to the South Jetty area and Coffenbury Lake (a well-marked junction). Note that the turnoff into the main camping area of Fort Stevens St. Pk. is located *before* the South Jetty turnoff; do not take this well-marked road. Before reaching the actual jetty area, watch for the signed turnoff to Coffenbury Lake, also part of the state park.

Coffenbury Lake. This beautiful fresh-water lake is best birded early in the morning during summer or migration periods. A trail winds completely around the quiet wooded lake. The west side is mostly thick coniferous forest, the east side marshy lowlands with brushy mixed forest. The area abounds with migrant warblers, vireos, flycatchers, thrushes, and the like, and the brushy growth is one of the best sites in Oregon to find a Wrentit during any time of year. Nesting waterbirds on the lake include Pied-billed Grebe, Green-backed Heron, Wood Duck, and Hooded Merganser. At the picnic grounds at the east side of the lake, listen for the distinctive *"carr, carr, carr, carr"* call of the rare Northwestern Crow. Most Pacific Northwest birders refuse to consider this bird as distinct from the American Crow, but as of this writing (1990), both the American Ornithologists Union and the American Birding Association still give the Northwestern Crow full specific status. This area is probably as far south as the species gets, and it best located during winter when juvenile Common Crows with similar calls are not present. Northwestern Crows are *extremely* difficult (and frequently impossible) to identify in the field; rely only on voice, and back it up with the species' smaller size (barely) and possibly its more labored and rapid wingbeats in sustained flight. Northwestern Crows should probably not be looked for south of Tillamook Head in southern Clatsop County. Other sites in Oregon where the species has occurred a number of times include the public boat basin in Hammond and along Sunset Beach between Seaside and Clatsop Spit.

The South Jetty of the Columbia River. To reach this area (known as *the* South Jetty among Oregon birders), simply follow the main road past the Coffenbury Lake turnoff — there are signs directing you to the South Jetty. From July to mid-May, this area is regularly checked by birders. Some remarkable species have occurred such as Yellow-billed Loon, Wilson's Storm-Petrel, Mongolian Plover, Spotted Redshank, Bar-tailed and Hudsonian Godwits, Curlew Sandpiper, Long-toed Stint, Black-throated Blue Warbler, Rose-breasted Grosbeak, and McKay's Bunting. The first area to check is the parking lot at the jetty's base (Parking Lot C). During high tide the entire estuary of the Columbia River fills up, and migrating shorebirds are forced onto the tiny flood plain just below this parking lot. These shorebird ponds cover a remarkably small area and are easily checked without a scope. During late September and October, large flocks of Pectoral Sandpipers frequently numbering in the hundreds stop here to rest; they are joined by a token Sharp-tailed Sandpiper or two each fall. Other rarities that occur more often here than anywhere else in Oregon include Ruff and Buff-breasted Sandpiper. During winter look for small numbers of Snow Buntings, Horned Larks, and Lapland Longspurs here and at the dunes along the actual mouth of the river (to the northwest of the shorebird ponds). Climbing up onto the jetty near the parking lot, look for migrant and/or wintering loons (Pacific are frequently the most abundant), grebes, Northern Fulmars, shearwaters, Brown Pelicans, cormorants, Brant, alcids, jaegers, gulls, and terns.

To reach the river's mouth and its open beach, hike due west from Parking Lot C for about a quarter of a mile. Thousands of gulls and terns gather here to rest; look for a few Arctic and Common Terns, Black-legged Kittiwakes, and Sabine's Gulls that frequently join them from late August through early

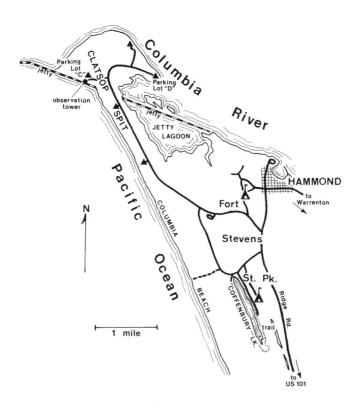

October. Also, any of the three jaegers are likely to appear when gull numbers peak during August and September. Dunlin, Sanderling, and especially Golden-Plover also favor these open beaches; the rare Snowy Plover is occasionally encountered here, also.

For a view of the quiet estuary backwaters, drive to Parking Lot D at the very end of the South Jetty Road. These quiet tidal waters are very good for waterfowl, including nesting Canada Geese and wintering Brant flocks. Bald Eagles and Peregrine Falcons are regular winter visitors here, preferring to perch and hunt from the old tressel across the water. Two rare arctic species that occur more frequently here than anywhere else in

Oregon are the Gyrfalcon and Snowy Owl. Look for them here or at the jetty by the shorebird ponds.

The potential for finding migrant passerines in the isolated brushy growth on outer Clatsop Spit has only recently been explored. So far, unusual species that have shown up (usually early in the morning following strong west winds) include Ash-throated Flycatcher, Mountain Bluebird, Black-and-White Warbler, Tennessee Warbler, Blackpoll Warbler, Black-throated Green Warbler, Black-throated Blue Warbler, Palm Warbler, and Rose-breasted Grosbeak!

Saddle Mountain State Park

Habitats: WF, BF, RR, FA
Elevation: 1400-3283'
Seasons: Sp • • • S • • • F • • • W • •

The turnoff to this park is located on US 26 some 66 miles
west of Portland. From the highway it is 7 miles to the
parking and picnicking area. A walk around the picnicking
grounds will produce such typical Coast Range species as
Chestnut-backed Chickadee, Golden-crowned Kinglet, Winter
Wren, Steller's Jay, Hutton's Vireo, and Pacific-slope Flycatcher. During winter and fall the picnic area is often visited
by Gray Jays from higher elevations. An exhilarating hike (3.5
miles one way, 1600' elevation gain) leads to the 3283' summit
of Saddle Mountain from the parking lot. The lower portion
of this trail passes through typical coastal forest of alder,
Douglas-fir, hemlock, and smaller stands of Sitka spruce. This
is excellent habitat for the beautiful Hermit Warbler; also look
and listen for Varied and Swainson's Thrushes, Hammond's
Flycatcher, and the seldom-seen Blue Grouse. The latter half
of the trail passes through open mountain meadows. Hummingbirds are quite common (almost exclusively Rufous), and
late in the summer it is good for migrating raptors. Black
Swifts have been reported during the fall, and Mountain Quail
are infrequently heard. The view of the Columbia River
Estuary from the summit is worth the strenuous hike in itself.

Ecola State Park/Cannon Beach

Habitats: RS, CE, FW, BR, WF, UR
Elevation: 0-400'
Seasons: Sp ••• S •• F •••• W •••

When entering Cannon Beach from the north, turn west off the highway just before crossing Elk Creek at the north end of town. This is Ecola Park Road; follow it for about 2.5 miles to the main park area. Ecola St. Pk. is probably the most scenic site on the Oregon coast; the view looking south from the observation point has appeared on innumerable calendars. The large rock just off the point is the home of a huge Common Murre colony. Other nesting waterbirds here include Brandt's and Pelagic Cormorants, Pigeon Guillemot, Western Gull, and Black Oystercatcher. Brown Pelicans are a common sight here during summer and fall. During the winter scope the rocky shoreline far below for Surfbird, Black Turnstone, Rock Sandpiper (very uncommon), and Harlequin Duck. Black Scoters are common in the surf just south of the main observation point.

The Cannon Beach sewage ponds should be checked for migrant waterfowl and gulls. To reach them, turn east on Second St. in downtown Cannon Beach. The boggy woods around the ponds are good for migrant and summering passerines, and Pileated Woodpeckers are seen here infrequently. Green-backed Herons and Wood Ducks nest around the more secluded wooded ponds, and wintering sparrow flocks (usually on the north side of the ponds) have yielded Swamp, White-throated, Harris', Tree, and Clay-colored Sparrows among the usual species.

At the south end of Cannon Beach, be sure to check Haystack Rock for nesting Tufted Puffins; this is one of the largest and most easily observed colonies in Oregon. Pigeon Guillemots and Pelagic Cormorants also nest here.

Nehalem Meadows

Habitats: FA, FW, BR, WF
Elevation: 10'
Seasons: Sp • • •   S • •   F • • • •   W • • • •

When heading south out of Nehalem on US 101, make the
first right (west) turn after crossing the Nehalem River. This
puts you on Tideland Rd., the main access to Nehalem
Meadows. Tideland Rd. winds around the meadows for about
5 miles to OR 52, then back to US 101; it makes a fascinating
and profitable loop for the birder passing through this part of
Tillamook County. Not far from the Nehalem River bridge on
Tideland Road are the Nehalem Sewage Ponds; ask permission
to enter. During a high tide, shorebirds from nearby Nehalem
Bay are forced onto these ponds. Among the typical species,
look for Golden-Plover, Baird's, Pectoral, and Semipalmated
Sandpipers, and Red-necked and Red Phalaropes, species
which appear every year. Bonus finds have included Sharp-
tailed and Buff-breasted Sandpipers, Ruff, and Wilson's
Phalarope. The rare Stilt Sandpiper occurs here virtually every
year during late August and September, making these ponds
the most reliable location in Oregon for the species. From late
fall through the winter, Black-shouldered Kites occur in the
fields across the road from the sewage ponds. Although
seldom seen during the summer months, the kites most likely
remain to nest in the area. Also check the ponds for waterfowl. Migrant geese are frequent drop-ins (an Emperor Goose
wintered once), and it is a haven for fresh-water ducks such as
Cinnamon and Blue-winged Teal, Lesser Scaup, and Ring-
necked Duck. Purple Martins are frequently seen here (they
nest along the river).

Throughout the entire meadow area, watch for wintering
Peregrine Falcons, Merlins, and other raptors; there are a
number of reports of Gyrfalcons from Nehalem Meadows.
Winter sparrow flocks (usually found around the various
farms) have hosted White-throated, Swamp, Clay-colored,
Harris, and Tree Sparrows among the abundant Golden-
crowneds, White-crowneds, and Songs. Palm Warblers have
occurred with some regularity. Also check the wintering gull

flocks, most which contain mainly Mew, Ring-billed, and California Gulls; Glaucous Gulls have occurred a number of times. In recent years, Cattle Egrets have been found during the winter, mainly from December to February; look for them around the dairies and cattle herds.

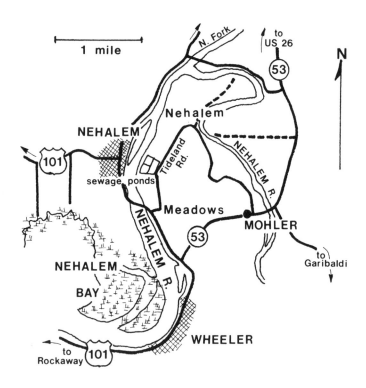

Northern Tillamook Bay

Habitats: CE, RS, OC, FW, FA, OB, BR, UR
Elevation: 0-20'
Seasons: Sp • • • • S • • F • • • • W • • • •

Being one of the state's largest estuaries, Tillamook Bay
warrents an entire day of birding to be thoroughly covered. In
conjunction with the Bayocean Spit area (see Site A-6), the
northern part of the bay can offer some of the best birding to
be found in the Pacific Northwest. Particular areas of note on
this part of the bay include the following:

Bay City Area. In the town of Bay City, turn west off US 101
onto Goose Point Rd.; follow this through a small residential
community (always bearing to the right) to the sewage
treatment facility. The two ponds are fenced off but are easily
scoped from the parking area at the end of the road. In recent
years these ponds have yielded such rare species as Redhead,
Little, Sabine's, and Franklin's Gulls, and Black-legged Kittiwake. Fresh-water ducks — Lesser Scaup, all three teal,
Hooded Merganser — are most easily found here. Purple
Martins occur infrequently, and the woodlands and brush of
the area are excellent for migrant and wintering passerines.

At the north end of Bay City, check the narrow finger of land
that juts into Tillamook Bay; this is where the Hayes' Oyster
Plant is located. This is a traditional wintering site for large
numbers of Black Turnstones and Surfbirds, as well as a few
Ruddy Turnstones. It is also a good site for close-up studies of
cormorants and Green-backed Herons.

Miami Cove and Garibaldi. The northeast corner of Tillamook
Bay is known as Miami Cove, and the community of Garibaldi
lies just west of that region. Access to scope the cove is
hazardous due to the narrow highway; the best viewing area is
just east of Garibaldi by the tall smoke stack. During a high
tide, look for grebes, loons, diving ducks, and Brant. At low
tide the entire cove empties and is excellent habitat for
shorebirds, gulls, terns, and herons. Bonaparte's Gulls seem to
favor this area, and patient searching has produced records of

Little and Sabine's Gulls among the flocks. A scope is highly recommended here.

In the town of Garibaldi, be sure to check the public boat basin for wintering water birds. Grebes (Red-necked, Horned, and Western) seem to favor this tiny harbor, and during fall the pelicans are amazingly tame. The waters around the boat basin are quite gravelly and thus attract migrant and wintering Harlequin Ducks, Black Scoters, and (rarely) Barrow's Goldeneyes.

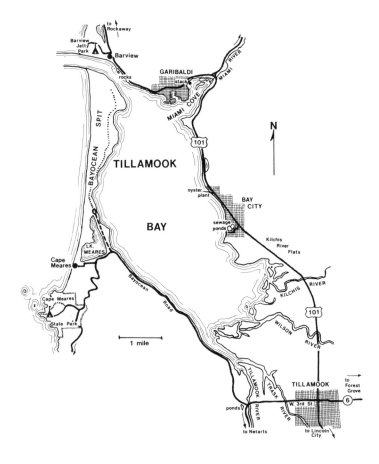

Just to the west of Garibaldi, US 101 passes a series of large rocks which should be checked out. Most of the year there are Harlequin Ducks here, and all three cormorants are easily studied. Brown Pelicans and Heermann's Gulls are common during late summer and fall. During winter watch for the usual Black Oystercatchers and assorted "rockpipers".

Barview Jetty County Park. This delightful park guards the entrance of the bay and offers the only access to the north jetty. About 0.5 miles north of the above-mentioned roadside rocks, turn left (west) into the park. The camping area here is especially productive during fall, spring, and winter for the passerines. Wrentits can be found any time of year, and Palm Warblers have wintered in the park a few times. The north jetty of Tillamook Bay is a great vantage point for scoping out the mouth of the bay. The channel should be scanned for wintering alcids; Ancient Murrelets and Cassin's Auklets have been found a number of times. Also watch for migrant loons, grebes, shearwaters, storm-petrels, gulls, terns, and even Red Phalaropes. The jetty has the usual complement of rock shorebirds including Rock Sandpiper during the winter.

Bayocean Spit

Habitats: CE, RS, OC, OB, BR, FW, FA
Elevation: 0-15'
Seasons: Sp • • • • S • • • F • • • • W • • •

In the town of Tillamook, head west on Third St., following
the signs for the Three Capes Scenic Route. About a mile after
passing the hospital on the west end of town, the road crosses
the Tillamook River. The meadowlands between the river and
the town along this road can be very productive during winter
and fall. Wintertime brings large numbers of wigeon to these
fields with a few Eurasian birds in each flock. Also watch for
the rare but increasingly more frequent Cattle Egret and Black-
shouldered Kite in any of the meadowlands in the Tillamook
area. During a very high tide from August through October,
shorebirds often congregate in the flooded or plowed fields of
this area. Golden-Plover and Buff-breasted Sandpiper are two
species that prefer this habitat. And, of course, every field has
its contingent of gulls from September to April that often
include Glaucous Gulls among the usual birds. Other coastal
meadows that should be searched during the winter are found
east of Tillamook on the road to Forest Grove (the Wilson
River Meadows) and south of town in the Tillamook Airport
area.

After the road crosses the Tillamook River west of town, take
the first right (northwest) turn, following signs to Cape Meares
(see next entry). Be sure to check the old log pond at this
junction for the secretive Green-backed Heron or Wood Duck.
The road now follows the upper reaches of Tillamook Bay,
offering excellent views of such birds as loons, grebes, cormorants, herons, ducks, and gulls. Bald Eagles are a frequent
sight along this stretch of road any time of year. About 5.5
miles from the above-mentioned junction is the gravel turnoff
to Bayocean Spit.

From early August to early October, Bayocean Spit is often the
hottest birding spot in the state. During a high tide, walk due
east to the exposed mudflats below the parking area. Tremen-

dous concentrations of peep sandpipers — mostly Westerns and Leasts — peak here during late August and early September. Flocks occasionally number in the tens of thousands and allow an amazingly close approach — often so close that binoculars are not necessary! Currently, Bayocean Spit is the most reliable site in Oregon for finding the rare Semipalmated Sandpiper; a few are reported from here every year during late August. Peeps aren't the only shorebirds present, though. Virtually anything can (and does) show up. Baird's and Pectoral Sandpipers, Black-bellied, Semipalmated, and Golden-Plovers, Whimbrel, Marbled Godwit, Dunlin, Sanderling, Red Knot, and Red-necked and Red Phalaropes are reported every fall. Such rarities as Bar-tailed and Hudsonian Godwits, Sharp-tailed, Curlew, Buff-breasted, and Stilt Sandpipers, Mountain and Mongolian Plovers, Rufous-necked Stint, and Ruff have all been well-documented at Bayocean Spit, some more than once! During late fall these same flats are good for Lapland Longspur and Horned Lark. The three mile walk out to the end of the spit is enjoyable but only of marginal interest birdwise. Expect the typical land birds found anywhere along the coast, but a few vagrant passerines are reported from the spit's forest each year. At the tip, on the ocean side, look for Snowy Plover anytime of year; they are most prevalent during the winter.

At the base of Bayocean Spit is another excellent birding hotspot, Lake Meares. Being a fresh-water lake adjacent to the open ocean, Lake Meares attracts unusual birds quite regularly. Such "fresh-water" species as Black Tern, White Pelican, American Avocet, Eared Grebe, Redhead, and Yellow-headed Blackbird have occurred here. Large concentrations of Ring-necked Ducks and scaup (both species) winter here, along with smaller numbers of goldeneye, Bufflehead, Canvasback, and dabbling ducks. Tufted Ducks have appeared in these huge rafts at least once. And during a very high tide, shorebirds swarm onto Lake Meares' north end when water levels are low enough to expose the grassy flats. Buff-breasted and Curlew Sandpipers, Ruff, and Rufous-necked Stint have been sifted out of the large flocks of typical species in this area.

Cape Meares State Park

Habitats: RS, OC, WF, BR
Elevation: 350'
Seasons: Sp • • • S • • F • • • • W • • •

This is one of the most productive headlands for birding to be
found in Oregon. The entry road winds through an island of
old-growth Sitka spruce forest amid the clear-cut hillside
surrounding the park. A hiking trail also winds through this
habitat. Although seldom seen or heard, there is a resident
pair or two of Spotted Owls in this forest. From the parking
lot walk down to the lighthouse. On the way down, scan the
cliff sides from the fenced overlook on the right for nesting
Tufted Puffins. From the tip, scan the open ocean for numerous birds. From August to November, look for migrant
shearwaters, jaegers, terns, gulls, and kittiwakes. Alcids seem
to favor this headland; eight species have been reported
including such rarities as Cassin's Auklet (actually quite
common offshore, but rarely seen from land), Ancient Murrelet, and even Xantus' Murrelet (once). The largest rock just
off the cape's tip hosts a huge colony of Common Murres.

During migration, Cape Meares may be a good site for finding
vagrant warblers —Blackpoll and Black-throated Blue Warblers
and American Redstart have been reported so far.

Siletz Bay

Habitats: CE, OB, FA, RS, WF, BF, FW, UR
Elevation: 0-23'
Seasons: Sp • • • • S • • F • • • • W • • •

US 101 follows the eastern shore of Siletz Bay just south of
Lincoln City. Turn west at the southernmost traffic light in
Lincoln City just before crossing the Schooner Creek bridge
(51 St.). At the end of the road near Mo's Restaurant is a
public dock where the mouth of the bay can be observed. All
three species of regularly-occurring loons (and Yellow-billed
once), Red-necked and Horned Grebes, all three cormorants,
Brown Pelicans, various bay and sea ducks, and Common
Murres may be seen here. Gulls tend to congregate at the tip
of Siletz Spit and are easily observed from the dock. Most are
Westerns, Glaucous-wings, or hybrids thereof, but look for the
additional California, Ring-billed, Herring, Thayer's, and
(during fall) Heermann's. Caspian Terns frequently join the
flock during summer and fall.

Shorebirds are best studied at a mid tide; virtually all waders
leave Siletz Bay during a high tide because there are no
exposed mudflats then. In the small community of Cutler
City, just south of Lincoln City, turn west on 62nd St. and
follow it a few blocks west to a beach access area at Josephine
Young Memorial City Park. From here you can walk south
around Cutler City to the mouth of Drift Creek. From late
July to October, look for both yellowlegs, Short-billed Dowitchers, Ruddy and Black Turnstones, and even Wandering
Tattlers. Black-bellied Plover are particularly common here,
and during September and October there are usually a few
Golden-Plovers mixed in with them. The drier sandy areas
attract Semipalmated Plover, Baird's Sandpiper, and Whimbrel. Anywhere between Cutler City and Drift Creek look for
the uncommon Red Knot, Marbled Godwit, Willet, and
Pectoral Sandpiper. Green-backed Herons and Hooded
Mergansers are a regular sight along lower Drift Creek (west of
the US 101 bridge).

When tides are particularly high and fields are full of water,
many birds head for the Drift Creek meadowlands. To reach

this area, turn west off US 101 onto Drift Creek Rd. just south of Cutler City (check the sloughs and wet fields at this intersection). 0.5 miles from the highway, turn right (southeast) onto Gorton Rd. The best viewing is right from the car immediately after crossing Drift Creek. Shorebirds swarm in here when there is a very high tide; during winter and late fall most will be Black-bellied Plover, Black Turnstones, Dunlin, Least Sandpiper, and Long-billed Dowitcher, but watch for other less common species. One March, the flocks were joined by a Red Knot and a Mountain Plover! Cattle Egrets have occurred a number of times during winter, and flocks of wigeon usually have a Eurasian bird or two mixed in with them. There are good sparrow hedges along Gorton Rd., and a Palm Warbler occurred here at least once.

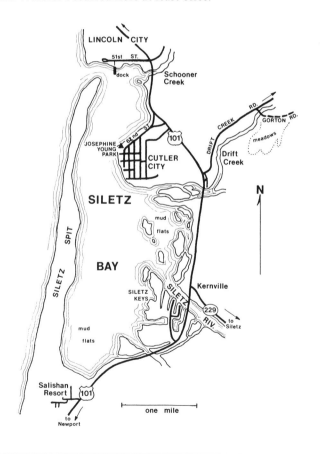

Boiler Bay State Wayside

Habitats: RS, OC
Elevation: 53'
Seasons: Sp • • • S • • F • • • W • • • •

This scenic headland is located on US 101 about 2 miles north of Depoe Bay. It is a favorite vantage point for observing migrating gray whales in spring, and for some reason it is among the best sites in Oregon for observing the truly pelagic birds from land. Birding here is very straightforward; simply set up your scope at the westernmost point of the observation area.

Boiler Bay is probably the best site in Oregon for watching winter alcids. Among the typical murres and guillemots, look for Marbled Murrelets, Rhinoceros Auklets, Cassin's Auklets, and even the elusive Ancient Murrelet. Rarities include Tufted and Horned Puffins and Xantus' Murrelet. Also look for wintering Red Phalaropes just off the foam line during bad weather. All three cormorants are easily seen any time of year, and the rocks on the south side of the park usually have wintering Black Turnstones, Surfbirds, Black Oystercatchers, and Rock Sandpipers.

During fall this is a good place to watch migrant Pacific Loons as they pass by in the hundreds. Brown Pelicans and Heermann's Gulls are almost always present from August through late October. Watch for shearwaters during fall; Sooties are regular well offshore, and Short-taileds are reported here annually, usually from November to March. Very rare species include Laysan Albatross, Buller's Shearwater, Black-vented Shearwater, and Mottled Petrel.

Yaquina Head Natural Area

Habitats: RS, OC
Elevation: 200-350'
Seasons: Sp • • •   S • • •   F • • •   W • •

The marked turnoff to Yaquina Head Natural Area and
Lighthouse is on US 101, 2.5 miles north of Newport. This
headland is best known for its easily viewed seabird colony,
consisting mostly of Western Gulls, Common Murres, and
Brandt's Cormorants. Nesting on the seaward side of the main
breeding rock west of the lighthouse are smaller numbers of
Tufted Puffins; they are usually seen flying to or from the rock
because their nesting burrows are not visible from the main-
land. Pigeon Guillemots also nest here, and Rhinoceros
Auklets, Marbled Murrelets, and even Ancient Murrelets are
occasionally seen from the head. Sooty Shearwaters migrate
by in the fall, and during strong west winds of winter, watch
for the occasional Northern Fulmar, Short-tailed Shearwater,
or Red Phalarope.

Yaquina Bay/Newport

Habitats: CE, OC, OB, RS, BR, UR, FA, WF, FW
Elevation: 0-50'
Seasons: Sp• • • • S • • • F • • • • W • • • •

One of Oregon's most heavily-birded areas, Yaquina (pronounced ya-QUIN'-uh; it's an American Indian word, not Spanish) Bay is worth exploring at a leisurely pace all day, any time of year. Some major sites that should not be passed up include the following:

The South Jetty. At the south end of the Yaquina Bay Bridge (hereafter, bay bridge) on US 101, turn west on the marked road to the Mark O. Hatfield Marine Science Center. This road loops around to the north, then to the east, passing under the bay bridge. Make the left (west) turn just before going under the bridge — this is the road to the South Jetty of Yaquina Bay. Where the road turns to gravel and joins the bay, scope the water for birds. From September to early May, thousands of scoters congregate here and just west of the bridge; viewing is best at a low tide. All three species are present, with Surf by far the most abundant, followed by White-winged, and then the uncommon Black Scoter; this is the general pattern of abundance throughout the state. Every winter there are up to five Oldsquaw to be found in the large duck concentrations here. Harlequin Ducks are easily found during winter and migration just below the road at the base of the jetty. Other species present here during this time of year include Western, Horned, and Red-necked Grebes, all three cormorants, Brant (lower tides), Greater Scaup, Common Goldeneye, Bufflehead, and Red-breasted Merganser. All three West Coast loons are easily found during winter in the channel west of the bay bridge, and the rare Yellow-billed Loon occurs more regularly here than anywhere else in Oregon. This species is reported about every other year on Yaquina Bay, generally from late October to March. During the late fall migration, look for Red Phalarope that are occasionally blown into the bay during storms. Brown Pelicans are easily found with their attendant Heermann's Gulls from late July to October, and the jetty itself supports a good number of "rockpipers".

Mark O. Hatfield Marine Science Center. Instead of turning west on the South Jetty Rd., continue under the bay bridge to the parking area of the Marine Science Center (hereafter MSC). This facility is operated by Oregon State University out of Corvallis and contains an excellent public interpretive center, museum, and viewing aquarium, all free of charge. Be sure to check in at the MSC for the latest birding news from the Yaquina Bay area.

This is the best shorebird area on Yaquina Bay; during high tide the area just east of the MSC often has the only exposed mudflats on the entire bay. During migration anything can show up, but the wintering shorebirds will be Black-bellied Plover, Dunlin, Sanderling, and a few Long-billed Dowitchers. Yaquina Bay is unique among northern Oregon estuaries with its wintering Willets and Whimbrels; small numbers can usually be seen on the flats behind the MSC. Also congregating on these flats at high tide is an incredible variety of gulls and terns when these birds are migrating. Among the regular ten or twelve species, look for the occasional Black-legged Kittiwake, Glaucous Gull, Sabine's Gull, Common Tern, or Arctic Tern. Yaquina Bay has hosted some of Oregon's rarest larids such as Little Gull, Ross' Gull, and Elegant Tern. Migrant jaegers (usually Parasitic) may occasionally join the gull flocks.

The shrubby growth and stunted pines around the MSC are excellent for migrant passerines, especially during the fall. The past ten years have seen records of Ash-throated Flycatcher, Say's Phoebe, Tropical Kingbird, Mountain Chickadee, Northern Mockingbird, Sage Thrasher, Prairie Warbler, White-throated Sparrow, Harris' Sparrow, Bobolink, and Orchard Oriole from this area. During late fall and winter, the brushy area just east of the MSC buildings is probably the best place in Oregon to find a Palm Warbler.

Sally's Bend and Upper Yaquina Bay. At the north end of the bay bridge, make an immediate east (right) turn that takes you down the hill to Newport's Old Town waterfront. Staying on the main road, continue through town and you will be on the old highway, heading toward the town of Toledo, some 10 miles up river from Newport. This is an excellent drive during a winter high tide when bay ducks, loons, Brant, and gulls head far up the bay. Bald Eagles are a regular sight here, and Green-backed Herons may be found on the quieter backwaters. A particularly worthwhile viewing area is at the huge LNG tank just east of Newport. After passing the mill on the bayshore, turn right on a gravel road that leads to a public viewing and fishing dock at the base of the LNG tank. Most of the local wintering waterbirds can be seen in the cove just east of the dock. This is a good spot to scope out the large numbers of American Wigeon for a Eurasian bird. At this point (about 3 miles upriver from Newport), the bay takes an abrupt curve to the south (as does the old highway) — this is the area known as Sally's Bend.

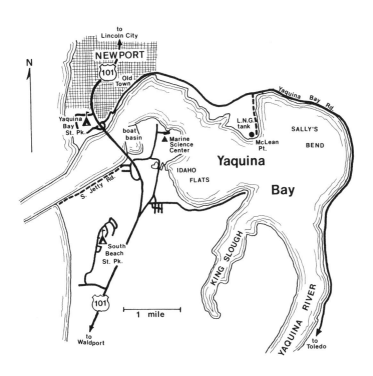

Seal Rock State Park

Habitats: RS
Elevation: 0-100'
Seasons: Sp • • S • F • • • W • • •

The main parking lot of this small park is located about 8 miles south of Newport's Yaquina Bay bridge. Seal Rock is most noted for its wintering population of rock-inhabiting birds. Especially prevalent are the flocks of Black Turnstones and Surfbirds. During migration check for Wandering Tattlers here, and the winter flocks often have a Ruddy Turnstone or two mixed in. The local and uncommon Rock Sandpiper is most reliable in Oregon at this site — there are usually 2-5 birds found in the flocks, especially at the southern tide pool areas of the park. A good pull-out to scope for these birds is located on the west side of US 101 about 0.5 miles south of the park's main entrance. Other good birds to watch for during winter include cormorants, Harlequin Ducks, Black Scoters, Oldsquaws (rare), and assorted gulls. As the name suggests, this park is well-known for its herds of harbor seals and sea lions.

Region B
South Coast

Harlequin Duck

Siuslaw River Estuary

Habitats: CE, FA, OB, OC, RS, WF, BR
Elevation: 0-20'
Seasons: Sp • • • • S • • • F • • • • W • • • •

To reach the main birding area here, head south on US 101 out of Florence. About 0.75 miles south of the Siuslaw River bridge, turn west on the marked South Jetty Rd. After the South Jetty Rd. turns north, pull into the third parking lot on the west side of the road (the lot with public rest rooms). During fall and winter, the low grassy floodplain due east of this parking lot should be checked out, providing water levels are low enough to permit access on foot. About 200 yards from the road, the shrubs and tall grasses give way to low sedges and sandy flats. This area is a magnet for migrant shorebirds, especially such uncommon species as Golden-Plover, Pectoral and Baird's Sandpipers, both yellowlegs, as well as all the regularly-occurring species. Rarities have included Buff-breasted Sandpiper (up to 14 birds one fall!), Ruff (a number of records), Sharp-tailed Sandpiper, and Stilt Sandpiper. Horned Lark and American Pipits also occur during fall, and Lapland Longspurs have been reported. In winter and spring, water levels are generally at their highest on this floodplain. Access is frequently impossible, but bring a scope to observe the large winter flocks of Tundra Swans. Other waterfowl are also common during migration — teal, wigeon, Canada and White-fronted Geese, and other species. Also during winter, watch for the raptors — occasional Black-shouldered Kites, Merlin, Peregrine Falcon, and Short-eared Owl have shown up.

The mouth of the Siuslaw River is reached by continuing north on the South Jetty Rd. Just before reaching the end of the road, watch for a sandy cove on the right with a parking area. Gulls and migrant terns favor these flats. Mixed flocks of Common and Arctic Terns ("Commic Terns") have been seen here, especially during bad September storms. Other species of note have included Black-legged Kittiwake, Red-necked and Red Phalarope, and even Elegant Tern (once). The jetty itself is good for observing loons, grebes, Brown Pelicans, cormorants, scoters, Harlequin Duck, and the occasional alcid.

To reach the North Jetty of the Siuslaw, head north on Rhododendron Dr. in Florence toward Heceta Beach. The North Jetty Rd. is located 1.5 miles north of the Coast Guard Station. Before reaching the jetty itself, there are a number of pull-out areas which offer good views of the lower estuary. Species seen from the north jetty will be much the same as those listed above for the south jetty.

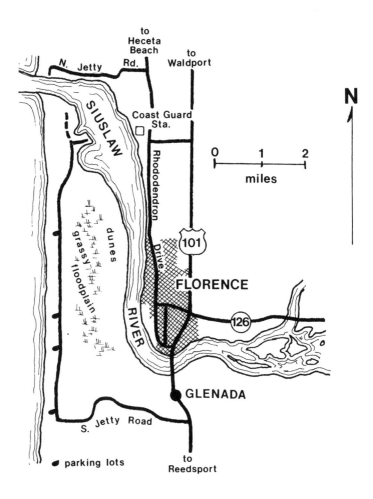

Mouth of Siltcoos River

Habitats: CE, OB
Elevation: 5'
Seasons: Sp ● ● ●   S ●   F ● ● ●   W ● ●

This is a good shorebird spot that is easy to check out. About 7.25 miles south of the Siuslaw River bridge in Florence, turn west off US 101 onto Siltcoos Beach Rd. About 0.5 miles west of the bridge leading into Waxmyrtle CG, there is a pull-out area where a gravel road heads off to the north. Park here and walk the path southward for a few yards to the estuary mudflats. The actual outflow of the Siltcoos River varies from time to time, but there is good shorebirding on the narrow mudflats anywhere between the gravel pull-out and the river mouth. Along with the more expected species, this site has produced Buff-breasted Sandpiper, Stilt Sandpiper, Semipalmated Sandpiper, Red Knot, Wilson's Phalarope, and Willet. Snowy Plover may be found along the nearby open sandy beach.

Coastal Douglas County

Habitats: FW, WF, OB, CE, RS, OC, UR
Elevation: 0-35'
Seasons: Sp • • • • S • • • F • • • • W • • •

Coastal Douglas County offers little access to areas that are
undoubtably rich in birdlife, but a few stops are recommended
when passing through this area. Numerous lakes and wooded
ponds can be seen alongside US 101, but the only one that
merits a stop — especially if you are county listing — is
Tahkenitch Lake. About 5 miles south of the Lane-Douglas
County line, US 101 parallels an arm of this large forested
lake; turn into the Tahkenitch Lake CG here. Most of the
local nesting species can be found here; watch (and listen) for
Western Tanager, Purple Finch, Warbling Vireo, Wilson's
Warbler, Varied Thrush, Chestnut-backed Chickadee, Steller's
Jay, Band-tailed Pigeon, Swainson's Thrush, Winter Wren, and
other species. Hutton's Vireos can be sifted out of the wintering flocks of chickadees, kinglets, and nuthatches, but the
species is more easily found during spring when it is on
territory. Tahkenitch Lake is also home to a few summering
Ospreys; they are frequently seen from US 101 along the
lakeshore.

South of Tahkenitch Lake, the estuary of the Umpqua River
offers the best birding opportunities in coastal Douglas Co.
Tantalizing views of the expansive estuary can be seen all
along US 101; good roadside pull-outs for scoping the birds
are found just south of Gardiner and on Bolon Island — use
caution when parking on the shoulder of US 101. During
migration and winter, watch for Tundra Swans, Canada Geese,
Brant, wintering ducks, Great Blue Heron, Great Egret (at
times quite common), Bald Eagle, Northern Harrier, and other
species. The boat basin at Winchester Bay (at the southern
end of the estuary) is one of the most productive and easily-
reached birding sites in this area. This harbor (known as
Salmon Harbor) is home to wintering Western and Horned
Grebes, all three loons, Brown Pelican, all three cormorants,
scaup, goldeneye, Bufflehead, Red-breasted Merganser, and
other water birds. The area just west of Salmon Harbor often
has resting flocks of gulls and terns, especially during migra-

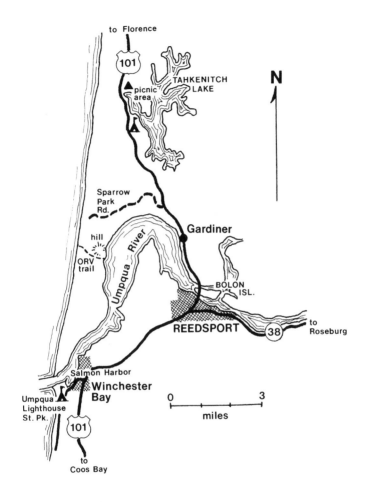

tion. Umpqua Lighthouse St. Pk. offers camping and access to the south jetty of the Umpqua River. Marbled Murrelets are frequently seen off this jetty during fall and winter.

To explore the tidal flats of the Umpqua River Estuary requires a full day and real determination. The best shorebird area is found in the northwest corner of the estuary, an area that is quite inaccessible by car. To reach the general area, turn west off US 101 about 2 miles north of Gardiner onto Sparrow Park

Rd. (also recognized as Douglas Co. Rd. 247); this road is located immediately north of the paper pulp mill complex. Sparrow Park Rd. heads west and stops just short of the ocean beach, thus entering the Oregon Dunes Nat'l. Recreation Area. Check this stretch of beach for the inconspicuous Snowy Plover. About 1.0 mile south of where Sparrow Park Rd. reaches the beach, look for two posts in the dunes that mark a very rough ORV road. Follow this road to the east and eventually to the extensive mudflats of Winchester Bay. Be sure to time your arrival at the flats with low tide for the best birding — it's about a two hour hike from the end of Sparrow Park Rd., down the beach, and east on the ORV road to the estuary.

Coos Bay/Cape Arago Area

Habitats: CE, RS, OB, OC, FA, WF, UR, BR, BF, FW
Elevation: 0-220'
Seasons: Sp • • • •   S • • •   F • • • •   W • • • •

Oregon's largest estuary, Coos Bay offers some of the most
enticing birding opportunities to be found anywhere in the
Pacific Northwest. Habitats vary from open sandy beaches,
rocky headlands, tidal mudflats, and coastal salt marshes to
dense coniferous forest, open coastal meadowland, and
suprisingly productive residential areas. The cities of Coos
Bay, North Bend, Empire, and Charleston offer ample opportunities for gas, good, and lodging; camping facilities are
found at the numerous state parks of the area, especially in the
Cape Arago region.

The North Spit. This area offers secluded sandy beaches and
dunes closed to vehicular traffic. North of the Bay Bridge,
turn west and take the causeway to Horsfall Beach St. Pk.
Jordan Cove is the tiny inlet just west of the causeway; bear
left after crossing the railroad tracks to view the cove, good for
migrant shorebirds, gulls, and terns. From Horsfall Beach it is
about a 10 miles hike (one-way) to the end of the North Spit.
This remote area is one of the last strongholds of the Snowy
Plover. Occasional winter suprises on the North Spit have
included Snowy Owl, Lapland Longspur, and Snow Bunting.

Simpson-Ferry Road Park. Located at the south end of the Bay
Bridge, this wooded park serves as an island of valuable
habitat in the residential sprawl of the North Bend-Coos Bay
metro area. It is especially productive for migrant and wintering passerines. A Black-and-White Warbler wintered here
once, and the park has a tendency to attract other rare
overwintering warblers, finches, and hummingbirds, and it is
a great site for the usual summering passerines.

Pony Slough. A small finger of Coos Bay itself, Pony Slough is
truly a hot spot for shorebirds. To reach the best viewing area,
turn west on Virginia Ave. in North Bend and head toward the
local airport. About 1.5 miles west of US 101, turn north on
Marion St., a rough gravel road that dead-ends at a public boat

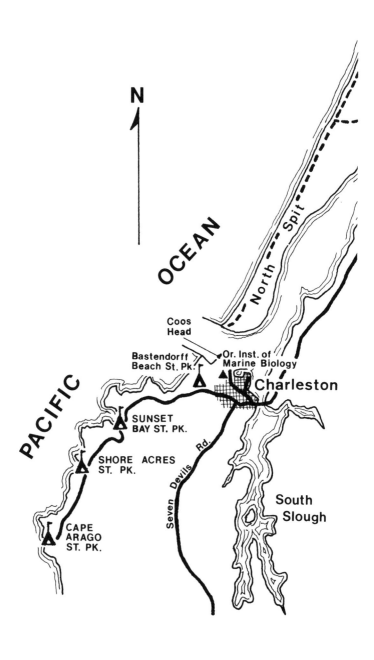

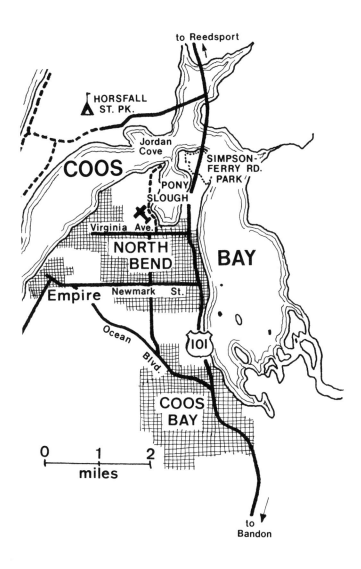

to Reedsport

HORSFALL
ST. PK.

Jordan
Cove

COOS

SIMPSON-
FERRY RD.
PARK

PONY
SLOUGH

Virginia Ave.

NORTH
BEND

BAY

Empire

Newmark   St.

Ocean

Blvd.

101

COOS
BAY

0   1   2
miles

to
Bandon

launch. Many Great Egrets use Pony Slough during fall and winter, and this is the only Oregon site that regularly hosts wintering Snowy Egrets as well (usually one or two Snowies per winter). Thousands of American Wigeons (a few Eurasians as well), Pintails, Gadwalls, both scaup species, Buffleheads, and Ruddy Ducks utilize the slough during winter and migration periods. These birds attract wintering raptors including Bald Eagles, Merlins, and Peregrine Falcons. The flats near the airport are the best site for shorebirds; this part of Coos Bay hosts one of the state's largest concentrations of wintering shorebirds. Thousands of peeps, Black-bellied Plover, Long-billed Dowitchers, Dunlin, Sanderling, and even Whimbrel are joined by smaller numbers of Marbled Godwit, both yellowlegs (Lesser <u>extremely</u> rare during winter), Short-billed Dowitcher, Ruddy and Black Turnstones, and even the occasional Long-billed Curlew. Migration periods bring even larger numbers and a greater variety of shorebirds. During a particularly high tide, the airport runway adjacent to Pony Slough often hosts resting shorebirds when major concentrations are present on the bay. Golden-Plover especially seem to favor this area. During winter look for sparrow flocks, Horned Larks, Northern Shrikes, and even Lapland Longspurs. Unusual finds here include Loggerhead Shrike, Mountain Bluebird, Palm Warbler, and Lark Bunting, so don't pass up the runway area.

Charleston Area. This attractive fishing town located a little south and west of North Bend deserves an hour or so of thorough coverage. The small boat basin in town is good for migrant and wintering loons, grebes, cormorants, Brant, and salt-water ducks. Gull concentrations are particularly impressive, and it is good for Brown Pelicans. A Magnificent Frigatebird even appeared here one spring. The nearby Oregon Institute of Marine Biology (at the west end of town, adjacent to the boat basin) offers good passerine birding. Anna's Hummingbirds are common all year at the Institute's feeders, but they are outnumbered by Rufous during spring and summer. Allen's should be looked for here. A gravel road leads up the hill behind the Institute toward the Coos Head Naval Station; a marked nature trail that goes to the Institute's bird sanctuary begins just before the Naval Station. This is good for the local nesting passerines such as Varied Thrush, Hermit and Wilson's Warblers, Red Crossbill, Western Tanager, Pacific-slope Flycatcher, Wrentit, and Winter Wren.

Shore Acres State Park. Without a doubt, Shore Acres is one of Oregon's most beautiful state parks. The botanical gardens here are very good for hummingbirds, most notably Anna's and Rufous, but Allen's occurs here (rarely) at the northern-most point of its normal range. The grounds also attract many warblers, vireos, flycatchers, tanagers, finches, and thrushes during migration. In 1974, a Prothonotary Warbler was found here, so check each and every migrant possible. Just below the lookout point to the north of the gardens are rocky tidal areas frequented by Surfbirds, both turnstones, and Black Oystercatchers.

Cape Arago and Simpson Reef. Located to the immediate south of Shore Acres St. Pk., these two headlands are scenic but of marginal interest for birding. Migrant loons, grebes, gulls, Brown Pelicans, and cormorants are rarely joined by the less frequent shearwaters, storm-petrels, Black-legged Kittiwakes, alcids, or jaegers. The Simpson Reef lookout is frequented by basking Harbor Seals and the occasional Elephant Seal.

Bandon Area

Habitats: CE, OB, UR
Elevation: 0-70'
Seasons: Sp ● ● ●   S ● ●   F ● ● ● ●   W ● ●

This estuary — the mouth of the Coquille River — has hosted some of Oregon's most spectacular shorebird finds in recent years including Mongolian Plover, Bristle-thighed Curlew, Bar-tailed and Hudsonian Godwits, Rufous-necked Stint, and Buff-breasted, Curlew, and Sharp-tailed Sandpipers! The best viewing areas vary according to the tide. During the highest tide, when most of the estuary fills up, head to the river's mouth. A good spot is reached by heading west on First St. (Scenic Beach Loop Dr.) in the town of Bandon; about 1 mile west of town is a sandy flat area with seaweed-covered rocks and pilings. This is good for the larger shorebirds during a high tide — look for Black Oystercatcher, Whimbrel, Marbled Godwit, and Willet resting on the rocks. Farther along the Scenic Beach Loop Dr. are viewpoints overlooking the large offshore rocks of Coquille Point. These are the summer home of nesting Western Gulls, Pelagic Cormorants, Pigeon Guillemots, and, if you look closely, Tufted Puffins.

The best shorebird area is found along Riverside Rd. which heads north and east from Bandon, paralleling the lower river as far as US 101. About 0.75 miles northeast of the sewage treatment plant in Bandon, pull over onto the left side of Riverside Rd. and follow the trail down to the marshy flats. This is where most of the rarities have occurred. The viewing here is best at a mid to nearly high tide; a scope is almost a necessity. Across the river from this point watch for large flocks of dowitchers, Dunlin, and peeps; Golden-Plover, Red Knot, Semipalmated Sandpiper, and Long-billed Curlew occur here almost every year. Black-shouldered Kites have also been seen in the dunes across the river.

A third viewing area for shorebirds is reached from the north side of the estuary. Just north of the US 101 bridge, turn west onto Bullard's Beach St. Pk. Rd. and follow the signs to the lighthouse. 1.3 miles from the highway turn left when you reach the first dune area. Another 1.5 miles turn left onto a small gravel road that leads down to a bend in the estuary. These flats are especially good for the Marbled Godwits during a mid-tide, and both Bar-tailed and Hudsonian have been found here more than once.

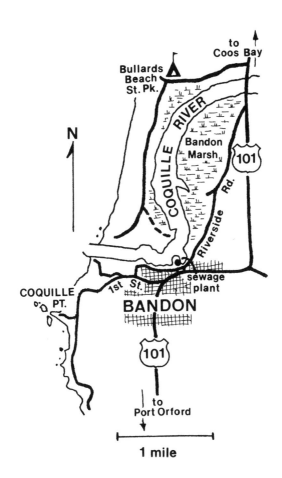

Cape Blanco State Park

Habitats: RS, OC, OB, WF
Elevation: 200'
Seasons: Sp • • • S • • F • • • W • •

The marked turnoff to Cape Blanco is located on US 101, just south of the Sixes River crossing (and the town of Sixes). The main birding attraction of Cape Blanco is the lighthouse and Coast Guard Station, located at the end of the road about 6 miles from US 101. Check any open brushy areas along this road for the tiny Allen's Hummingbird, a relatively common species; but be aware that Rufous also occur here. Seabird viewing from Cape Blanco is poor to fair, depending on viewing conditions, time of year, and whatever you're using to look at birds with. Immediately offshore is the Blanco Reef and numerous rocks (part of the Oregon Islands NWR system), so most pelagic species such as shearwaters, jaegers, alcids, and terns remain far west of the cape. The offshore rocks do support nesting cormorants, murres, and gulls, and Cape Blanco is good for watching migrant waterfowl, loons, and grebes pass by. The real attraction of Cape Blanco, however, is the chance of finding vagrant warblers during migration in spring and fall. So far, patient observers have turned up such species as Black-and-White Warbler, Blackpoll, American Redstart, Magnolia Warbler, and Black-throated Blue Warbler. Most of these vagrants are found in the early morning following a night of steady winds coming off the ocean.

Coastal Curry County

Habitats: FA, RS, CE, WF, BR, UR
Elevation: 0-1750'
Seasons: Sp • • •   S • •   F • • •   W • •

The mouth of the Rogue River offers some of the only coastal meadow habitat on the southern Oregon coast. The small boat basin at Wedderburn, on the north side of the river, is good for wintering grebes, ducks, and occasionally even alcids. Gulls and terns frequently loaf on the sandy flats. At the south end of the US 101 bridge, turn east to explore the meadows up the Rogue River. Specialties to look for in this part of Oregon include the local Black Phoebe and the Red-shouldered Hawk.   The phoebe is usually seen around rural houses and bridges where it nests; the species is resident along the southern Oregon coast roughly north to Cape Blanco. The Red-shouldered Hawks are frequently found in more wooded areas where they enjoy hunting from inconspicuous perches. This species is also most common in Oregon along the coastal areas north to about Cape Arago. Other unique species to watch for in the coastal meadows of Curry County include California Quail, Scrub Jay, Western Bluebird, and Lesser Goldfinch; although rather frequent south of Cape Blanco, these species are extremely rare on the coast north of that headland.

Other good roads that enter the coastal meadowlands of Curry County can be found at Hunter Creek (about 1.5 miles south of Gold Beach) and at Pistol River (about 9 miles south of Gold Beach).

Brookings

Habitats: UR, FA, RS, OB, CE
Elevation: 0-130'
Seasons: Sp • • •   S • • •   F • • •   W • • •

The Brookings area of south Curry Co. is best known among
Oregon birders for three things — Red-shouldered Hawk,
Allen's Hummingbird, and Black Phoebe. All three species are
seldom reported north of Cape Blanco, and in recent years the
area around the mouth of the Chetco River has proven to be
one of the most reliable sites for these birds. Red-shouldered
Hawks have been seen along west Benham Rd. in the town of
Harbor, on the south shore of the Chetco. This road intersects
US 101 about 1.25 miles south of the river. Red-shouldered
Hawks prefer the lightly-wooded coastal meadowlands that
many Red-tailed Hawks avoid. West Benham Rd. also takes
you down to the Brookings-Harbor boat basin and the mouth
of the Chetco River — a good place to study loons, grebes,
pelicans, cormorants, and diving ducks. Sport Haven Co. Pk.,
at the road's end, is good for migrant and wintering gulls and
terns. Rarities here have included Black-legged Kittiwake,
Common Tern, and Elegant Tern. Another good drive
through Red-shouldered Hawk habitat is along the South Bank
Chetco River Rd., reached by turning north at the southeast
end of the US 101 bridge.

At the northwest end of the US 101 bridge, make the first
north turn and enter Azalea St. Pk.   This beautiful day-use
park is a sure bet during summer for the Allen's Hummingbird, a species present from March through at least September.
Allen's Hummingbirds are best found during April, May, and
June when the males are in full plumage and performing their
unique courtship flight; this display flight is often the best
way to tell Allen's from the nearly identical Rufous Hummer,
which is also found here. A third species, the larger Anna's
Hummer, is also common — it also remains through the
winter.

In central Brookings (west of Azalea St. Pk.), turn south off US
101 on Center St. to explore the Mill Beach area. There are

some log ponds near the end of the road that have produced Black Phoebe in the past; also check the sewage treatment plant to the south near Chetco Point.

At the very northwest end of Brookings is Harris Beach St. Pk. The camping area is good for local passerines (a guaranteed Wrentit), and the park offers a good view of offshore Goat Island. This inaccessible rock is home to nesting seabirds including Common Murre, Pigeon Guillemot, Tufted Puffin, and Western Gull. Goat Island is part of the inaccessible Oregon Islands NWR, a string of nesting rocks and islands that stretch from Tillamook Head to the California border.

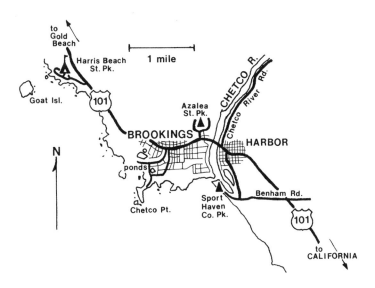

Region C

Willamette Valley
Western Cascades

Acorn Woodpecker

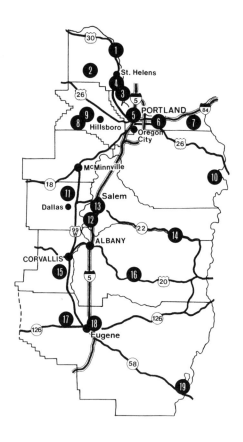

Trojan Nuclear Power Plant Grounds

Habitats: FW, BF, BR, WF
Elevation: 18'
Seasons: Sp • • •   S • • •   F • •   W • • •

Regardless of your views on nuclear power, the grounds around Trojan should be visited for the rich birdlife found there. This area, much of it open to public access, is located about 45 miles north of Portland on the east side of US 30.

An interpretive nature trail heads north from the visitor center to a public viewing blind that overlooks one of the area's numerous sheltered backwater ponds. These sloughs are traditional wintering areas for the rare Trumpeter Swan. The species still occurs here, but it is greatly outnumbered by the Tundra Swan. Other wintering birds to look for include Great Blue and Green-backed Herons, Canada Goose, Wood Duck, Common Goldeneye, and Common and Hooded Mergansers. Osprey and Bald Eagles are frequent migrants. Typical marsh birds found here include American Bittern, Ruddy Duck, Virginia Rail, Sora, and Marsh Wren. South of the visitor center, across the main road, there is a series of small quiet ponds surrounded by deciduous woods and small tracts of lawn. Wigeon flocks that winter here usually have a few Eurasian birds mixed in. Resident passerines include chickadees, Bushtit, nuthatches, both kinglets, Bewick's and Winter Wrens, Steller's and Scrub Jays, Hutton's Vireo, and Varied Thrush. During summer, look for Black-throated Gray Warbler, Black-headed Grosbeak, Northern Oriole, Warbling and Solitary Vireos, Western Tanager, Cedar Waxwing, Red-breasted Sapsucker, Swainson's Thrush, Pacific-slope Flycatcher, and Purple Finch.

Vernonia

Habitats: FW, WF, BF, UR, BR
Elevation: 600'
Seasons: Sp • • •   S • • •   F • •   W •

Located at the southeast corner of town just off OR 47 is the hard-to-miss Vernonia Log Pond. This former lumber mill property now serves as a city park with public access. A dirt road encircles the pond and offers excellent birding during the summer. Pied-billed Grebes abound on the marshy pond, and occasional migrant ducks may drop in from time to time. Belted Kingfishers are common, and the pond is regularly visited by five species of swallows (a sixth, the Purple Martin, has occurred a number of times during migration). The heavy deciduous woodlands around the pond are home to Rufous Hummingbird, Pacific-slope Flycatcher, Steller's Jay, Black-capped and Chestnut-backed Chickadees, Bushtit, Warbling Vireo, Purple Finch, Black-headed Grosbeak, Black-throated Gray Warbler, Purple Finch, and Cedar Waxwing.

Washington Elementary School is located west of the log pond in Vernonia, also on OR 47. A side road just east of the school heads south to the sewage treatment plant. Although fenced off, the ponds are still visible from outside the compound. An old railroad right-of-way leads east from the school area through the brushy fields with boggy willow stands. Such locally uncommon species as House Wren, Lazuli Bunting, Yellow Warbler, Yellow-breasted Chat, and Lesser Goldfinch occur here.

Sauvie Island

Habitats: FA, FW, BR, BF, WF
Elevation: 5-15'
Seasons: Sp ● ● ●   S ● ●   F ● ● ● ●   W ● ● ● ●

Lying at the confluence of the Columbia and Willamette Rivers, this large island is one of Oregon's most important wintering areas and migration stops for migrant waterfowl. Tens of thousands of Canada Geese winter here, mostly birds of the dusky, lesser, and Taverner's races. Many other waterfowl species abound, and it is one of very few staging and wintering areas in western Oregon for Sandhill Cranes. Numbers of wintering raptors can be astounding, especially Bald Eagles and buteo hawks. A few choice spots on the island serve as migration stops for shorebirds, and some rather suprising species have occurred. The numerous brushy areas, oak woodlands, conifer stands, and dense patches of riparian growth support a wide variety of smaller land birds, especially during migration and winter.

Land ownership on Sauvie Island is roughly split in half; the northern part is mostly ODFW land, while most of the southern half is privately owned. During hunting season (November through March), most of the ODFW land is closed to public entry except by permit, but much of the best birding during this season can still be done from public access roads. It goes without saying that care should be taken not to trespass on private property.

To reach Sauvie Island, take US 30 north from Portland. The only road access to the island, the Sauvie Island Bridge, is about 10 miles north of downtown Portland. There is a small general store at the east end of the bridge, and checklists, maps, and other wildlife information are available at ODFW headquarters on the island.

To observe wintering or migrating waterfowl, drives around Gillihan Loop Rd., along Oak Island Rd., and the north reaches of Reeder Rd. are recommended. A spotting scope is almost a necessity to scan over the huge flocks of Canada Geese for the rare Emperor or Ross' Goose or Brant. Major concentrations of Snow and White-fronted Geese are usually found in the vicinity of Rentenaar Rd. and on Sturgeon Lake, just east of Oak Island. In addition to waterfowl, Oak Island Rd. also hosts a large number of wintering Sandhill Cranes.

During August, September, and early October, Coon Point and Racetrack Lake are the major shorebird spots on Sauvie Island. Among the typical species, such rarities as Sharp-tailed, Curlew, Stilt, and even Buff-breasted Sandpipers have occurred (but don't expect them). Semipalmated Sandpipers now occur at one or both of these sites every fall. Coon Point is also a major wintering area for Bald Eagles; as many as 20 may be seen from the view point on the dike.

The farmland that can be viewed from Gillihan Loop and Reeder Rd.'s is the best area to look for wintering gull flocks; up to 12 species have been reported from the island. The old (but still active) livestock feed plant at the southern tip of the island attracts huge numbers of gulls and blackbirds. Large flocks of Thayer's Gulls winter here, and Glaucous and Western Gulls occur annually. Rusty and Tricolored Black-birds have been found among the large blackbird flocks here and elsewhere on the island, usually during the winter. Sparrow flocks at this plant should definitely be checked; Harris' and Swamp have popped up more than once.

Sauvie Island is probably the best location in western Oregon for studying winter sparrow flocks. The main site for these birds is along Rentenaar Rd. at the north end of the island. Among the large concentrations of Golden-crowned, White-crowned, Song, Fox, Lincoln's, and even Savannah Sparrows, one should look for the more unusual species. Swamp and White-throated Sparrows winter here annually. Other good winter finds on Sauvie Island have included Harris', Brewer's, Chipping, Vesper, Tree, and Clay-colored. The wet, boggy sloughs along Rentenaar Rd. are the most reliable location to find the secretive Swamp Sparrow in Oregon, generally from November to March. Up to 5 of these sparrows have wintered here at once.

Raptors abound on Sauvie Island, especially in the more open areas from October through March. Most will be Red-tailed

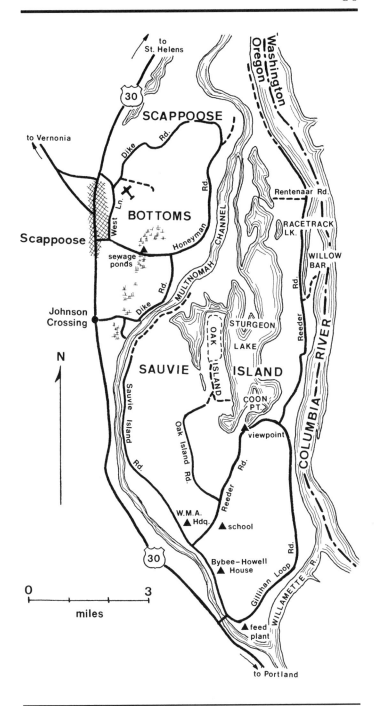

and Rough-legged Hawks, Northern Harriers, and American Kestrels, but Cooper's and Sharp-shinned Hawks, Merlins, and even Peregrine Falcons appear most winters. Rarities have included Ferruginous and Swainson's Hawks, Prairie Falcon, Gyrfalcon, Golden Eagle, and Black-shouldered Kite. The locally diminishing Short-eared Owl is still a regular winter visitor and rare nester on Sauvie Island.

For deep-water birds, scan the Columbia off the east side of the island. Loons, grebes, cormorants, and diving ducks are likely. This is also an excellent area to observe gulls when fish runs occur on the Columbia River.

Summer birdlife on Sauvie Island is much less dramatic, and the island can seem very quiet from May to early August. Typical nesting land birds include Wood-Pewee, Pacific-slope Flycatcher, Bushtit, Black-capped Chickadee, White-breasted Nuthatch, House and Bewick's Wrens, Cedar Waxwing, Warbling Vireo, Black-headed Grosbeak, Savannah Sparrow, Western Meadowlark, and Northern Oriole. Summering or nesting water birds to watch for include Pied-billed Grebe, American Bittern, Green-backed Heron, Wood Duck, Virginia Rail, Sora, and Common Snipe. Good areas for summer birding include the Sauvie Island School on Reeder Rd.; the trail around Oak Island; Willow Bar on the island's east side; the willow woods at Coon Point; and the marsh and woodlots at the historic Bybee-Howell House.

Scappoose Bottoms

Habitats: FA, FW, BR, BF
Elevation: 6-10'
Seasons: Sp • • • S • • F • • • W • • •

In the small community of Johnson Crossing (south of
Scappoose), turn east onto Dike Rd. off US 30. This is about
0.75 miles north of the Columbia-Multnomah Co. line. Dike
Rd. continues east and north, winding through Scappoose
Bottoms; eventually it joins Honeyman Rd., where you can
turn west onto Columbia Rd. to check the flooded fields and
ponds adjacent to the Scappoose Sewage Treatment Plant.
This immediate area often has wintering Great Egret and
Green-backed Herons, and the small pond just north of the
road supports a wide variety of wintering ducks. Such scarce
inland species as Barrow's Goldeneye, Greater Scaup, and even
Surf Scoter have occurred here. Back at the Dike Rd.-Honey-
man Rd. intersection, continue east on the latter road to
farther explore the open farmland. Honeyman Rd. continues
around Scappoose Bottoms until joining West Lane, just north
of Scappoose near the airport. At Scappoose, you may return
to US 30.

Most of Scappoose Bottoms consists of low-lying pastures and
farmland. Wintering and migrant goose flocks can appear
anywhere, and the area is well-known for its wintering raptors.
Up to 20 buteos can be seen on a swing through the area,
mostly Red-tailed and Rough-legged Hawks. Wintering
Swainson's and Ferruginous Hawks have occurred (very
rarely), and Bald Eagles are a frequent sight in the taller trees
along Multnomah Channel. Very rare, but reported more
than once, is the beautiful Black-shouldered Kite. Because
most of the land is privately owned and posted as such, there
are few opportunities to examine the local passerines. The
best sites include the upland brushy areas and mixed oak/
Douglas-fir woods along the side roads at the north end of the
airport. Look for Black-headed Grosbeak, Northern Oriole,
American Goldfinch, Red-breasted Sapsucker, wrens, White-
breasted Nuthatch, chickadees, and wintering sparrows in
these areas.

Portland

Habitats: UR, FA, BR, WF, BF, FW
Elevation: 10-1000'
Seasons: Sp • •   S • •   F • • •   W • • •

Oregon's largest city offers some good birding for those who
know where to look. Portland's park system includes a
number of "natural state" reserves that should serve as models
for other metropolitan areas. The following birding sites are
among the most popular in the greater Portland area. Specific
directions are not presented here; it is best to use this guide in
conjunction with a Portland city road map.

Pittock Bird Sanctuary. This small forested sanctuary, located
in Portland's West Hills on Cornell Rd., is the headquarters of
the Audubon Society of Portland. The Society maintains a
visitor center here, complete with active bird feeders, a wildlife
rehabilitation center, and one of the best book and gift stores
operated by any Audubon Society. Also pick up checklists,
maps, brochures, and the latest birding news here. The
sanctuary itself is mainly dense coniferous forest land that
occupies a steep ravine. A series of well-maintained foot trails
leads throughout the property. Most of the local breeding
birds of this habitat occur here — Band-tailed Pigeon, Rufous
Hummingbird, Vaux's Swift, Pacific-slope Flycatcher, Steller's
Jay, Chestnut-backed Chickadee, Bewick's Wren, Varied
Thrush, Swainson's Thrush, Warbling and Hutton's Vireos,
Black-throated Gray Warbler, Western Tanager, and Black-
headed Grosbeak are typically encountered along the trails.
A small pond below the visitor center supports summering
Wood Ducks and the occasional migrant Great Blue Heron.

Forest Park. Located in extreme northwest Portland, Forest
Park is the largest city park in the United States. Habitats
found here (and their associated birds) are very similar to
those at the Pittock Sanctuary — dense forest of Douglas-fir,
western red cedar, big-leaf maple, and red alder. There are no
public facilities in Forest Park, but a lengthy trail system offers
a good sampling of the local flora and fauna. Forest Park can
be especially good for nighttime owling. Screech, Great

Horned, Pygmy, Saw-whet, and even Long-eared have all been reported.

Oaks Bottom Park. Located in southeast Portland along the Willamette River, Oaks Bottom is a spectacular birding site throughout the year. The park consists mainly of marshy wooded river bottoms interspersed with brushy areas. Great Blue Herons, the official city bird of Portland, nest in a rookery on Ross Island, just west of Oaks Bottom; these birds are very common in the wetter areas of the park. During migration check the woodlots for numerous warblers, vireos, flycatchers, thrushes, and finches. Nesting species of interest include Wood Duck, Spotted Sandpiper, Green-backed Heron, Screech-Owl, Willow Flycatcher, swallows, and Bushtit. During winter check the sparrow flocks found in the blackberries — White-throated and Swamp have both appeared more than once, and wintering Orange-crowned Warblers are always exciting. Winter raptor searches usually turn up American Kestrels, Sharp-shinned or Cooper's Hawks, and sometimes even a Merlin. One winter a Red-shouldered Hawk took up residence along the railroad tracks near the river.

Crystal Springs Rhododendron Test Gardens. This park with a beautiful collection of rhododendrons and azaleas is located a few blocks east of Oaks Bottom, near Reed College. During winter this is one of the best places to study waterfowl in the state. The local tame Mallards and "barnyard" ducks are joined by good numbers of wigeon (always a few Eurasian present), Lesser Scaup, Bufflehead, Canvasback, and Ruddy Ducks. Less common species include Canada Goose, Greater Scaup, Gadwall, Common Goldeneye, Hooded Merganser, and Green-winged Teal. Pied-billed Grebes winter in good numbers, and a few remain through the summer on the quieter backwaters and ponds. Wood Ducks are a major attraction, even for non-birders, and there are few places where the species allows such a close approach. Winter passerine flocks are worth checking out. Orange-crowned Warblers are recorded here virtually every winter on the Portland Christmas Bird Count, and other winter rarities have included Hermit Warbler and Black-throated Gray Warbler. Green-backed

Herons are frequently encountered in the less disturbed backwater areas any time of year.

Marine Drive. A drive along this road between I-5 and Troutdale can be quite productive from September to May. Following the Columbia River, Marine Dr. is a good route to use when looking for deep-water birds such as loons (three species have occurred), grebes, diving ducks, geese, gulls, and terns. The pilings located along the river just east of the I-205 bridge support nesting Purple Martins during the summer. Where Marine Dr. passes the Portland International Airport, look for open-country birds such as Rough-legged and Red-tailed Hawks, falcons, gulls, Horned Lark, and Northern Shrike during the winter. The airport area has also turned up some rarities such as Western Kingbird, Say's Phoebe, Sage Thrasher, Loggerhead Shrike, Harris' Sparrow, and Lapland Longspur.

Tryon Creek State Park. Located in extreme southwest Portland just north of Lake Oswego, Tryon Creek is yet another hillside park occupied mainly by dense Douglas-fir forest. In addition to the typical birds of this habitat, Tryon Creek is good for wintering Anna's Hummingbird and Band-tailed Pigeon. An excellent visitor center with interpretive displays, checklists, maps, and trail guides is located near the main parking lot.

Lower Sandy River

Habitats: WF, BF, RA, FA, FW
Elevation: 20-510'
Seasons: Sp ● ● ●   S ● ● ●   F ● ● ●   W ● ●

On the east side of the Sandy River, exit off I-84 to enter Lewis and Clark State Park, a good stop for local nesting birds. Habitat here is mostly riparian river bottoms with extensive cottonwood forests. From April to September, expect such species as Vaux's Swift, Rufous Hummingbird, Downy Woodpecker, Western Wood-Pewee, Willow Flycatcher, five species of swallows, Scrub Jay, Black-capped Chickadee, House and Bewick's Wrens, Cedar Waxwing, Warbling Vireo, up to eight species of warblers, Black-headed Grosbeak, Brewer's Blackbird, Brown-headed Cowbird, Northern Oriole, and American Goldfinch. In the extensive stands of cottonwood, look and listen for the Red-eyed Vireo, a very rare local summer bird in Western Oregon. Lazuli Bunting may be found in the more open brushy areas north of the Interstate, and the Sandy River itself supports Common Merganser, Spotted Sandpiper, and Belted Kingfisher in the vicinity of Lewis and Clark Park.

Continuing south along the old Crown Point Scenic Highway, watch for Dabney St. Pk., some 2.75 miles from Lewis and Clark St. Pk. Also situated along the Sandy River, Dabney Park is more heavily forested with stands of Douglas-fir and other conifers. Woodland species are more likely to be found here than at Lewis and Clark Park. During spring and summer look for Ruffed Grouse, Band-tailed Pigeon, owls, Red-breasted Sapsucker, Hammond's Flycatcher (migrant), Steller's Jay, Chestnut-backed Chickadee, Red-breasted Nuthatch, Brown Creeper, kinglets, Solitary and Hutton's Vireos, Townsend's and Hermit Warblers (migrants), Black-throated Gray Warbler (nests), Western Tanager, and Purple Finch. Wintertime often bring birds from even higher nesting areas — Hairy and Pileated (rare) Woodpeckers, accipiters, Varied and Hermit Thrushes, Pine Siskin, Red Crossbill, and Evening Grosbeak. From Dabney Park the Crown Point Scenic Highway continues east and enters the Columbia River Gorge.

Oxbow County Park, located about 3 miles upriver from
Dabney St. Pk., is best reached via Troutdale, back at the
beginning of the Scenic Highway. In Troutdale, head due
south on Troutdale Rd. for about 4 miles, then turn east on
S.E. Division. After 1.5 miles, Division merges with Oxbow
Parkway, which veers off to the southeast. Follow this road
down into Oxbow Park, about 4 miles from the Troutdale Rd.
This county park is situated in the scenic Sandy River Gorge,
and it offers unique birding for an area so close to a major city.
The day-use picnicking area is located at the northwest part of
the park and offers mixed conifer-broadleaf forest and riparian
floodplain. The camping area is set in deep old-growth and
second-growth Douglas-fir forest. A series of trails winds
throughout the large park; checklists, maps, and other information can be obtained at the park headquarters near the
entrance. There is a nominal entry fee and an additional
camping fee if you wish to stay overnight.

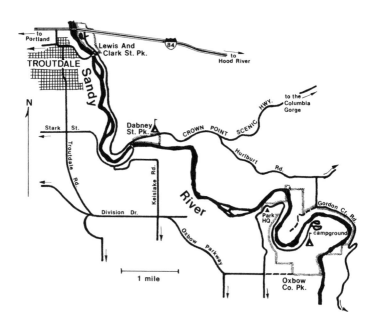

The Sandy River is scenic and often rough as it passes through Oxbow Park; this is a good place for migrant Harlequin Ducks during May. Common Merganser and Mallard nest in the park. Also look for Belted Kingfisher, Spotted Sandpiper, Rough-winged Swallow, and Dipper along the river. Oxbow is particularly well known for its nesting Ospreys, which can be seen anywhere in the park. The most common nesting area is among snags near the campground. Passerines of note include Steller's Jay, Olive-sided and Hammond's Flycatcher, Swainson's and Varied Thrushes, Solitary Vireo, Black-throated Gray and Townsend's (migrant) Warblers, Wilson Warbler, Western Tanager, Chipping Sparrow, and Pine Siskin. During winter, such "mountain" rarities as Gray Jay, Townsend's Solitaire, and even Cassin's Finch have occurred. Check the flowering plants at the headquarters buildings for summer hummingbirds — most will be Rufous, but Anna's and Calliope have also been found. The headquarters area has riparian habitat for Screech-Owl, and Pygmy, Great Horned, and Saw-whet can be heard anywhere in the park. Unfortunately, there is not nearly enough old-growth forest in Oxbow Park to support Spotted Owls.

Larch Mountain

Habitats: WF, BR, FA, RR, BF
Elevation: 800-4055'
Seasons: Sp • • • S • • • F • • • W • •

Located about 45 miles east of Portland, Larch Mountain is a popular day-use area most famous for its spectacular vista of Mt. Hood and the other peaks of the northern Cascades. This alone is worth a trip to the site, but Larch Mountain is also the closest site to the Portland area for finding mountain birds.

From the town of Corbett, continue east on the Columbia Gorge Scenic Highway toward Crown Point St. Pk. About 2 miles east of Corbett, take the right (southeast) turnoff onto the marked Larch Mountain Rd. Follow this well-maintained, paved road to the mountain's summit, a distance of about 15.5 miles from Corbett.

At an elevation of 4055', Larch Mountain is covered with dense forests of Douglas-fir, red cedar, western hemlock, and even grand and subalpine fir. From May to mid-June is the best time for birding when most passerines are in full song. Larch Mountain is a sure bet for finding the beautiful Hermit Warbler. But be aware that the very similar Townsend's Warbler appears here at the higher elevations, and the sound-alike Black-throated Gray Warbler may occur in broadleaf or mixed forest at the lower elevations. Other common summer species near the parking area and picnic grounds at the summit include Steller's Jay, Chestnut-backed Chickadee, Winter Wren, Hammond's and Olive-sided Flycatchers, Hermit and Varied Thrushes, Evening Grosbeak, Western Tanager, Pine Siskin, and Chipping Sparrow. Occasionally, birds of the higher, more easterly mountains drift over to this area, especially during late summer and fall. Calliope Hummingbirds have been seen at the Larch Mountain viewpoint at least three times, and territorial Townsend's Solitaires may also be found in the open areas at the summit. Rare wanderers have included Cassin's Finch, Mountain Chickadee, Mountain Bluebird, and Williamson's Sapsucker. Gray Jays may be encountered anywhere on Larch Mountain, but check the picnic area first.

About 5 miles below the summit on Larch Mountain Rd. there is much logging activity. Just after entering the Mt. Hood N.F. from the west on Larch Mountain Rd., turn right (south) on either N.F. Rd. 1509 or N.F. Rd. 20 to explore the open clear-cut areas for the rich birdlife. These roads are blocked by gates arout 3 or 4 miles from their junction with Larch Mountain Rd.; the gates mark the northern boundary of Portland's Bull Run Watershed, an area closed to the public. Between the gates and the main road are numerous pull-outs and spur roads that offer excellent birding opportunities during spring and summer. Check the clear cuts and the bordering forest for such local species as Mountain Quail, Band-tailed Pigeon, Common Raven, Willow Flycatcher, Western Bluebird, House Wren, MacGillivray's Warbler, and Lazuli Bunting. Long thought to be extremely rare west of the Cascades Crest, the Dusky Flycatcher has been reported on territory in these clear cuts a number of times. Townsend's Solitaires also nest here in small numbers.

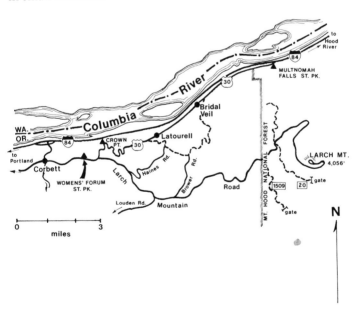

Scoggins Valley Park

Habitats: FW, WF, BF, BR, FA
Elevation: 350'
Seasons: Sp • • •   S • • •   F • • • •   W • • •

Take OR 47 south from Forest Grove about 6 miles to Scoggins
Valley Rd. on the west. Follow the signs to Scoggins Valley
Park, another 4 miles or so from the highway. The park's
main road circles Henry Hagg Lake, a large man-made reservoir surrounded by coniferous and mixed forest. A series of
hiking trails also circles the lake, and there are a number of
picnic grounds, boat landings, and view points that offer good
birding opportunities.

At the dam end of the lake look for the deep-water species
such as loons, grebes, Double-crested Cormorant, diving
ducks, and Common Mergansers. Every winter these typical
birds are joined by rarities such as Pacific or Red-throated
Loons, Red-necked Grebe, scoters, or even Oldsquaw. Large
rafts of Ring-necked Ducks, Canvasback, and Lesser Scaup
regularly winter on the lake. At the north reaches of the lake
look for concentrations of Mallard, Pintail, Green-winged Teal,
and American Wigeon (with the token 2 or 3 Eurasians mixed
in). Particularly good birding areas at the north end of the
lake include the mouths of Tanner and Scoggins Creeks.
During low water there are extensive mudflats at these sites
that are good for shorebirds and gulls. Hooded Mergansers
and Green-backed Herons seem to prefer these quiet backwater
areas, the latter species mainly in summer. The boat landing
on the lake's west shore is a good place to scope over the inlet
of Scoggins Creek, probably the best area for water birds.
Ospreys are regular migrants over the lake, and Bald Eagles
occasionally take up residence during the winter.

Owling around the lake can be very productive most any time
of year. Great Horned and Screech-Owls are common, and
Saw-whet and Pygmy-Owls are frequently encountered
(heard). In recent years Long-eared Owls have been discovered nesting in the lakeside woods; they seem to prefer the
drier Douglas-fir/oak/ash woods interspersed with open fields
on the northeast side of the lake.

Good land birding can be found throughout the park, but outstanding sites during migration and summer include the woods at the handicap-access dock (the west end of the dam) and at Scoggins Creek picnic area. The latter site features a good variety of migrant warblers, vireos, flycatchers, Western Tanagers, Black-headed Grosbeak, and the like. Dippers may be seen along the rougher stretches of the creek, and a territorial Red-eyed Vireo summered here one year. Band-tailed Pigeons favor the open woods along the creek at this site during the summer.

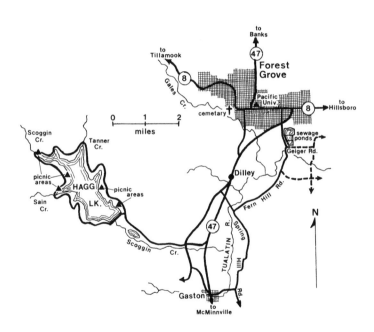

Forest Grove

Habitats: UR, FW, BF, FA
Elevation: 175'
Seasons: Sp • • • S • • F • • • • W • • •

The Forest Grove sewage ponds are reached by heading south on OR 47 from its junction with OR 8 in Forest Grove; less than a mile from this intersection, turn south onto Fern Hill Rd. and look for the sewage ponds and facility immediately after crossing the railroad tracks. Although they are posted for no trespassing, birders are welcome during business hours after checking in at the main office. Although at their best during migration, these ponds offer excellent birding any time of year. The center pond (there are three) and the extensive marsh east of it support nesting or summering species that are very local elsewhere in this part of Oregon. Look for Gadwall, Blue-winged and Cinnamon Teal, American Wigeon, Ruddy Duck, American Bittern, Virginia Rail, Sora, Yellow-headed Blackbird, and Marsh Wren. Wilson's Phalaropes appear most springs and occasionally spend the summer. During migration the ponds attract an amazing variety of shorebirds if waterlevels are low enough. More then 20 species have been reported including such rarities as Golden and Black-bellied Plovers, Black-necked Stilt, Ruddy Turnstone, and Semipalmated, Stilt, and Sharp-tailed Sandpipers! Unusual gulls and terns are reported almost annually — Caspian Tern and Bonaparte's Gull are almost annual visitors, and rarities such as Western Gull, Sabine's Gull, and Common, Forster's, and Arctic Terns have occurred.

Winter brings large numbers of Tundra Swans (and a few Trumpeters each year) and Canada Geese to the ponds and nearby farm fields. Hundreds of ducks occur from late September through April (as long as the water doesn't freeze), and grebes, loons, cormorants, and non-Canada geese may be found then as well. Geiger Rd., bordering the ponds on the south, is lined with dense hedge rows that shelter large wintering sparrow flocks; among the typical Golden-crowned, White-crowned, Song, Lincoln's, and Fox, look for smaller numbers of Savannah and White-throated Sparrows each year.

Records of Lark, Tree, Clay-colored, Harris', and Swamp
Sparrows have also come from these Geiger Rd. brush patches.
These sparrows, along with large numbers of goldfinches
(Lessers are uncommon), siskins, blackbirds, finches, juncos,
and other winter passerines, attract a variety of raptors this
time of year. Accipiters, Northern Harriers, Red-tailed Hawks,
and American Kestrels are regulars, and Bald Eagles, Merlins,
Rough-legged Hawks, and Northern Shrikes are infrequently
reported.

In the town of Forest Grove itself, check the mature groves of
oak trees at Pacific University for the northernmost permanent
colony of Acorn Woodpeckers known. The university grounds
are also good for migrant passerines and wintering accipiters.

At the western end of Forest Grove, OR 8 (Pacific Ave.) veers to
the north; continue due west instead, past the junior high
school, to Forest View Cemetery, a good spot for wintering
songbirds and the attendant raptors that feed on them. The
cemetery sits on a hill that overlooks extensive fields to the
west.

Timothy Lake

Habitats: WF, FW, BR
Elevation: 3217'
Seasons: Sp • • S • • • • F • • • • W •

From Estacada, head east on OR 224 about 28.5 miles to Ripplebrook CG. Turn east here and follow Mt. Hood N.F. Rd. 57 as it parallels the Oak Grove Fork of the Clackamas River; Timothy Lake is approximately 15 miles from Ripplebrook CG on this road. Upon reaching Timothy Lake, N.F. Rd. 57 follows the lake's southern shore some 3.25 miles to N.F. Rd. 42, sometimes called the Oregon Skyline Rd. By turning left at this junction, you may proceed to US 26 (Mt. Hood Highway), another 8 miles or so to the northeast.

Timothy Lake serves as an amazing magnet for migrating waterbirds, including some very surprising species. During fall, from late July to October, look for loons, grebes, cormorants, geese, and diving ducks that frequently drop in. Timothy Lake has hosted all four species of Oregon loons, including one of the state's only inland record of a Yellow-billed Loon! Other rarities have included Surf and White-winged Scoters, Oldsquaw, Greater Scaup, and Red-necked Grebe. The four campgrounds on the lake's south shore (Pine Point, Hoodview, Gone Creek, and Oak Fork) offer the best viewing opportunities for migrant waterbirds — be sure to bring a scope for the best results.

There are excellent hiking opportunities around Timothy Lake that will give a good sampling of the local summer passerines. The fifth shoreline campground (Meditation Point, on the north shore) is reached only by foot, about 1.5 miles from the dam along the popular Oregon Skyline Trail (see map). This trail closely follows the north shore, while the famous Pacific Crest Trail parallels the east shore. Typical forest species to expect along these trails include Rufous Hummingbird, Pileated and Hairy Woodpeckers, Hammond's Flycatcher, Steller's Jay, Chestnut-backed Chickadee, Varied and Hermit Thrushes, kinglets, vireos, Hermit and Townsend's Warblers,

Western Tanager, finches, and Evening Grosbeak. The campground at Little Crater Lake, just northeast of Timothy Lake, is excellent for species that nest in wet meadows — Spotted Sandpiper, Nashville Warbler, Lincoln's Sparrow, and White-crowned Sparrow are among these species.

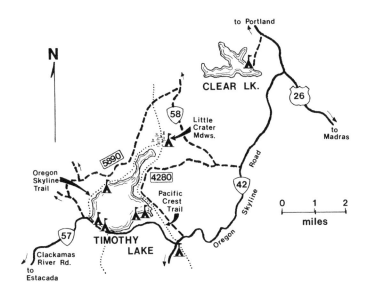

Baskett Slough National Wildlife Refuge

Habitats:	FA, FW, BF, RA, BR
Elevation:	190-420'
Seasons:	Sp • • • S • • F • • • • W • • • •

Baskett Slough NWR is located a mile west of US 99W, just north of the town of Rickreall (this is about 9 miles west of Salem on OR 22). There are two main access roads into the refuge. The first is Smithfield Rd., about 3.5 miles north of Rickreall off US 99W. The second is Coville Rd., 2 miles north of Rickreall, also off US 99W. Smithfield Rd. enters the northern, more upland regions of the refuge. At the intersection of Smithfield and Livermore Rds. is a large grain storage structure with ornamental trees and brush around it. Check this area for wintering sparrows, finches, blackbirds, chickadees, and other small birds. On the south side of Smithfield Rd., across from the building, is a gated hiking trail that leads onto the refuge. This short trail heads up to Morgan Lake, probably the best birding site on the refuge. Birders are permitted to hike the trail to Morgan Lake from May to early September (consult the refuge manager at Finley NWR or the hunting pamphlets for exact dates of closures). During August, check the lake for migrant shorebirds, gulls, and terns (rare). Among the typical species here are both yellowlegs, Long-billed Dowitcher, Semipalmated Plover, Western and Least Sandpipers, Baird's Sandpiper, and Red-necked Phalarope. Rarities have included Stilt and Semipalmated Sandpipers, Red and Wilson's Phalaropes, and Common and Forster's Terns.

Coville Rd. cuts through the center of Baskett Slough NWR; along with OR 22 on the south border of the refuge, this is the best area for scoping winter goose concentrations. The two viewpoints at the west end of Coville Rd. and the two on OR 22 are the best areas to look for the "non-Canada" species among the large flocks. It should be noted that there is much interchange of geese between Baskett Slough, Ankeny, Finley, and even Sauvie Island refuges; therefore, if an Emperor

Goose or some other rare species occurs at one refuge, it very well may appear at one of the other three locations the next day or later that week. Also located on Coville Rd. is a hunter's check station with an adjacent parking lot. In recent winters this has been a good sparrow area; White-throated and Swamp Sparrows have occurred here. A dirt road leads north from the parking lot to a hiking trail in the upland woods. This is open all year.

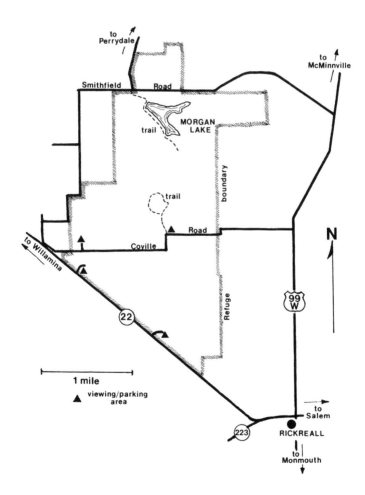

Ankeny
National Wildlife Refuge

Habitats: FA, BF, FW, RA, BR
Elevation: 170-300'
Seasons: Sp • • • S • • F • • • • W • • • •

Along with Baskett Slough and William L. Finley NWR's, Ankeny was established in the 1960's as a preserve for the threatened Dusky Canada Goose. These refuges combine open pastures and farm fields with brushy upland habitats and deciduous woodlots. Although still best known for its wintering geese, Ankeny NWR also attracts a wide variety of other species.

To reach Ankeny, head south on I-5 from Salem to the Ankeny Hill Exit (about 6 miles). The refuge is located about 1.5 miles west of this exit on Wintel Rd. About 2.5 miles from the I-5 exit on Wintel Rd. are two public parking areas, one north of the road and one on the south side. The north lot is a good vantage point for scoping the fields. The south lot has a nature trail (the only one on the refuge) that covers upland woods, fields, and brushy areas. This trail, open to the public from May through September, is good for the local nesting birds: California Quail, Mourning Dove, Wood-Pewee, Scrub Jay, Bushtit, White-breasted Nuthatch, House and Bewick's Wrens, Black-throated Gray, Yellow, Orange-crowned, and MacGillivray's Warblers, Black-headed Grosbeak, and Purple Finch. Acorn Woodpeckers can be found in the oaks, and Lesser Goldfinch occur throughout the refuge.

A good touring route for exploring the refuge (especially during winter when much of the area is closed to the public) is to take Wintel Rd. west to Buena Vista Rd.; follow Buena Vista Rd. northeast to its intersection with Ankeny Hill Rd.; then continue south on Ankeny Hill Rd. and back to the I-5 Interchange. This route takes the birder through the best viewing areas possible during the winter. The parking lot at the north end of Ankeny Hill Rd. is one of the best sites for scoping out the winter goose flocks. Most of the birds will be the Dusky Canada Goose, but look for small numbers of White-fronted and Snow Geese as well. Patient scoping has paid off with the discovery of wintering Brant, Ross' Geese, and even Emperor Geese in recent years. Another good site for scanning the fields is at the parking area on Buena Vista Rd. just southwest of its intersection with Ankeny Hill Rd. Not only do geese congregate here, but it is a good place to check wintering wigeon flocks for the handsome Eurasian species. Dunlin and smaller numbers of Long-billed Dowitchers also favor this area during fall and winter.

Be sure to watch for wintering raptors throughout Ankeny NWR. Bald Eagles favor the north area near the Willamette River while Red-tailed and Rough-legged Hawks, the two smaller accipiters, Merlin, Northern Harrier, and even Short-eared Owl may occur anywhere. The many brushy patches and hedgerows along the roads harbor wintering sparrow flocks, mostly White-crowns and Golden-crowns. Open areas also support American Pipit, Horned Lark, and Savannah Sparrow.

As with most federal refuges, Ankeny is closed to public entry from September through May, but the above-mentioned roads and parking areas stay open.

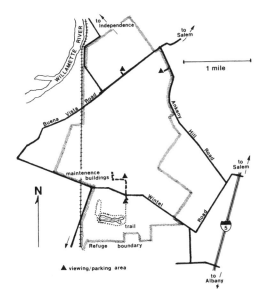

Salem

Habitats:	UR, FA, BR, FW, BF, WF
Elevation:	160'
Seasons:	Sp ••• S •• F ••• W ••••

Oregon's scenic capital city is graced with some very productive birding areas, including a number of sites within fifteen minutes driving time from the city center. An oasis for wintering birdlife in the greater Salem vicinity can be found in the area of the municipal airport.

Cascade Gateway Park. This combination of manicured parkland and undeveloped natural areas is located at the intersection of I-5 and OR 22. The park contains two small lakes, oak groves, open grassy areas, and thick riparian growth along Mill Creek. The north lake is wooded and frequently harbors Hooded Merganser, Wood Duck, Green-backed Heron, and other species of quiet backwater ponds. A short trail starts in the picnic area and winds around this lake; during winter, look for chickadee hordes, sparrows, nuthatches, woodpeckers, and even the occasional warbler (an amazing Black-and-White Warbler wintered here one year). Spring migrants include the typical Willamette Valley species — tanagers, flycatchers, warblers, vireos, thrushes, etc. Along Turner Rd. just north of the park entrance is a large gravel pit which usually holds water. During winter it is good for diving ducks, grebes, and other deep-water species.

McGilchrist Pond. Located on McGilchrist Rd. near its intersection with 25th St., this large pond is a tremendous wintering area for waterfowl, and large concentrations of gulls gather here at dusk to spend the night on the pond — up to ten species have been reported including Western, Glaucous, and Bonaparte's. It also attracts deep-water birds such as Double-crested Cormorants, Western and Horned Grebes, goldeneyes, scaup, Canvasback, and even scoters (rare).

There is much undeveloped grassy and brushy land around the Salem Airport, just west of Cascade Gateway Park. This is particularly good for wintering raptors such as Red-tailed and

Rough-legged Hawks, accipiters, and Short-eared Owls. Winter sparrow flocks here hold much potential and should be checked thoroughly.

Minto-Brown Island Park. This park is situated in the wet floodplain of the Willamette River; it is reached via River Rd. about 1.25 miles south and west of downtown Salem. During winter flocks of Canada Geese use the area for feeding and are occasionally joined by White-fronts or Snows. Nesting birds in this brushy riparian area include Wood Duck, Green-backed Heron, Virginia Rail, Common Snipe, Mourning Dove, and various passerines.

Detroit Lake

Habitats: WF, FW, BR, BF
Elevation: 1569'
Seasons: Sp • • • S • • • F • • • W •

Straddling the county line, Detroit Reservoir was constructed in 1953 for flood control along the Santiam River. It is easily reached via OR 22 some 46 miles southeast of Salem. This is a deep-water lake, completely surrounded by dense coniferous forests of Douglas-fir, hemlock, red cedar, and grand fir. It is very popular with boaters, waterskiiers, and other tourists during the summer months, but the area offers good birding all year round. The dam is located at the west end of the lake; this is a good spot to pull out and scope for deep-water birds including migrant loons, grebes, cormorants, and diving ducks. Black Swifts have been seen hawking insects high over Detroit Reservoir during adverse May and June weather. Most waterbirds of the lake can be scoped from the various pullouts along OR 22 and at Lakeshore St. Pk. at the lake's northeast corner. Good landbird areas include Hoover CG, reached by turning south off OR 22 in Idanha onto Blowout St. Follow this road across the river and continue west about a mile to the camping area. Also in Idanha, take the first turnoff to the south at the west end of town; this unnamed side road leads down to a fine riparian area just below the highway.

A recently discovered birding area, among the best in Marion County, is the marshy region known as Santiam Flats. To reach this popular area, turn south off OR 22 into the town of Detroit; turn left (southeast) on Detroit Ave., one block from the highway. Follow this unpaved road through the woods for a quarter-mile or so to its end at Santiam Flats. This boggy forest edge area is particularly attractive to late spring and early summer migrants. Some remarkable finds here have included Yellow-headed Blackbird, Gray, Dusky, and Ash-throated Flycatchers, Sage Thrasher, and Mountain Bluebird.

Summer birds of the forest surrounding Detroit Reservoir include Hammond's Flycatcher, Solitary Vireo, Hermit and Varied Thrushes, Chestnut-backed Chickadee, Townsend's and

Hermit Warblers, Western Tanager, Purple Finch, Pine Siskin, and Evening Grosbeak. The riparian areas and open woods along the lakeshore are home to such species as Rufous Hummingbird, House Wren, Swainson's Thrush, Yellow Warbler, Warbling Vireo, White-crowned Sparrow, and Lincoln's Sparrow.

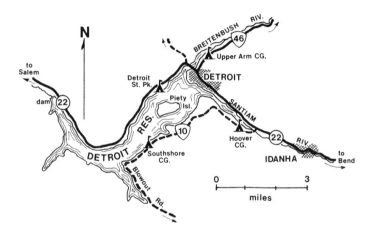

William L. Finley
National Wildlife Refuge

Habitats: FA, FW, RA, BF, BR, WF
Elevation: 250-520'
Seasons: Sp • • • •   S • •   F • • •   W • • •

Along with Baskett Slough and Ankeny NWR's, Finley NWR is mainly a waterfowl refuge, but it still offers a unique variety of Willamette Valley birding habitats. During hunting season (late September through April) most of the refuge is closed to the public to protect the wintering flocks; the main roads are still open, however, and offer excellent birding opportunities.

The northeast entrance to the refuge is located off US 99W, about 12 miles south of Corvallis; the southeast entrance is also off US 99W, another 3.5 miles farther south. At the northeast corner of the refuge is an extensive field area with low brushy growth. This is prime winter raptor habitat, and Red-tailed, Rough-legged, Cooper's, and Sharp-shinned Hawks and Northern Harrier are frequently reported from here. This area has infrequently supported a small number of wintering Black-shouldered Kites in recent years which have even nested on the refuge; check at refuge headquarters for recent kite sightings. Short-eared Owls may also be seen in these fields, and the denser stands of brushy growth have harbored wintering Long-eared Owls.

Farther west along this main refuge road is the headquarters complex where checklists, maps, and the latest birding news may be obtained. The headquarters area itself is good for the local summering species and wintering passerines. Typical nesters throughout the refuge include Northern Oriole, Black-headed Grosbeak, House Wren, Bewick's Wren, White-breasted Nuthatch, Purple Finch, Orange-crowned Warbler, and other birds of deciduous-riparian habitats. Western Bluebirds may be seen in the open areas, especially during the winter. Hiking trails starting near headquarters lead to major marshy areas, namely Brown Swamp and Cabell Marsh. These and McFadden Marsh at the southeast entrance are good for the local nesting marsh and swamp species — Pied-billed Grebe, American Bittern, Wood Duck, Green-backed Heron, and Virginia Rail, to name a few.

During periods of low water, check the east and south edges of Cabell Marsh and McFadden Marsh for migratory shorebirds; these two sites offer the only good wader habitat on the refuge.

Farther along the main access road west of headquarters are good hiking trails that lead through drier upland habitat. Along these trails look and listen for some of the more local

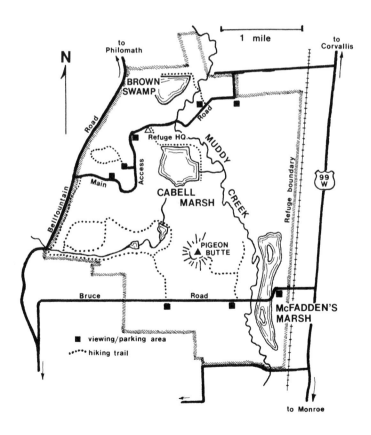

Willamette Valley species such as Mountain Quail, Ruffed
Grouse, Lazuli Bunting, Willow Flycatcher, Acorn and Lewis'
Woodpeckers, and MacGillivray's and Yellow Warblers.

Winter waterfowl viewing — especially large flocks of geese —
is best in the open flat country at the south end of the refuge.
Large flocks can be viewed from the roads near the town of
Bellfountain and along Bruce Rd. Among the thousands of
Canada Geese there are usually a few token White-fronted and
Snow Geese. Rarities that show up from time to time include
Brant, Ross' Goose, and Emperor Goose.

Foster Reservoir

Habitats: FW, WF, RA
Elevation: 650'
Seasons: Sp • • • S • • • F • • • W • •

Located east of Sweet Home, Foster Reservoir is a pleasant spot to visit for a sampling of the typical avifauna of the Cascades' west slope. The large lake is located along the Santiam River less than a mile above the town of Sweet Home. US 20 follows the lake's south shore, and the north shore is reached via north River Dr. out of Sweet Home.

Almost entirely surrounded by dense second-growth forests of Douglas-Fir, Foster Reservoir also includes some mixed riparian growth and deciduous woodland along the river inlets. Typical summering species to be encountered anywhere around the lake include Swainson's Thrush, Black-headed Grosbeak, Western Tanager, Pacific-slope Flycatcher, Band-tailed Pigeon, Hutton's, Warbling, and Solitary Vireos, Wilson's, Orange-crowned, and MacGillivray's Warblers, Vaux's Swift, Rufous Hummingbird, and the usual mixed flocks of chickadees, creepers, nuthatches, and wrens. Foster Lake CG (formerly known as Sunnyside CG), located at the inflow of the Middle Fork Santiam River, offers more riparian growth mixed in with the conifers — Red-eyed Vireos have been found here a number of times during the summer.

Water birds are best observed from the dam area. Osprey are frequent summer visitors, and Common Merganser nest on Foster Reservoir. On wilder stretches of the Santiam River upstream from the reservoir, look for migrant Harlequin Ducks — they usually appear in this part of Oregon during May. Dippers are also year-round residents along the Santiam River. Also check the lower part of Foster Reservoir for Green-backed Heron (summer), wintering goldeneyes and Bufflehead, Hooded Merganser, and Ruffed Grouse and Mountain Quail. Rough-winged Swallows nest below the dam, and Purple Martins have appeared rarely.

Another 4.5 miles or so up the Middle Fork Santiam River from Foster Reservoir is the larger, more undeveloped Green

Peter Reservoir. This artificial lake supports much the same birdlife as that found on Foster Reservoir, but because the coniferous forest is more extensive, expect such species as Blue Grouse, Pileated Woodpecker, Hammond's Flycatcher, Steller's and Gray Jays, Townsend's and Hermit Warblers, and Hermit Thrush.

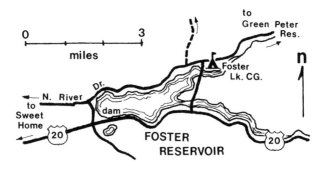

Fern Ridge Reservoir

Habitats: FW, BF, FA, WF, BR, UR
Elevation: 370-400'
Seasons: Sp • • •   S • • •   F • • • •   W • • • •

Located just west of US 99W, Fern Ridge Reservoir offers the
Eugene-based birder an easily reached wildlife area that can be
quite productive during the appropriate seasons. Habitats
found here are typical of the Willamette Valley wetland areas
— cattail marshes, brushy fields, canary grass, alder and willow
thickets, Douglas-fir groves, oak-covered upland areas, and
adjacent farmland. Main avian attractions include thousands
of wintering waterfowl (including geese and swans), winter
raptors, and migrant shorebirds and gulls. Passerine birds are
widespread and typical of most inland western Oregon birding
sites.

To reach the dam area — one of the best parts of the reservoir
for water birds — head west on Clear Lake Rd. out of Eugene.
A scope is highly recommended, especially during low water
periods when acres and acres of mudflats are exposed all
around the lake. Shorebird migration at Fern Ridge can be
spectacular during the fall. Among the usual species such
rarities as Golden-Plover, Sanderling, Short-billed Dowitcher,
Semipalmated Sandpiper, and even Stilt and Sharp-tailed
Sandpipers have been reported. Good scoping sites for
shorebirds and gulls include the south end of Shore Ln.; the
Richardson Point St. Pk. area; the west end of Royal Ave.; the
area just west of Perkin's Peninsula St. Pk.; and the peninsula
north of Zumwald Park.

Wintering raptors can be observed anywhere in the area. In
general, Sharp-shinned and Cooper's Hawks prefer the more
wooded areas, such as Krugur Park below the dam, while Red-
tailed and Rough-legged Hawks and Northern Harriers are
common in the open fields. Bald Eagles occasionally patrol
the shoreline during winter, and the smaller owls — Screech,
Saw-whet, and Pygmy — may occur in the denser oak woods.
In recent years the very rare Red-shouldered Hawk has been
reported wintering in the Fern Ridge area, preferring the wet

alder-oak woodlots shunned by most Red-tails. The local but increasingly more frequent Black-shouldered Kite occasionally establishes communal roosts in the reservoir area; one recent concentration numbering around 25 birds has been at the west end of Royal Ave.

Passerines around Fern Ridge are best observed at the three parks near the dam; the woods along Fir Butte Rd. west of the lake; Perkins Peninsula; and Zumwald Park. Nesting species include Black-headed Grosbeak, Yellow Warbler, Common Yellowthroat, Northern Oriole, Rufous-sided Towhee, Purple Finch, Warbling Vireo, American and Lesser Goldfinches, Cedar Waxwing, and Brown-headed Cowbird. These birds are joined by even more species during migration, especially flycatchers, warblers, vireos, and thrushes. Wintertime is well known for its amazingly varied sparrow flocks. Among the usual Fox, Song, White-crowned, and Golden-crowned, look for the less common Lincoln's, White-throated, and Savannah Sparrows. Such rarities as Harris', Brewer's, Tree, and Swamp Sparrows have occurred. Grasshopper Sparrows used to nest (in very small numbers and seldom every year) in the brushy areas of Fern Ridge Reservoir and in the Cantrell Rd. area, but they have not been present for years.

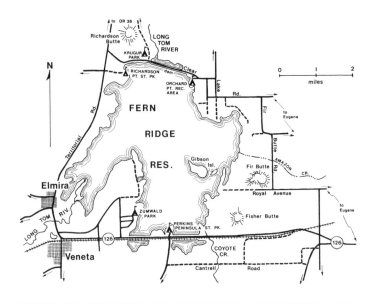

Eugene Area

Habitats: UR, FA, FW, BR, WF
Elevation: 420-500'
Seasons: Sp • • •   S • •   F • • •   W • • • •

The greater Eugene area offers some remarkable sites for birdwatchers limited to a metropolitan area. Due to the complex street and road layout, directions to these sites are generalized; the interested visitor should consult a city map for thorough directions.

Spencer Butte. This undeveloped forested hill lies south of town just off Willamette St. An excellent hiking trail less than a mile in length leads from the parking area, through Douglas-fir and mixed conifer-broadleaf forests, up to the grassy open summit with a spectacular view. Summer birds are typical of the western Oregon forests — Vaux's Swift, Rufous Humming-bird, Pacific-slope Flycatcher, Steller's and Scrub Jays, Black-capped and Chestnut-backed Chickadees, Red-breasted Nuthatch, Winter Wren, Swainson's Thrush, Varied Thrush, Warbling Vireo, Western Tanager, Purple Finch, and Pine Siskin. Watch for the local Mountain Quail, more often heard than seen, and the resident two or three Pileated Woodpeckers are infrequently heard. Hermit Warblers nest in the conifers, and Townsend's Solitaires have occurred during spring at the summit. Hutton's Vireo is an easy species to find on Spencer Butte, especially during summer.

Skinner Butte. This more developed park is located in the heart of Eugene, along the south shore of the Willamette River. It is very similar to Spencer Butte in habitat types and associated birds, but there is a paved road to the summit (Skinner Butte Loop) and the general aspect of this park is less wild and more manicured. In addition to the species listed above, listen for Pygmy-Owls among the more common Screech. Purple Martins are frequent visitors from nesting sites at Fern Ridge Reservoir and are sometimes seen feeding above the city. Wrentits have also been reported from Skinner Butte.

Alton Baker Park. This typical riverside city park is located in the central part of Eugene along the Willamette. It is part of a series of parks that make up the Willamette Greenway Park System stretching from Eugene to Portland. Alton Baker Park contains brushy, weedy garden plots along Day Island Rd. that attract an amazing variety of sparrows and other seed-eaters during the winter. Among the usual species are a few White-throated and Savannah Sparrows each winter. Rarities in this area have included Clay-colored, Chipping, Swamp, Lark, Harris', and Grasshopper Sparrows, Indigo Bunting, and Dickcissel. The nearby Autzen Stadium parking area hosted one of Oregon's only records of Black-backed Wagtail!

Danebo Pond. Located west of Eugene just outside the city limits, this small seasonal pond is full of water during winter and spring. During late summer and fall it may have wet mudflats that have attracted numerous shorebirds. Danebo Pond is located on Danebo Rd. about a mile north of OR 126. A gravel path leads from Danebo Rd. to the pond, offering access to a number of wetland habitats. Waterfowl that have been found here include such uncommon species as Cinna-mon and Blue-winged Teal, Gadwall, Northern Shoveler, and Canvasback (winter). Yellow-headed Blackbirds have been reported during summer, and a walk along the slough may kick up a Green-backed Heron. Good marsh species found here include American Bittern, Marsh Wren, Sora, and Virginia Rail.

Mahlon Municipal Airport. The general area of Eugene's airport is reached via Green Hill Rd., northwest of the city. This vast open land of farm fields, hedgerows, and isolated stands of trees is one of the most profitable birding areas during winter. The open fields around the runways attract winter raptors such as the ever-present Red-tailed and Rough-legged Hawks, Northern Harrier, accipiters, Short-eared Owl (local in summer), Merlin, and Northern Shrike. Rarities have included Prairie and Peregrine Falcons, Gyrfalcon, Snowy Owl, and (a number of winters) Burrowing Owl.

Salt Creek/Waldo Lake

Habitats: WF, FW, DF, RR
Elevation: 3500-5420'
Seasons: Sp • • S • • • • F • • • W •

Nestled on the crest of the Cascades, this area is reached via OR 58 east of Oakridge. From Oakridge, OR 58 follows the beautiful Salt Creek Canyon some 21 miles or so to Salt Creek Falls. This is the first major stop for birding.

Pull into the first roadside parking area just east of the 800-ft. long highway tunnel on OR 58. Take the lower trail about 150' to a viewpoint that overlooks Salt Creek Falls. At 286 ft., this is the second highest waterfall in Oregon. In birding circles, Salt Creek Falls is known as the only reliable site in Oregon for finding a Black Swift. These birds are seen flying around and even into the plummeting main waterfall where they probably nest. They are best observed in the early daylight hours or toward dusk as much of their day is spent on the wing at tremendous altitudes. Salt Creek CG and a secondary, much lower waterfall are located near the highway just upstream from the the main falls. Don't pass up the CG, as reports of Northern Waterthrush and White-winged Crossbill have come from here.

Continuing east on OR 58, take the north turnoff onto Willamette N.F. Rd. 5897, 2.5 miles east of Salt Creek Falls. This leads to beautiful Waldo Lake, one of the largest natural bodies of water in Oregon. At an elevation of 5414', Waldo Lk. is surrounded by dense forests of fir, hemlock, lodgepole pine, and Douglas-fir. The three campgrounds on the east shore all offer excellent birding when they are not too over-crowded with campers, fishermen, and boaters. The west side of Waldo Lk. is undeveloped and accessible only by boat or on foot. A well-maintained 20-mile trail encircles the lake; shorter, less strenuous hikes have trailheads located all along Rd. 5897. Of particular interest to birders is the 2-mile (one-way) hike to Bobby Lake; the trailhead is located on Rd. 5897 about 5.5 miles north of OR 58. Birds sighted along this trail during August include Gray Jay, Mountain Chickadee, Northern Goshawk, and a Black-backed Woodpecker at the lake itself.

About 6.5 miles north of OR 58 on Rd. 5897 is the entrance to Shadow Bay CG on Waldo Lake's east shore. The other two CG's, Islet and North Waldo, are located at the very northeast corner of the lake, another 6 or 7 miles north of Shadow Bay. From June to October, expect such species as Steller's and Gray Jays, Mountain and Chestnut-backed Chickadees, Hammond's and Olive-sided Flycatchers, Common Raven, Hermit and Varied Thrushes, Solitary Vireo, Yellow-rumped, Townsend's,

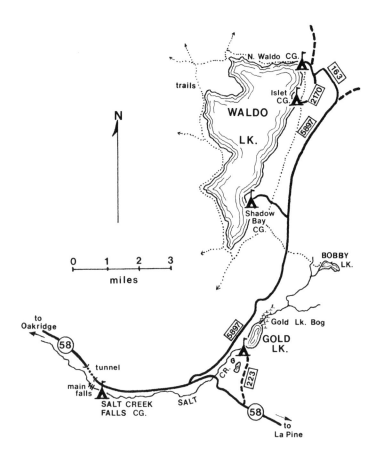

and (local) Hermit Warblers, Dark-eyed Junco, Western Tanager, and Evening Grosbeak. When the irruptive White-winged Crossbill appears in the Oregon Cascades, the Waldo Lake area seems to get more than its fair share of reports.

Even farther east on OR 58, another 2 miles or so from Rd. 5897, is Willamette N.F. Rd. 223 to the north This gravel road leads to Gold Lake, another unique area of interest to the naturalist. In addition to the typical species mentioned above, Gold Lake is known for its sporadic summering Solitary Sandpipers. The undeveloped Gold Lake Bog Research Natural Area, located at the lake's northeast corner, is the home of these birds. Since the late 1970's, two or three birds have been seen along the nature trail leading into the bog. The sandpipers are very territorial to any intruders, and they are highly suspected of nesting in the area. If this is true, Gold Lake would be the only known nesting site for Solitary Sandpipers in the lower 48 states!

Region D
Southwest Oregon

Blue-gray Gnatcatcher

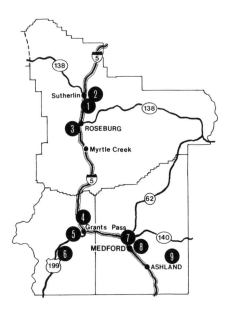

Sutherlin-Winchester Area

Habitats: FA, FW, BR, WF, BF
Elevation: 450-519'
Seasons: Sp • • •   S • •   F • • •   W • •

To explore this valley area, exit I-5 at the north Sutherlin exchange, and head west on OR 138. The first stop is at Fords Pond, located alongside OR 138 about 1.5 miles west of the interstate. This large abandoned log pond now serves as a community fishing spot. The marshy borders support nesting Pied-billed Grebe, Green-backed Heron, various ducks, and occasionally Purple Martins. During migration and winter, the typical flocks of Mallard, American Wigeon, Northern Shoveler, Green-winged Teal, Lesser Scaup, and Ring-necked Duck are often joined by rarer species such as Double-crested Cormorant, goldeneyes, scoters, Greater Scaup, grebes, and phalaropes. At the east end of the pond is a small cattail marsh which has yielded Sora, Virginia Rail, and Marsh Wren in May.

In the town of Sutherlin, head south on US 99W (east of the railroad tracks) to Hastings Ave.; turn west on that road and cross the railroad tracks. There are two log ponds here that have yielded Green-backed Herons and Wood Ducks. Spotted Sandpipers also nest here, and Purple Martins are occasionally seen.

Continue south on 99W out of Sutherlin to explore a leisurely alternate route to I-5. This secondary highway parallels the interstate from Sutherlin to Winchester, a 5 or 6 mile drive. This route gives ample opportunities to pull off the road an explore the brushy riparian creek bottom of the valley. Summer species of note include Rufous and Anna's Humming-birds, Red-breasted Sapsucker, Scrub Jay, House and Bewick's Wrens, Yellow, Wilson's, and Orange-crowned Warblers, Yellow-breasted Chat, Black-headed Grosbeak, and sparrows. Mountain Quail are occasionally encountered in this valley during the winter.

Just north of the town of Winchester there is another large log pond that should be scoped out. Much of what appears on Fords Pond can also be seen here, but don't pass it up because that lost Oldsquaw or Tufted Duck may have dropped in. About a mile north of Winchester on US 99W, look for the unmarked and unnamed gravel road to the west that passes under the interstate highway. This road leads to an excellent vantage point for scoping the pond.

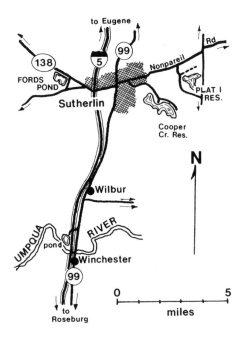

Plat I Reservoir

Habitats: FW, FA, BF, RA
Elevation: 590'
Seasons: Sp • • • S • • F • • • W • • •

To reach this shallow water impoundment on Sutherlin Creek, head east from Sutherlin on the Nonpareil Rd. (Douglas Co. Rd. 19); about 4 miles east of I-5, turn south on Plat I Rd. The boat launch near the dam is the only public access to the lake itself, but Plat I Rd. circles the lake and offers good birding in the surrounding farm land, brushy areas, and open woodland. During periods of low water, check for migrant shorebirds at the inlet of Sutherlin Creek on the east side of the lake. Gulls may also be found resting on the flats during spring or fall. Passerines of the area include the typical species of the riparian areas of western Oregon — warblers, flycatchers, Northern Oriole, Black-headed Grosbeak, Cedar Waxwing, Lazuli Bunting, House and Bewick's Wrens, etc. Winter raptors can be worth checking out because there are a number of Black-shouldered Kite reports from here, and Northern Goshawks may move down from the higher mountains.

Roseburg

Habitats: UR, FW, BR
Elevation: 455'
Seasons: Sp • • • S • • F • • • W • •

When passing through Roseburg on I-5, take the Garden
Valley Blvd. Exit (north of the Umpqua River) and follow that
road to the west. Less than a mile from the interstate, turn
south on Stewart Parkway; this leads to the productive birding
area of Stewart Park. The relatively undeveloped northern part
of this park offers typical species of the riparian areas and
open fields. Look for Cedar Waxwing, Black-headed Grosbeak,
House Wren, warblers, Warbling Vireo, Swainson's Thrush,
flycatchers, and various sparrows. Lesser Goldfinches may be
seen here, and the short nature trail has faithfully hosted a
territorial pair or two of Anna's Hummingbirds for a number
of years.

Also check out the Umpqua Community College campus
during spring and fall migration. Located on College Dr., east
of I-5 and south of Garden Valley Blvd., the campus grounds
are a great place to watch migrant warblers, vireos, thrushes,
sparrows, and numerous other passerines.

Merlin Rest Area

Habitats: CH, BF
Elevation: 1150'
Seasons: Sp • • •   S • • •   F • • •   W • •

The rest area on the north-bound (east) side of I-5 one mile north of the Merlin Exit is a good stop for birders with little time to explore southwest Oregon. Although not guaranteed, all three of the "California specialties" occur here, especially during the summer — Plain Titmouse, Blue-gray Gnatcatcher, and California Towhee. The gnatcatcher is, of course, most likely to be found in patches of ceanothus shrubbery. The titmouse is most often encountered foraging in small flocks throughout the stands of oak; it may be found any time of year. Other summer species of interest to be found here include Rufous and Anna's Hummingbirds, Acorn and Lewis' Woodpeckers, Ash-throated Flycatcher, White-breasted Nuthatch, House Wren, Lazuli Bunting, and Lesser Goldfinch (often outnumbering the American Goldfinch).

The best birding opportunities are found along the quiet frontage road just to the east of the rest area; to drive this road, leave the north-bound lane of I-5 at the Merlin Exit and continue north on the east side of the interstate. This paved frontage road is a dead-end.

Whitehorse County Park

Habitats: BF, WF, RA, FW, FA
Elevation: 860'
Seasons: Sp ● ● ●   S ● ●   F ● ● ●   W ● ●

In the town of Grants Pass, head west on 'G' St. Just outside
of town, turn south on Lincoln Rd. to join Lower River Rd.
About 6 miles west of town along this road is Whitehorse Co.
Park, located on the north shore of the Rogue River. Whitehorse Park can be birded all year, but restrooms and other
facilities are closed during the winter. The park offers a variety
of mostly passerine birding habitats. The higher ground near
the park entrance (camping area) is upland mixed woodland
— watch for the typical chickadees, warblers, Hutton's Vireo
(quite common, especially during summer), Swainson's and
Hermit Thrushes, Wood Pewee, wrens, and Black-headed
Grosbeak during the appropriate times of the year. Closer to
the river there are riparian and ash woods near the picnic area;
these woods support Red-breasted Sapsucker, Yellow-breasted
Chat (common during summer), Yellow Warbler, flycatchers,
Scrub Jay, Bushtit, House Wren, and other species. The
seldom-seen Wrentit is an uncommon resident here, and both
Plain Titmouse and Black Phoebe have occurred. A walk down
to the Rogue River may yield summering Osprey (they nest
across the river), Spotted Sandpiper, Belted Kingfisher, Com-

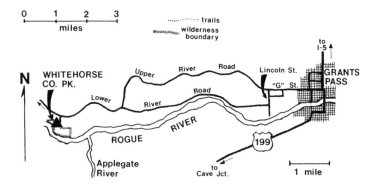

mon Merganser, Mallard, and five species of swallows. During fall and summer there are exposed sand bars just east of the park where the Applegate joins the Rogue; check here for migrant shorebirds, ducks, and other waterbirds.

The open fields along Lower River Rd. are good for summering Western Kingbird, Lazuli Bunting, Lesser Goldfinch, and sparrows. During winter, watch for Great Egrets along the road, especially in the vicinity of the dairies and farms just east of the park.

Lake Selmac County Park

Habitats: WF, BF, FW, RA
Elevation: 1390'
Seasons: Sp • • • S • • • F • • • W • •

Nestled in the Deer Creek Valley of western Josephine County, Selmac Lake offers the birder a good sampling of coniferous forest bird communities. Typical species that can be found at the picnic grounds and the campground include Steller's Jay, Band-tailed Pigeon, Pygmy, Saw-whet, and Screech Owls, Varied and Swainson's Thrushes, Hermit, Townsend's, and Black-throated Gray Warblers, Pacific-slope Flycatcher, Western Tanager, and Solitary Vireo. Shier, off-the-road species include Ruffed and Blue Grouse, Mountain Quail, Pileated Woodpecker, and Hammond's Flycatcher. Osprey are frequent migrants, some remaining to nest. The lake itself supports breeding Spotted Sandpiper, Hooded Merganser, Bufflehead, Green-backed Heron (rare), Dipper, and Ring-necked Duck.

To reach this park, head southwest from Grants Pass on US 199 for about 20 miles. Turn left (east) onto Lakeshore Dr.; the lake is 2 miles from US 199.

Lower Table Rock/ Tou Velle State Park

Habitats: CH, BF, RA, FW, FA, RR
Elevation: 1230-2044'
Seasons: Sp • • • •   S • • •   F • • •   W • •

In downtown Medford, take Table Rock Rd. northward; Tou Velle St. Pk. is located on the Rogue River about 4.5 miles north of the Medford Airport on this road. This popular riverside park has excellent riparian habitat with the appropriate summering species: Northern Oriole, Black-headed Grosbeak, Downy Woodpecker, Yellow Warbler, Warbling Vireo, Pacific-slope and Willow Flycatchers, Purple Finch, and American Goldfinch. Lesser Goldfinchs are quite common in this part of Oregon. Both Plain Titmouse and California Towhee occur somewhat regularly in the brushy oak woods of the park. Turn west on Kirtland Rd. just south of the state park to visit the local sewage ponds. These are visible from the road and offer the best habitat for waterfowl and shorebirds during the appropriate seasons. The small pump house often has a nesting Black Phoebe; this is one of the more reliable sites to see the species in Oregon.

To reach Lower Table Rock, continue north and west on Table Rock Rd. from Tou Velle Park. About 3.5 miles from park turn left (west) onto Wheeler Rd.; the parking area and trailhead are located on the west side of this road, less than a half-mile from Table Rock Rd. Owned and preserved by The Nature Conservancy, Lower Table Rock is a dry, mostly deciduous habitat with oaks, pine, and much brushy growth. Especially note the patches of ceanothus; this is prime Blue-gray Gnatcatcher habitat. Also present year-round are the two other southwest Oregon specialties — the California Towhee and Plain Titmouse. Other summering species to watch for include Anna's Hummingbird, Acorn and Lewis' Woodpeckers, Ash-throated Flycatcher, Bushtit, House, Rock, Canyon, and Bewick's Wrens, Western Bluebird, Lazuli Bunting, and

Purple Finch. Poorwill may be heard calling at night. During the fall this butte is an excellent site for observing migrant raptors; Turkey Vultures can be quite common at times, and Prairie Falcons have also occurred.

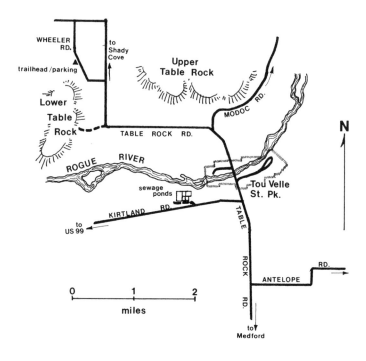

Roxy Ann Butte

Habitats: CH, BF, RR, UR
Elevation: 1550-3571'
Seasons: Sp • • •   S • • •   F • • •   W • •

This city park (Prescott Park) has traditionally yielded most of the local nesting birds of note in southwest Oregon. To reach the area, take the Barnett Rd. exit off I-5 at the south end of Medford. Follow Barnett Rd. east for about 2 miles to north Phoenix Rd. where you turn north. Another 0.75 miles or so, turn right (east) on Cherry Ln. This rural road offers excellent habitat for the dry chaparrel species — especially the sprightly little Blue-gray Gnatcatcher. Check the more extensive stands of ceanothus for this inquisitive species. California Towhees are also common here. At Hillcrest Rd. (which Cherry Ln. intersects), turn east and go about 0.5 miles to the Roxy Ann Butte Rd. This rough, unimproved gravel/dirt road is good for walking; it is about 2 miles to the butte's summit. All along the road watch for the typical summering species including the gnatcatcher, California Towhee, and Plain Titmouse. Anna's Hummingbirds are quite common, and Black-chinned Sparrows nested here one year, the only Oregon occurrence of this southern sparrow. Poorwills are relatively common and can be heard at night near the gravel pit at the top.

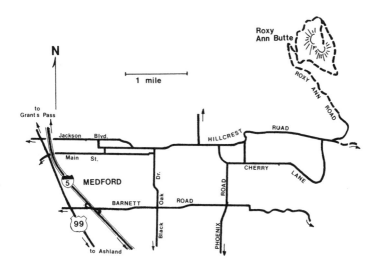

Hyatt and Howard Prairie Reservoirs

Habitats: FW, DF, FA, RA, BF
Elevation: 4525-5016'
Seasons: Sp • • • S • • • F • • • W • •

Averaging around 5000' in elevation, these two artificial lakes offer the birder scenic mountain habitat that is easily accessible. Both lakes are sites of recreation resort facilities, and as such, the birding can be rather poor during the busy summer season. Productive habitats can still be found, however, including a combination of extensive open meadowlands interspersed with stands of dense forest. To reach the popular area, exit I-5 at the south Ashland Exit (Exit 14). Head east almost a mile to Dead Indian Rd. Follow this major thoroughfare east about 17 miles to the Howard Prairie Lake Resort sign.

One of the highlights of this area is the handsome Great Gray Owl. This is one of only six or seven easily accessible areas in Oregon where this elusive species is consistently seen. The best method for locating an owl is to drive the numerous side roads off Dead Indian Rd. and the Howard Prairie Resort Rd. Especially check those roads that border open meadowlands along the east side of both lakes. Areas of regular sightings include the junction of Dead Indian and Howard Prairie Resort Roads; the turnoff to the lake's marina, and along the East Side Hyatt Lake Rd. Remember that the more isolated and remote the meadows, the better the chances for finding an owl.

If you don't find an owl, enjoy the other summer birds. The forests of the area support Blue and Ruffed Grouse, all three accipiters, Three-toed and Black-backed Woodpeckers (lodgepole pine), Varied Thrush, Mountain Bluebird, Hermit Thrush, Solitary Vireo, Hermit and Townsend's Warblers (learn their remarkably similar songs!), Hammond's Flycatcher, Chipping Sparrow, and Lincoln's Sparrow.

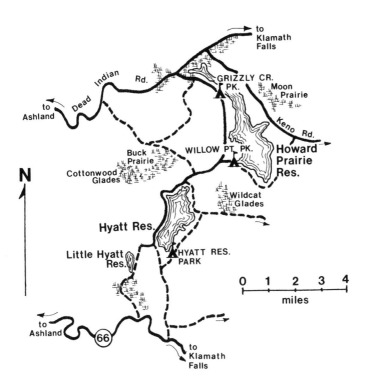

Region E
Northcentral Oregon

Calliope Hummingbird

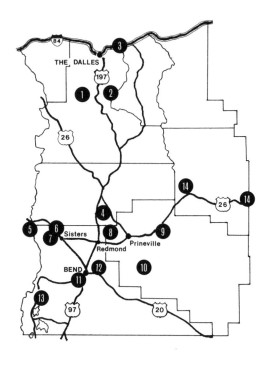

White River Wildlife Management Area

Habitats: DF, FA, BR, RA, FW
Elevation: 1400-2265'
Seasons: Sp • • • S • • • F • • • W • •

Set aside in 1953 for wintering deer herds, this ODFW land offers a unique habitat area for birding. Although difficult to locate, Wild Turkeys are the main attraction for birders in the White River area. Introduced in 1961, these birds constitute the largest and oldest population of the species in Oregon. In recent years, turkeys have increased their numbers to such an extent that they have been reported all the way from Hood River to the southern reaches of Warm Springs Indian Reservation. The birds prefer the mixed pine-oak woodlands so prevalent throughout the WMA; they are generally found at higher elevations during the summer on the western reaches of the WMA. Also check the secondary roads and trails in the adjoining Mt. Hood N.F.

One site worth checking for local birdlife is Rock Creek Reservoir, located about 6 miles west of the town of Wamic on White River Rd. (this becomes N.F. Rd. 48 upon entering Mt. Hood N.F.). Nearby is the newer (and more heavily utilized) Pine Hollow Reservoir, just northwest of Wamic. These are the only substantial bodies of water in the area, and thus they serve as magnets for any migrant waterbirds.

The uncommon Lewis' Woodpecker is a regular bird in the pine-oak habitat, and White River is one of the better places to find the species during the summer. Other nesting species include Northern Oriole, Yellow Warbler, Lazuli Bunting, House Wren, Black-headed Grosbeak, and Lark Sparrow. The drier canyon regions east of the WMA near Tygh Valley support Prairie Falcon, Chukar, Canyon and Rock Wrens, and Loggerhead Shrike.

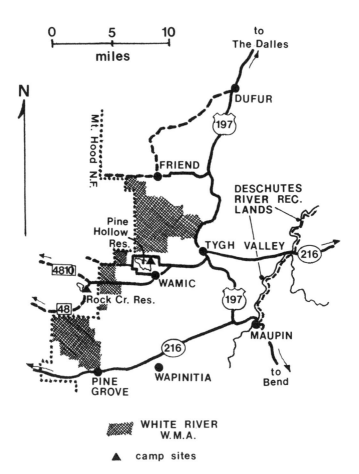

Deschutes River Recreation Area

Habitats: RR, SS, FW, RA
Elevation: 790-845'
Seasons: Sp • •   S • •   F • •   W •

When heading south on US 197, turn left (east) immediately after crossing the Deschutes River in Maupin. This gravel road closely follows the east bank of the Deschutes for ten miles or so to Sherar's Bridge. Here the road joins OR 216, and you can continue from there to Grass Valley (19 miles east) or to Tygh Valley (5 miles west).

This gravel road between Maupin and Sherar's Bridge (locally but unofficially known as the Deschutes River Rd.) is an excellent way to explore the dry canyonlands so typical of the Deschutes River Recreation Lands. Be sure to watch for rattlesnakes when exploring the area on foot. Ring-billed and California Gulls are common sights during summer as they cruise up and down the river from their nesting colony at the mouth of the Deschutes. Osprey are common migrants, and Mallards and Common Mergansers nest on quieter stretches of water. Spotted Sandpiper nests are easily found. The rugged cliffs are home to Prairie Falcon, Rock and Canyon Wrens, American Kestrel, Rock Dove, and Common Raven, and calling Poorwill have been heard at least once. The dense riparian growth and occasional trees along some parts of the Deschutes support such summer species as Western Kingbird, Say's Phoebe, Lazuli Bunting, Northern Oriole, Black-headed Grosbeak, Warbling Vireo, and House Wren. Yellow-breasted Chats are quite common, but more often heard than seen. Also, watch for the beautiful Chukar, one of the few birds that remain through the winter.

Deschutes River State Park

Habitats: FW, RA, NG, SS
Elevation: 100'
Seasons: Sp • • •   S • •   F • •   W • •

This small park at the confluence of the Deschutes and
Columbia Rivers provides a good rest stop off I-84 for the
travelling birder, and there are restroom facilities as well as
campsites located here. This is mostly an arid rocky canyon
area, and the water of the river supports a sparse riparian
growth that is important to the local birdlife. A short trail
follows the Deschutes River's eastern shore, offering the best
birding opportunities. Typical passerines of the area include
Yellow and Wilson's Warblers, House and Bewick's Wrens,
American Goldfinch, Song Sparrow, Black-headed Grosbeak,
and Lazuli Bunting. The nearby steep ravine walls support
both Rock and Canyon Wrens, as well as "wild" Rock Doves,
American Kestrels, and the occasional Prairie Falcon. Nesting
or summering waterbirds include Canada Goose, Common
Merganser, Spotted Sandpiper, and Belted Kingfisher. There
are a number of small islands and river bars located near the
mouth of the Deschutes — these areas, many which are
managed by ODFW, are important nesting sites for California
and Ring-billed Gulls and Caspian Terns.

Haystack Reservoir

Habitats: FW, FA, NG
Elevation: 2848'
Seasons: Sp ••• S• F••• W••

This lake is easily found just off US 97, about 18 miles south of
Madras. Situated in the dry Crooked River National Grassland,
Haystack Reservoir is a major resting site for migrant loons,
grebes, waterfowl, gulls, terns, and, when waterlevels are low
enough, shorebirds. The scant riparian growth lining parts of
the shore may yield some interesting migrant landbirds — a
Yellow-billed Cuckoo was found here one fall. During spring
and fall and even into winter (if the water remains unfrozen)
look for the uncommon Barrow's Goldeneye among the more
abundant waterfowl species.

Santiam Pass Area

Habitats: WF, DF, FW, BR, RA, AL
Elevation: 3980-4650'
Seasons: Sp • •   S • • • •   F • • •   W •

Located alongside OR 22 (the Santiam Pass Highway) just west
of the Linn/Deschutes Co. line, Lost Lake is the most easily
birded of the Cascades Lakes. In a half-hour the visiting birder
can get a good sample of the local avifauna at this elevation.
The forest at the entrance is alive with such species as Cassin's
Finch, Western Tanager, Pine Siskin, Yellow-rumped Warbler,
Steller's and Gray Jays, Mountain Chickadee, Hermit Thrush,
Solitary Vireo, and Chipping Sparrow. Two species of interest
to most visitors are the beautiful Hermit Warbler and the local
Barrow's Goldeneye. The former species abounds in the
campground from late May to August and is quite tame. The
goldeneye is easily found on the lake itself where it is the most
common nesting species of waterfowl. Black-backed and
Three-toed Woodpeckers have been found in the surrounding
pine forest, but their nesting sites are seldom reliable from
year to year.

About 4 miles west of Lost Lake on US 20 is Santiam Pass itself.
Just east of Lost Lake, turn south on the well-marked road to
Hoodoo Ski Bowl. The ski area is located about 0.8 miles from
US 20; keep to the left (east) at this point to continue on to
scenic Big Lake. Prior to reaching Big Lake itself, the gravel
road passes through the extensive Airstrip Burn of 1967.
Composed of thousands of dead lodgepole pine snags (and a
number of live trees as well), this burn area is well-known for
nesting Black-backed and Three-toed Woodpeckers. Throughout most of the Oregon Cascades, the Black-backed is the
commoner of the two species, but both have been reported
from this area. Also watch for Mountain Bluebird,
Townsend's Solitaire, MacGillivray's Warbler, and Red
Crossbill.

Big Lake lies nestled in a hollow at the base of Mt. Washington (7,794'). Although it is a popular summer spot for fishing and camping, Big Lake is still far enough off the highway that most people pass it up. Surrounded by pine and fir forest, this lake is good for the high-elevation birds. The campground at the west side of Big Lake is a sure bet for Gray Jay, Townsend's Warbler, Western Tanager, and Cassin's Finch. Other regular summer species include Olive-sided and Hammond's Flycatchers, Mountain Chickadee, Hermit Thrush, Solitary Vireo, Hermit Warbler, Pine Siskin, and Evening Grosbeak. The raucous Clark's Nutcracker is easily found around the lake and at the nearby ski area.

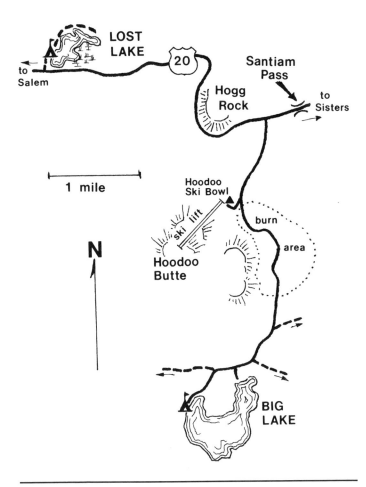

Indian Ford Campground

Habitats: DF, RA, JW
Elevation: 3239'
Seasons: Sp ● ● ● S ● ● ● ● F ● ● W ●

This site is located just off US 20 about 5 miles west of Sisters.
From mid May to early September is the best time to visit.
The large ponderosa pines (especially on the northwest side of
Indian Ford Creek, which flows through the campground)
almost always yield a pair or two of White-headed Woodpeck-
ers. Also look for Williamson's (pines) and Red-naped (aspens)
Sapsuckers here. The generally more western Red-breasted
Sapsucker occurs infrequently here, and hybrids between it
and the closely related Red-naped have been noted as well!
Warblers and vireos abound along the creekside brush —
MacGillivray's, Orange-crowned, Townsend's, and Yellow
Warblers, Comon Yellowthroat, and Warbling and Solitary
Vireos are sure to be found. The creek is also a good place for
finding Pygmy-Owls.

Away from the riparian growth, the campground is dominated
by pine, sage, and juniper. Pygmy Nuthatch and Green-tailed
Towhee are easily found here. Also in these drier areas look
for Dusky and Hammond's Flycatchers, Red Crossbill, Cassin's
Finch, House Wren, and other interesting species.

Cold Springs Campground

Habitats: DF, RA, FW, JW
Elevation: 3422'
Seasons: Sp • • •   S • • • •   F • • •   W • •

To reach this quiet campground, take OR 242 west from Sisters
about 4.5 miles. Or, head east on US 20 one mile from Indian
Ford CG (see previous entry) and turn south (right) on a
marked gravel road (Deschutes N.F. Rd. 1012). Cold Springs
offers much the same birding fare as Indian Ford, but it is still
worth the time to check out. Vagrants such as Rose-breasted
Grosbeak and Tennessee Warbler have been found here, and it
is excellent for Red-naped Sapsucker and White-headed
Woodpecker. This is a great place to study the *Empidonax*
flycatchers (especially Dusky and Hammond's), and watch the
dry pine-sage-juniper areas for Gray Flycatcher, Pygmy
Nuthatch, and Green-tailed Towhee.

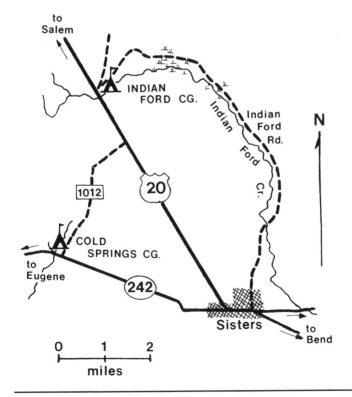

Smith Rock State Park

Habitats: RR, JW, RA
Elevation: 2400-3000'
Seasons: Sp • •   S • • •   F • •   W •

This beautiful park of towering walls and scenic oasis-like vegetation lies at the western reaches of the Ochoco Mountain system. The park is located 8 miles north of Redmond; in the town of Terrebonne, turn east on Wilcox Ave., and follow that road for about 2.5 miles to the park entrance on the north.

Although it is better known for its rock climbing opportunities, Smith Rock also offers some interesting birding.   Prairie Falcons and Common Ravens nest on the cliff faces across the canyon from the parking area. Canyon and Rock Wrens are easily found anywhere in the park, and the juniper-sagebrush habitat frequently has Say's Phoebe, Ash-throated Flycatcher, Savannah and Lark Sparrow, and migrant warblers, flycatchers, vireos, and tanagers. During winter the area harbors Townsend's Solitaires, Mountain Bluebirds, and tons of Black-billed Magpies. Occasionally, migrant White-throated Swifts will remain through the summer to nest.

A trail leads from the parking area down to the Crooked River at the bottom of the canyon. The riparian growth along the river has yielded Black-headed Grosbeak, Northern Oriole, Yellow-breated Chat, and Lazuli Bunting.

Ochoco Reservoir/ Ochoco Mountains

Habitats: FW, RA, DF, FA, JW, RR, WF
Elevation: 3130-4020'
Seasons: Sp • • • S • • • • F • • • W • •

Located about 6 miles east of Prineville on US 26, Ochoco
Reservoir was constructed in 1921 to provide irrigation water
for the arid farmland in the area. Much of the shoreline
around the lake is privately-owned, and public access is greatly
restricted. About midway along the north shore along US 26
is Ochoco Lake St. Pk., which includes picnic grounds, a
camping area, and a good vantage point for scoping out the
lake. Recreational use on the lake can be ridiculously heavy
during summer, but good water birds may be found during
spring, fall, and, as long as the water remains unfrozen,
winter. Most of the habitat surrounding the lake is open dry
rangeland; the west end of the reservoir has steep, rugged cliff
faces that support Violet-green and Cliff Swallows, Canyon
and Rock Wrens, and such raptors as Golden Eagle and Prairie
Falcon.

Farther along US 26, about 6.5 miles east of the reservoir, turn
right onto the Ochoco Ranger Station Rd. (Ochoco N.F. Rd.
22); at this intersection US 26 veers off to the northeast while
Rd. 22 continues following Ochoco Creek. The riparian
growth along the creek bottom can be very productive during
summer. Watch (and listen) for Black-headed Grosbeak,
Lazuli Bunting, House Wren, warblers, Willow and Dusky
Flycatchers, and American Goldfinch. Hummingbirds can be
quite conspicuous, most of which will be Calliope or Rufous;
watch for the much rarer Black-chinned in this area.

Another 8 miles or so east of the US 26 junction, look for the
Ochoco Ranger Station and CG, a very good summer birding
spot. If you missed Calliope Hummingbird earlier along
Ochoco Cr., you should find them here. At the confluence of
Ochoco and Canyon Creeks, just east of the Ranger Station,
search the dense riparian growth for the secretive Veery, an
"eastern" species that reaches the western limits of its range

here in the Ochoco Mountains. They are easy to hear, but seeing one is often a different story. The mixture of pine forest, riparian creek-side growth, and open meadows offer a wide variety of summering birds in the Ranger Station area. In the ponderosa pines look for White-headed Woodpecker, Williamson's Sapsucker, Northern Goshawk, Pygmy and White-breasted Nuthatches, Mountain Chickadee, Solitary Vireo, and Cassin's Finch. Red Crossbills are common throughout the area, and excellent studies of the local fly-catchers are possible.

Owling in this part of the Ochocos may yield some interesting results. Western Screech-Owls are found along the creek bottoms while Great Horneds can be heard anywhere. Saw-whet Owls prefer the more heavily forested areas, and even Flammulated Owls have been heard in the more extensive stands of ponderosa. Walton Lake CG, another 5 miles or so east of the Ochoco Ranger Station on Rd. 22, has had territo-rial Flammulated Owls during June and July.

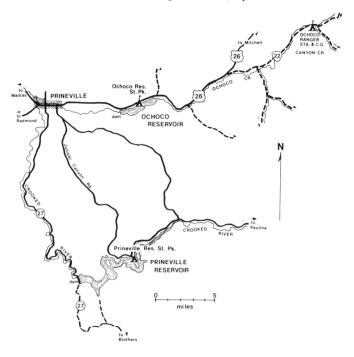

Prineville Reservoir

Habitats: FW, SS, RR, RA, NG
Elevation: 3235'
Seasons: Sp • • • S • • F • • • W • •

Located in the dry desert country of Central Oregon, Prineville
Reservoir is a magnet for all forms of wildlife. Birding is best
at two sites on the lake. Take OR 27 south from Prineville
about 19 miles to reach the dam. This end of the lake has
rugged cliff faces and slopes that attract Golden Eagle, Prairie
Falcon, Raven, Rock Wren, and Canyon Wren. Poorwill have
been heard calling from this area at night in July. Chukar may
also be seen any time of year. Migrant loons, grebes, gulls,
terns, and other water birds are most likely to be seen at this
end of the lake.

To reach the east end of the lake (Prineville Reservoir St. Pk.),
take a marked county road (Juniper Canyon Rd.) southeast
from Prineville for 16 miles to the park. The inlet to Prineville
Reservoir is located just east of the park; this area is marshy in
spots and supports nesting Pied-billed Grebe, Canada Goose,
Mallard, Cinnamon Teal, Redhead, Virginia Rail, and Coot.
During spring and fall low water periods check this end of the
lake for migrant shorebirds, gulls, and terns. The surrounding
terrain is mainly sagebrush uplands with interspersed juniper
woodlands. Brewer's, Lark, and Vesper Sparrows are quite
common here, and Sage Thrasher, Loggerhead Shrike, Say's
Phoebe, and Common Nighthawk round out the list of
summering species.

During winter, nomadic flocks of Mountain Bluebirds,
Townsend's Solitaires, and American Robins wander widely
throughout Central Oregon, and the Prineville area often
hosts these birds. This is a particularly good area for the local
Pinyon Jay; although a resident species in the juniper forests,
this often inconspicuous bird tends to wander widely, usually
forming flocks during the winter. A good area to look for the
jays is along OR 27 between Prineville Res. and the tiny town
of Brothers, located some 20 miles south of the lake. Also
watch for the local Ash-throated and Gray Flycatchers in
juniper-sage woodlands of this region.

Bend

Habitats: UR, JW, RA, FW, FA, DF
Elevation: 3596'
Seasons: Sp • • • S • • • F • • • W • •

Located almost in the center of Oregon, the Bend area offers excellent birding in the unique juniper uplands of this region. Using the city itself as a central base, the following sites offer the best birding for visitors with little time to spare:

Robert Sawyer State Park. Situated along the beautiful Deschutes River, this is one of the most profitable birding sites in the county. It is located in northern Bend about a block west of US 97, approximately .75 miles south of the US 97-US 20 junction. A walk along the river during May will yield such summering species as Spotted Sandpiper, Common Night-hawk, Vaux's Swift, Belted Kingfisher, Bank and Rough-winged Swallows, Pygmy Nuthatch (pines), House Wren, Yellow Warbler, and Warbling Vireo. This park and the next site are fantastic places to study the confusing *Empidonax* flycatchers during migration — Willow, "Western" (either Pacific-slope or Cordilleran), Dusky, Hammond's, and Gray are all regular visitors, with the Willows and occasionally the "Westerns" remaining to breed. Sawyer Park is particularly good for migrant warblers. Osprey are a frequent sight along the river here, and when the flowers are in bloom look for Rufous, Calliope, and Anna's Hummingbirds.

Tumalo State Park. This popular camping and picnicking area is located just north of Bend along US 20; like Sawyer Park, it is situated along the Deschutes River and its birdlife is similar to that mentioned above, specializing in riparian and open ponderosa pine forest species.

Mirror Pond. This is actually an artificially widened section of the Deschutes River found in the center of Bend. It is an excellent place to observe wintering and migrant waterfowl. Barrow's Goldeneye tend to gather here during late fall and winter, and such uncommon species as Gadwall, Shoveler,

Ruddy Duck, Wood Duck, Redhead, and Hooded Merganser may winter here as long as the water remains unfrozen. Small numbers of wild Canada Geese and feral Mute Swans nest here and frequently travel up and down the Deschutes River.

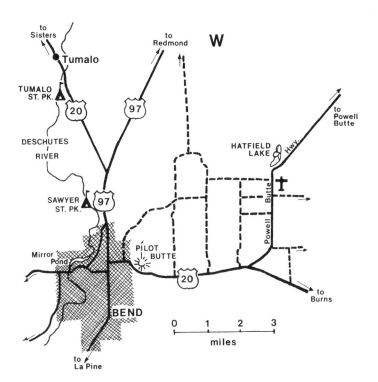

Hatfield Lake

Habitats: FW, JW, FA
Elevation: 3600'
Seasons: Sp • • •   S • •   F • • •   W •

Hatfield "Lake" is actually the settling pond complex of Bend's sewage treatment plant. As such it is fenced off and posted for no trespassing. Birders are welcome, however, and be sure to check in with any personnel that may be present during your visit.

To reach Hatfield Lake, take US 20 east from Bend and pass Pilot Butte. About 4.5 miles east of the US 97-US 20 junction in town, turn north (left) at the traffic light onto Powell Butte Highway — this takes you toward the Bend Municipal Airport. Continue northward, passing the airport on the east side of the road. 4.0 miles from US 20 turn northwest (left) onto the unnamed access road to the ponds. Drive one mile to the barricade and park.

There are three main ponds that comprise Hatfield Lake, and water levels vary according to the season. Due to the large size of the ponds and the distance between them, a spotting scope is highly recommended. These ponds are well known as Eastern Oregon's most profitable shorebird location. During the fall migration (July through late September), typical migrant waders include both yellowlegs, Western, Least, Baird's, and Spotted Sandpipers, Long-billed Dowitcher, Semipalmated Plover, and Wilson's and Red-necked Phalaropes. Smaller numbers of such species as Solitary and Pectoral Sandpipers, and Black-bellied Plover are found almost every year, and some real "ultra-rarities" have occurred — Whimbrel, Semipalmated Sandpiper, Black-necked Stilt, Red Knot, Sanderling, Dunlin, Short-billed Dowitcher, and Red Phalarope. The ponds also attract migrant gulls and terns each fall, and surprises in this group have included Common, Forster's, Arctic, and Black Terns and Sabine's Gull!

Up to 27 species of waterfowl have occurred on Hatfield Lake, and there are numerous reports of loons, grebes, cormorants, and other water birds. During the winter these ponds often attract respectable numbers of Barrow's Goldeneyes if the water remains unfrozen.

Land birds can be few and far between at Hatfield Lake. Swallows are abundant during migration with Banks being quite common along with the regular species. Spring and fall migration may also see a heavy movement of sparrows through the area, and the mudflats attract numbers of American Pipits.

Cascades Lakes Highway

Habitats: DF, WF, FW, BR, RA, RR, JW
Elevation: 4300-5500'
Seasons: Sp • • S • • • • F • • • W • •

To reach the birding area of this highway (officially recognized as Deschutes N.F. Rd. 46), head west out of Bend on Century Dr., the main road to Bachelor Butte Ski Area. After passing the ski area (about 25 miles west of Bend), the first lake for which the highway was named is encountered on the south side of Rd. 46 — Sparks Lake. From here, the Cascades Lakes Highway veers due south, joining OR 58 about 40 miles to the south. This entire route offers excellent birding over a two or three day excursion. Elevations range from 4338' at Wickiup Reservoir to nearly 7000' on some of the nearby buttes and peaks. Habitats available for sampling include high-elevation fir forest, dry ponderosa pine forest, brushy areas, and riparian growth along creeks. No fewer than 15 lakes can be visited, offering birding that ranges from poor to excellent. In this account, only those sites with good access, unique habitats, and noteworthy birding results are covered.

The Northern Lakes   The smaller, more northern lakes along the highway offer birds of the higher-elevation habitats. Elk Lake, Lava Lake, Little Lava Lake, and Sparks Lake are situated in forests of ponderosa and lodgepole pine, hemlock, sub-alpine fir, and grand fir. Summer bird species here may include Townsend's, Yellow-rumped, and Hermit (local) Warblers, Gray and Steller's Jays, Red-breasted Nuthatch, Hermit and Varied Thrush, and Hammond's Flycatcher — all species which are harder to find at the south end of the highway where elevations are lower and forests are drier. Other species such as Northern Goshawk, Red Crossbill, Mountain Chickadee, Hairy Woodpecker, Vaux's Swift, Dusky Flycatcher, and Western Tanager are likely to occur anywhere along the 40+ mile stretch of road. Short hikes into the region of the northern lakes can turn up some of the more local birds. Sparks, Hosmer, Cultus, and Little Cultus Lakes in particular have produced sightings of Three-toed and Black-backed Woodpeckers, including birds at nest holes. Remember that these two species are found almost exclusively in stands of lodgepole pine. The areas of fir and larch are home to Townsend's and Hermit Warblers, the latter species being much less common here east of the Cascades Crest. Also listen for the mournful whistle of the Varied Thrush in this type of forest. The campground at Lava Lake has been somewhat consistent for finding Pygmy Owl, and the extremely rare Pine Grosbeak has also occurred here.

Crane Prairie Reservoir. The southern, larger lakes generally offer more interesting birding. Crane Prairie Reservoir is particularly well-known for its ODFW Osprey nesting area, established in 1970. The lake is full of large dead snags which are favored by these birds for nesting and perching. An official Osprey Point Observation Trail with interpretive displays and signs is located along the southwest shore of the lake. Other good sites for viewing these birds are at Rock Cr. CG on the lake's west side, and at Crane Prairie CG in the northeast corner. Small numbers of Bald Eagles also nest in these high-country lakes, but not on Crane Prairie due to the large concentration of very territorial Ospreys.

Wickiup Reservoir. Wickiup Reservoir, the largest lake along this highway, is probably the most heavily used lake in the Deschutes N.F. Because of this it can be rather "birdless" at times except for the typical summering passerines. Later in the season (mid-September to whenever the lake freezes over), however, Wickiup Reservoir can be a remarkable site for migrant waterbirds. Species seldom found on the Cascades Lakes that have been reported here include Common and Red-throated Loons, grebes, Double-crested Cormorant, White Pelican, migrant geese, Tundra Swans, diving ducks (even an Oldsquaw!), gulls, and terns. The five campgrounds and the dam (on the east side) offer the best viewing.

Davis Lake. Davis Lake, located just south of Wickiup Reservoir, is the best birding site along the Cascades Lakes Highway. Nearly every species recorded at all these lakes has been seen at Davis Lake. Much of the lake's shoreline is lined with wet meadows, marshes of cattail and tule, and brushy riparian growth. These quiet, relatively undisturbed areas support nesting populations of such local species as Western and Eared Grebes, Sora, Virginia Rail, Wilson's Phalarope, and even Forster's and Black Terns. Summering ducks include Ring-necked Duck, Lesser Scaup, Cinnamon Teal, and (rarely) Hooded Merganser. The most productive viewing areas are found between East Davis Lake CG and the mouth of Odell Creek; at the very north end of the lake off the west side road (Deschutes N.F. Rd. 4660); and at the undeveloped camping area at the mouth of Ranger Creek, also reached via Rd. 4660.

In the early 1970's, American Redstarts were discovered nesting in the mixture of riparian growth and pine woods near the mouth of Odell Creek. Their occurrence at Davis Lake is now sporadic (*i.e.*, not every year), but it is worth the time to listen for their distinctive song at west Davis Lake CG, east Davis Lake CG, and along lower Odell Creek.

The north end of Davis Lake has been dammed by a lava flow nearly a mile wide and two miles long. This unique area supports unique birds — look for Poorwill, Rock Wren, Mountain Bluebird, Clark's Nutcracker, and even Brewer's Sparrow here. Also bordering Davis Lk. in this area are some interesting pine forests mixed with scrubby growth of ceanothus and manzanita — the haunt of such species as Pygmy Nuthatch, Green-tailed Towhee, Fox Sparrow, Gray and Dusky Flycatchers, Nashville Warbler, Townsend's Solitaire, and White-headed Woodpecker.

From Davis Lake continue south on N.F. Rd. 46 (Cascades Lakes Hwy.) about 6 miles to the Crescent Cut-off Rd. (N.F. Rd. 61). From here, head west to OR 58 or go east to Crescent Creek CG and the Gilchrist/Crescent area.

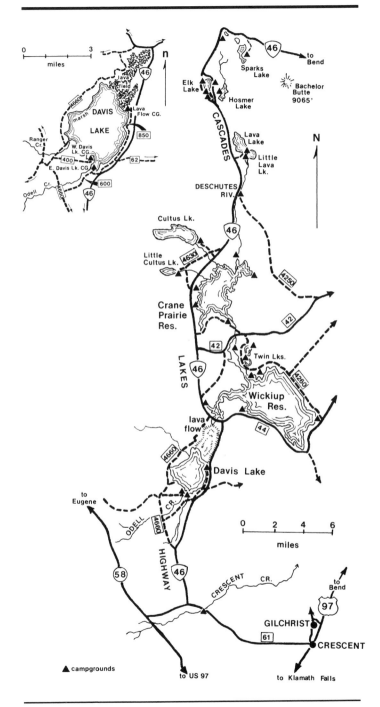

Region E, Northcentral Oregon

John Day Fossil Beds National Monument

Habitats: SS, RR, NG, RA, FW
Elevation: 2250-3300'
Seasons: Sp • •   S • • •   F • •   W •

Consisting of small parcels of land scattered throughout this part of Oregon, the John Day Fossil Beds are better known for their unique geological features rather than their birdlife. The best areas for birding include the small Sheep Rock Unit of the monument; this is located at the junction of US 26 and OR 19, about 5 miles west of Dayville. This is the site of scenic Picture Gorge, best known for its small (and not always present) population of White-throated Swifts. The canyon is also home to Rock and Canyon Wrens, Prairie Falcon, Golden Eagle, and the occasional Chukar. During winter, Bald Eagles often visit the John Day River areas of the monument, and gallinaceous birds — Ring-necked Pheasant, California Quail, and (rarely) Gray Partridge — tend to congregate on the roadsides.

Located about 2.5 miles north of the US 26 junction on OR 19 is the Cant Ranch of the John Day Fossil Beds Nat'l. Mon.. This rustic ranch house now serves as a public visitor center with displays, brochures, maps, and other information. The ornamental trees and brush planted here serve as habitat for local nesting passerines such as Lazuli Bunting, Northern Oriole, Yellow Warbler, Yellow-breasted Chat, Cedar Wax-wing, House Wren, and other riparian species. The potential for finding "eastern" vagrants at the ranch house during migration is certainly not to be ignored. A short interpretive trail to the scenic Sheep Rock Overlook begins at the ranch house.

Region F
Southcentral Oregon

Least Bittern

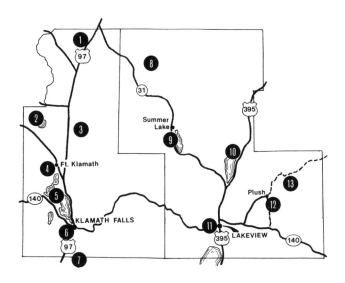

Little Deschutes River Area

Habitats: DF, RA
Elevation: 4450'
Seasons: Sp ● ● ● S ● ● ● F ● ● W ●

Located on OR 58 about 4.5 miles northwest of the US 97 junction, Little Deschutes CG has been a traditional site for Northern Waterthrush, an extremely local and rare species in Oregon. The stretch of the Little Deschutes River between the campground and the town of Gilchrist is the best area to find the species. A good road to drive in search of this species is Deschutes N.F. Rd. 100, just south and west of Crescent. Another specific site where a number of waterthrushes have been found on territory is along the side road that parallels US 97 between the towns of Gilchrist and Crescent. This is a marshy, brushy stretch of the above river where birds may be difficult to observe — learn the waterthrush's distinctive song, but try not to use voice recordings any more than necessary.

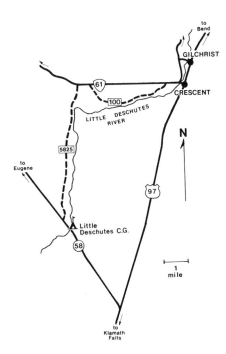

Crater Lake National Park

Habitats: WF, DF, RA, AL, RR, FW
Elevation: 4200-8926'
Seasons: Sp • •   S • • •   F • • •   W •

Although spectacular with its majestic scenery, Oregon's only
national park is of marginal interest for birds. It is easily
reached via three different entrances, two (the western and the
southern along OR 62) which are open all year. Crater Lake is
good for observing the high-elevation species from the
roadside and campgrounds. Especially look for Gray Jay,
Clark's Nutcracker, and the elusive Rosy Finch. The first two
species are easily found in major, above-timberline visitor
areas such as Rim Village and the park headquarters. The Rosy
Finch is harder to locate. They are usually seen during
summer on the highest peaks including Llao Rock, Applegate
Peak, Dutton Ridge, Garfield Peak, and Vidae Ridge. Also
check the caldera rim itself (best viewed by boat). During
winter they form large flocks and wander widely throughout
the lower open areas of the park, especially the Pumice Desert
north of the lake.

Typical nesting species of the dominant lodgepole and pine-
hemlock forest that covers most of the park include Blue
Grouse, Black-backed and Three-toed Woodpeckers,
Hammond's Flycatcher, Steller's Jay, Mountain Chickadee,
Red-breasted Nuthatch, Hermit Thrush, Townsend's Solitaire,
Yellow-rumped and Townsend's Warblers, Pine Siskin, and
Chipping Sparrow.

The southern and eastern portions of Crater Lake Nat'l. Pk.
harbor extensive stands of ponderosa pine forest. Look for the
associated bird species here — White-headed Woodpecker,
Williamson's Sapsucker, Dusky Flycatcher, Pygmy Nuthatch,
Nashville Warbler, Red Crossbill, Green-tailed Towhee, and
Fox Sparrow.

The lake itself is deep (at 1,932 feet, the deepest in North America) and lacks any kind of littoral zone; therefore, it is not very attractive to waterbirds, but Osprey and Bald Eagles are occasionally found. During late summer and fall the park may be a good place for observing migrant raptors.

Winter in Crater Lake Nat'l. Pk. is quiet and beautiful. Few birds remain except for Clark's Nutcrackers, Gray Jays, Common Ravens, and a few raptors.

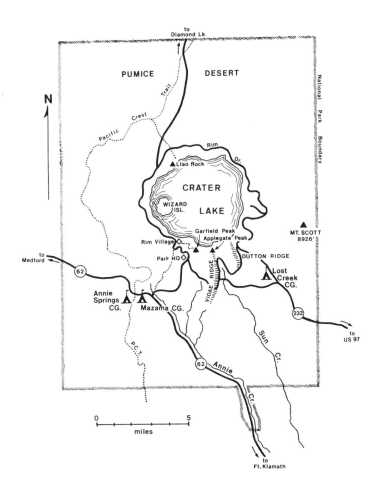

Klamath Forest National Wildlife Refuge

Habitats: FW, DF, FA, RA
Elevation: 4517-5200'
Seasons: Sp • •   S • •   F • •   W •

To reach Klamath Forest NWR, head north on US 97 from
Klamath Falls; 45 miles north of that town, turn east on Silver
Lake Rd. and continue on to the refuge entrance (6 miles from
US 97). This is an undeveloped refuge with no visitor facili-
ties; viewing is done from the car along the access roads. Most
of the refuge is covered with extensive tule and cattail
marshes. Typical summer species include White Pelican,
Double-crested Cormorant, Canada Goose, various ducks,
Ring-billed and California Gulls, Caspian, Black, and Forster's
Terns, American Bittern, Black-crowned Night-Heron, and
Virginia Rail and Sora. The extensive marshes most likely
support a good population of Least Bitterns even though the
species is rarely reported from here. Nesting Red-necked
Grebes and Ring-necked Ducks can be seen in roadside ponds
along the main road and Military Crossing Rd. to the north. A
good place to observe most of the water birds is in the Wocus
Bay area, located at the east end of the refuge. Access is best
along the Winema N.F. roads east of Wocus Bay, especially
N.F. Rds. 7602 and 690. The surrounding ponderosa pine
forests here support such interesting birds as Pygmy-Owl,
White-headed Woodpecker, Williamson's Sapsucker, Mountain Chickadee, Pygmy Nuthatch, Dusky and Gray (rare)
Flycatchers, Green-tailed Towhee, and Calliope Hummingbird.

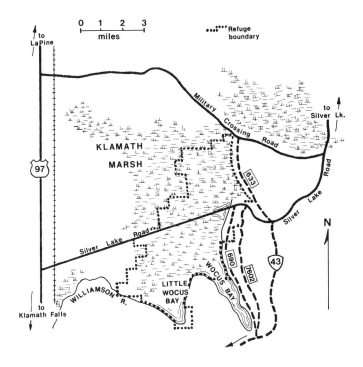

Fort Klamath Area

Habitats: DF, FA
Elevation: 4185'
Seasons: Sp • • S • • • F • • W •

The area between Agency Lake and Ft. Klamath is wet and grassy. In recent years this has been home to a surprising population of nesting Yellow Rails. Very rarely seen, these tiny secretive birds are best found after dark when their distinctive *"tick....tick....tick....tick"* call can be heard during the summer. Yellow Rails prefer the wet sedge meadows where the grasses are seldom more than three feet high. They readily answer tapes, *but use these sparingly and do not trample the fragile habitat* when searching for the rails. A particularly good site for the birds has been in the meadow immediately behind the Ft. Klamath National Historical Site interpretive sign just east of town. Other reports have come from the roadsides of Dixon Rd., Nicholson Rd., Weed Rd., and Seven-mile Rd.

Another specialty of this area is the magnificent Great Gray Owl. Although they occur throughout the forest-bordered meadowlands, a traditional site has been the Ft. Klamath dump and adjacent cemetery. To reach the dump, head north from the town of Klamath Agency on OR 62. About 6 miles north of that town, continue west on OR 62 toward Ft. Klamath. About 0.5 miles from this junction is the entry to the dump on the left.

Just north and east of Ft. Klamath is Kimball St. Pk., probably the most productive passerine birding site in this area. The park is famous for its underground source of the Wood River, and this amazing sight alone makes it worth a visit. A walk through the woodlands along the river should yield such nesting birds as chickadees, wrens, warblers, vireos, thrushes, finches, and sparrows.

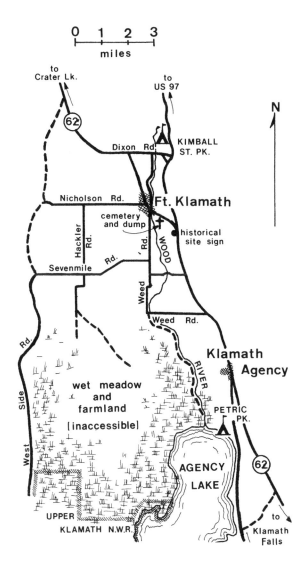

Upper Klamath Lake and National Wildlife Refuge

Habitats: FW, DF, WF, FA, BF, BR, RA, RR
Elevation: 4139-4200'
Seasons: Sp • • • S • • • • F • • • W • •

Huge Upper Klamath Lake offers some excellent birding opportunities, especially at the northern end and at Upper Klamath NWR. Along the eastern side of the lake, US 97 parallels the shore, offering good views at Hagelstein Park and Rattlesnake Point. Typical summering species to be found throughout the lake area include Western and Clark's Grebes, Great Egret, Great Blue Heron, Caspian, Forster's and Black Terns, White Pelican, Double-crested Cormorant, and Canada Goose. The Klamath Basin is unique in Oregon with its nesting (but local) Horned and Red-necked Grebes. An excellent access point to observe these local water birds is along the Link River in Klamath Falls at the very southeast corner of the lake. To reach the Link River, take the Oregon Ave. exit off US 97 in Klamath Falls. Go west on Nevada St. for 0.5 miles and follow the signs to Moore Park. There is a hiking trail here that follows the river.

Hagelstein Park is a good stop for the local summer passerines — Black-headed Grosbeak, Northern Oriole, Lazuli Bunting, Yellow Warbler, Western Wood-Pewee, Swainson's Thrush, etc.

At Modoc Point, US 97 splits off to the east; keep to the west toward Ft. Klamath on Modoc Point Rd. Where the highway crosses the Williamson River look for nesting Bank Swallows. A little farther north on the road is Henzel County Park, a good stop for checking the local nesting waterbirds on Agency Lake.

Upper Klamath NWR is difficult to explore as it is mostly wet marshland. It is reached via OR 140; about 27 miles northwest of Klamath Falls on this highway turn north on Rocky Point Rd. Follow the signs to Rocky Point Resort. This is one of the best sites in Oregon to find the shy and retiring Least Bittern. To see one of these birds, it is best to rent a canoe (or bring your own) from the resort; from here you can follow a marked canoe trail through the adjacent refuge. This is also a great place to observe breeding Red-necked Grebe and other wetland species. The bordering ponderosa pine forest around Upper Klamath NWR is good for the appropriate species such as White-headed Woodpecker, Pygmy Nuthatch, Mountain Chickadee, bluebirds, Dusky Flycatcher, and Green-tailed Towhee.

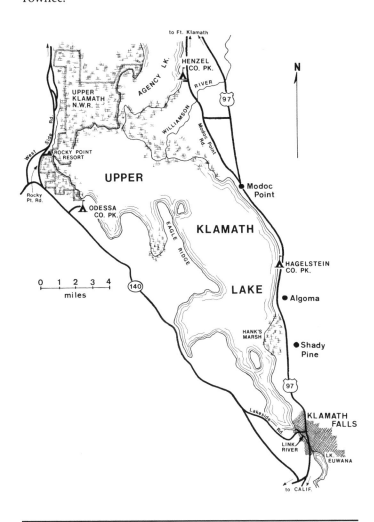

Klamath Wildlife Management Area

Habitats: FW, FA, BR
Elevation: 4093'
Seasons: Sp ● ● ●   S ● ●   F ● ● ●   W ● ●

Take US 97 south from Klamath Falls and cross the Klamath River. Proceed under the railroad crossing, then turn west on the first road (Miller Island Rd.). The WMA lies between US 97 and the Klamath River to the west. Managed as a migration resting area for waterfowl, Miller Island is mainly marshland interspersed with agricultural fields. Most of the state land is open to the public, but please avoid any areas that are posted as off-limits. And please avoid trespassing on adjacent (posted) private land.

Waterfowl numbers peak at Klamath WMA during early spring, from late February through April. The most notable species is the locally common Ross' Goose, a species found regularly at only a few select Oregon sites. Pure Ross' flocks often numbering in the thousands can be found anywhere on the WMA this time of year; also look for large numbers of Canada, White-fronted, and Snow Geese. Large concentrations of Tundra Swans are also present during February and March.

Also during early spring, search the cattail marshes and fields for the handsome but local Tricolored Blackbird, another specialty of the Klamath Basin. Shorebird migration during April and May can be interesting, and local nesters of note include Black-necked Stilt, American Avocet, and Wilson's Phalarope.

Lower Klamath
National Wildlife Refuge

Habitats: FW, SS, FA, BR
Elevation: 4080-4600'
Seasons: Sp • • • • S • • • F • • • • W • •

Although located mainly in California, this highly managed and farmed refuge is still worth visiting for the Oregon birder. Unlike the other refuges in the Klamath Basin, Lower Klamath is more visitor-oriented and offers a series of self-guided auto tours. Headquarters and a visitor center are located at nearby Tulelake NWR in California.

Of particular interest to Oregon birders is a drive along Stateline Rd., which begins about 0.3 miles south of the state border off US 97. Drive east on this road into the refuge; remember that the first 9 miles of Stateline Rd. are entirely

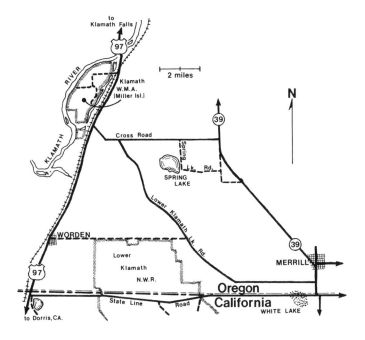

---

within California, but after that the road straddles the border all the way to OR 39 (a total of 19 miles from US 97 to OR 39). This route passes through dry upland habitats with intermittent marshes and alkali ponds. Summering species of note include American Bittern, Black-necked Stilt, Cinnamon and Blue-winged Teal, Snowy Egret, Black-crowned Night-Heron, American Avocet, Long-billed Curlew, and Wilson's Phalarope. The dry sage areas yield the typical desert species of the Great Basin such as Horned Lark, Sage Thrasher, Brewer's Sparrow, and Western Meadowlark.

About 5.5 miles west of Stateline Rd.'s junction with OR 39 is White Lake, an intermittent body of water that straddles the state border and is bisected by Stateline Rd. This is one of the best areas for birding — water levels permitting, White Lake is great for migrant shorebirds. Snowy Plovers have nested here, and during the winter months check the lake bed and surrounding fields for flocks of Lapland Longspurs (Chestnut-collared and McCown's have occurred here also).

Lower Klamath Lake Rd. (located just north of the refuge in Oregon) is a good secondary road to return to Klamath Falls on. Passing mainly through extensive irrigated farmland (actually the dry bed of Lower Klamath Lake), watch for migrant swans, geese (including Ross'), ducks, and Sandhill Cranes during spring and fall. Tricolored Blackbirds have been found at various cattail-lined ponds and marshes along this road and OR 39 north of Merrill. Spring Lake, located northwest of Merrill off OR 39, can be good for migrant shorebirds, gulls, and terns when water levels are adequate.

Fort Rock State Park/ Cabin Lake Campground

Habitats: SS, RR, DF, JW, RA
Elevation: 4340-4500'
Seasons: Sp • •   S • •   F • • •   W •

One mile north of the town of Fort Rock turn west into the state park. This impressive horseshoe-shaped rock formation is best known among birders for its easily observed White-throated Swift colony. Other nesting species along the towering cliffs include Violet-green and Cliff Swallows, Prairie Falcon, Rock and Canyon Wrens, and Rock Doves. The surrounding sagebrush areas support Horned Lark, Brewer's and Sage Sparrows, Sage Thrasher, Say's Phoebe, Green-tailed Towhee, and occasionally Gray Flycatchers.

About 10 miles north of the town of Fort Rock is Cabin Lake Ranger Station; the campground is located just beyond the RS. This is a transition area between the sagebrush flats and open pine-juniper woodlands and is remarkably profitable for the visiting birder. The main attraction here is the trickling spring with convenient observation blinds built nearby. During late summer and early fall these blinds are a great place to observe the elusive Pinyon Jay, a nomadic species that seldom occurs regularly at any other Oregon location. Other interesting species that may be found here include migrant warblers, flycatchers, and sparrows. Green-tailed Towhees, White-headed and Lewis' Woodpeckers, Pygmy Nuthatches, and Townsend's Solitaires may be seen in the surrounding woodland.

Summer Lake
Wildlife Management Area

Habitats: FW, SS, FA, RA, JW, RR
Elevation: 4150-4243'
Seasons: Sp • • • •   S • • •   F • • • •   W • •

The headquarters for this WMA is located in the town of
Summer Lake, one mile south of the post office on OR 31.
Check here for birding news, checklists, and maps of the
refuge. From headquarters, take Lint Canal Rd. east to enter
the refuge. Typical summering species include Black-crowned
Night-Heron, Great and Snowy (uncommon) Egrets, Cinnamon and Blue-winged Teal, Gadwall, American Avocet, Black-
necked Stilt, Willet, Forster's and Black Terns, Marsh Wren,
and Yellow-headed Blackbird. There is a small gull colony at
the north end of Summer Lake on the refuge which also hosts
a few nesting Caspian Terns. This end of the lake is also home
to nesting White Pelicans and Double-crested Cormorants. To
view the area, drive south off Lint Canal Rd. on Windbreak
Dike Rd.. The south end of the dike overlooks the lake and
the nesting island. Check the numerous alkali flats and ponds
throughout the refuge for migrant shorebirds and nesting
Wilson's Phalarope and Black-necked Stilt. Snowy Plover are
occasionally reported from appropriate habitat (alkali flats)
anywhere around the lake. Drier sagebrush flats in the area
support such species as Sage Thrasher, Brewer's, Sage, and Lark
Sparrow, Loggerhead Shrike, and Horned Lark.

During spring and fall, Summer Lake itself and the surrounding fields are a major resting area for thousands of migrant
waterfowl, especially Canada, White-fronted, and Snow Geese.
Ross' Geese occur in smaller flocks away from other geese,
mainly during spring (mid-March to April).

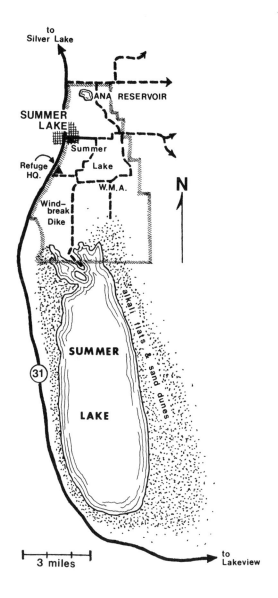

Abert Lake and Rim

Habitats: FW, RR, SS, NG, JW
Elevation: 4255-7600'
Seasons: Sp • • •   S • •   F • • •   W • •

Located adjacent to US 395 about 5 miles north of Valley Falls, Abert Lake is a valuable patch of bird habitat, especially during migration. Access for the visiting birder, however, is severely limited, and viewing must be done from the roadsides. This can be very risky along US 395, but a few gravel or dirt county roads at the north end of the lake offer access to the best birding areas. A dirt county road heads west from US 395 about 22 miles north of Valley Falls, at Abert Lake's north end. This road traverses the alkali flats and small marshes found in this floodplain. Look for summering Black-necked Stilt, American Avocet, Wilson's Phalarope, Cinnamon and Blue-winged Teals, and Black and Forster's Terns. Great and Snowy Egrets are occasionally seen here. Common summer birds likely to be seen on Abert Lake itself include Eared, Western, and Clark's Grebes and Ruddy Ducks. The alkali flats bordering the lake support one of Eastern Oregon's largest nesting populations of Snowy Plover; these are best observed at Abert Lake's north and east shores.

During spring, fall, and winter, Abert Lake hosts large numbers of visiting geese (Canada, White-fronted, Snow, and even Ross') and Tundra Swans along with thousands of other waterfowl. The lake is also a major resting place for south-ward-bound Wilson's Phalaropes, and up to 20 other shore-bird species can be reasonably expected during the fall.

Impressive Abert Rim rises 2500 ft. above the lake's east shoreline. During August, September, and early October, this steep escarpment produces thermals which are beneficial to migrating raptors, most notably Golden Eagles, Red-tailed, Rough-legged, Swainson's, and Ferruginous Hawks, and accipiters. Prairie Falcons and Ravens nest on the cliff faces, and White-throated Swifts are occasionally seen during migration. The top of Abert Rim is accessible only via ex-tremely rough jeep trails originating in the Fremont N.F. to the southeast. The topography is much like neighboring Hart Mountain — sagebrush flats interrupted by tiny stands of juniper and pine. An interesting site is Colvin Timbers, a remnant stand of ponderosa pine forest. Pygmy Nuthatch, Green-tailed Towhee, and Dusky Flycatcher have been reported from here, but the birding is hardly worth the effort of getting there.

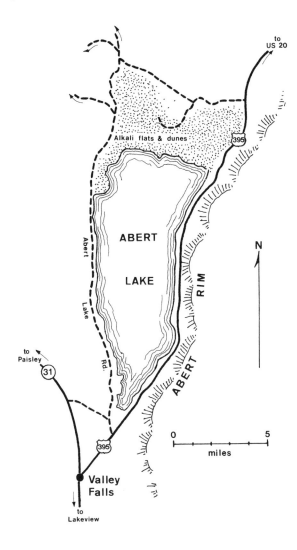

Lakeview

Habitats: FA, FW, UR, RA, BR, SS
Elevation: 5080'
Seasons: Sp • • •   S • •   F • • •   W •

Just north of greater Lakeview on US 395, turn west on
Missouri Rd., which veers off to the north and leads to Hot
Springs Pond, a large body of water adjacent to the scenic
Hunters Hot Springs Geyser. This very shallow seepage area is
a major shorebird spot for Lakeview — regular species include
Least and Western Sandpipers, Long-billed Dowitcher, both
yellowlegs, Spotted Sandpiper, Red-necked and Wilson's
Phalaropes, and Semipalmated Plover. Due to the local
geothermal activity, Hot Springs Pond remains unfrozen
during winter and often provides the only open water for
waterfowl in the vicinity. Although privately-owned, the
pond can still be birded by walking along the south border of
the property. Lakeview's sewage ponds are located south of
town, adjacent to Roberta Ave. between South 3rd and South
9th Streets. This area is fenced but can be adequately scoped
from the road. Look for migrant shorebirds here, especially
phalaropes. Small groups of Bonaparte's Gulls have oversum-
mered on the ponds a number of years, and it is a good place
to find a Barrow's Goldeneye during winter.

At the east end of Center St. in Lakeview, check the small city
park along Bullard Creek. This area is especially good during
winter when it attracts local passerines. Watch for sparrow
flocks, chickadees, finches, American Robin, Townsend's
Solitaire, and even waxwing flocks. Continuing east, Center
St. becomes Bullard Canyon Rd. after passing the park. This
wooded canyon with riparian growth along the creek is good
for local nesting species. Noteworthy summering birds
include Black-headed Grosbeak, Lazuli Bunting, Yellow-
breasted Chat, Yellow Warbler, and Warbling Vireo. A male
Black-chinned Hummingbird was seen on territory here one
summer, and the species should be expected again. Only the
first mile or two of this road is negotiable for most cars, and
even this stretch of road may be impassable sometimes.
Check at BLM or USFS offices in Lakeview for road conditions,
especially following rain or bad weather.

Warner Valley

Habitats: FW, FA, SS, RA, RR
Elevation: 4470-4490'
Seasons: Sp • • • S • • • F • • • W •

This extremely large wildlife area is a patchwork of land ownership including state lands, BLM property, and private property. As such, it is hard to bird, but the rich variety of wildlife makes Warner Valley a worthwhile place to visit.

Nestled at the base of Hart Mountain's dramatic west face (see next entry), Warner Valley's main attraction to wildlife is the chain of lakes which brings migrant waterbirds from miles around. There are ten major lakes that stretch some 40 miles from north to south: Bluejoint, Stone Corral, Campbell, Upper Campbell, Flagstaff, Mugwump, Swamp, Hart, Crump, and Pelican. Depending on local water conditions, the state of some lakes varies from dry alkali beds to permanant open water. The largest and most permanent include Hart and Crump.

The valley is best birded via a series of gravel roads beginning at the town of Adel. About 2 miles north of Adel on the road to Plush is the uppermost Warner Valley lake, Pelican Lake. Although tiny, it supports a large colony of nesting White Pelicans and Double-crested Cormorants. Pelican and nearby Crump Lakes are surrounded by wet grassy meadows and farm fields; they are among the most productive lakes for birding. Look for nesting Canada Geese, ducks, Sandhill Cranes (much more common during migration), rails, Long-billed Curlews, Willets, American Avocets, Black-necked Stilts (rare), Wilson's Phalaropes, and Forster's, Caspian, and Black Terns. During spring and fall, thousands of migrant geese use this end of the valley to rest and refuel — look for Snow, White-fronted, and even Ross' among the mostly Canadian flocks. Large numbers of migrant Tundra Swans also use this area, mainly during the fall; be alert for the possibility of finding a Trumpeter Swan among them.

Continuing on to the town of Plush, 18 miles north of Adel, the lakes become smaller, shallower, and less permanent. One mile north of Plush, the gravel road forks, one branch heading northeast to Hart Mountain Refuge, the other branch continuing northward along the west side of Warner Valley. The Hart Mountain branch gives excellent opportunities to scope out Hart Lake — good for grebes (including the local Clark's Grebe), ducks, gulls, and terns. About 10 miles northeast of Hart Lake this road climbs up to Hart Mountain, offering a spectacular view of the entire Warner Valley. By continuing northward on the westside road out of Plush — named Hogback Rd. — you get a better view of the drier, alkali-lined lower lakes (Flagstaff, Campbell, Bluejoint, etc.). These are particularly good for American Avocet, Wilson's Phalarope, and migrant shorebirds during spring and fall. These northernmost lakes, especially Bluejoint, occasionally have nesting Snowy Plover, a local and rare species anywhere in Oregon.

It is best to return to civilization by retracking to Plush and Adel; these towns offer the only services in the Warner Valley area. And be sure to check your gas tank and drinking water supply before leaving Plush!

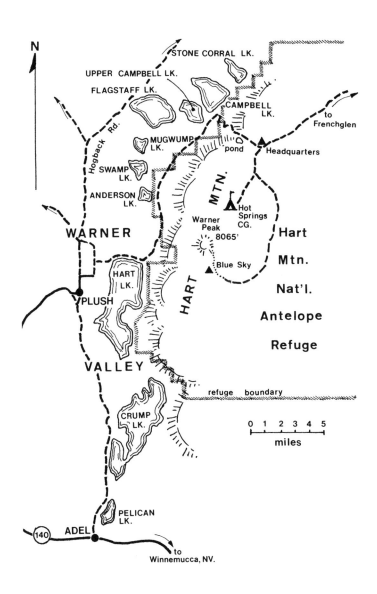

N

STONE CORRAL LK.

UPPER CAMPBELL LK.

FLAGSTAFF LK.

CAMPBELL LK.

to Frenchglen

MUGWUMP LK.

pond

Headquarters

SWAMP LK.

MTN.

ANDERSON LK.

Hot Springs CG.

Warner Peak 8065'

Hart

WARNER

Mtn.

Blue Sky

Nat'l.

HART LK.

Antelope

PLUSH

Refuge

HART

VALLEY

refuge boundary

CRUMP LK.

0 1 2 3 4 5
miles

PELICAN LK.

140 ADEL

to Winnemucca, NV.

Hart Mountain National Antelope Refuge

Habitats: SS, RR, JW, DF, NG, RA
Elevation: 4500-8065'
Seasons: Sp • • • S • • F • • • W •

Established mainly as a reserve for remnant herds of American pronghorn antelope, Hart Mountain is one of Oregon's most isolated refuges. As such, it receives very few visitors, but those who do venture over the miles of gravel roads for birding may be rewarded with some very unusual finds.

To reach Hart Mountain from Lakeview, take US 395 north for 5 miles to OR 140; turn east here and go 29 miles to the small town of Adel. In Adel, head north to the equally quaint town of Plush, a drive of about 18 miles. There is only one main road heading out of Plush to the northeast; about 25 miles from the town along this gravel road is refuge headquarters. This gravel road continues east from the refuge, eventually reaching Frenchglen, some 47 miles from refuge headquarters.

It should be noted that the roads to Hart Mountain are accessible to the average car only from mid-May through October; winter wash-outs are common, especially on the road between headquarters and Frenchglen. Be sure to fill the gas tank in Plush, Adel, or Frenchglen; these towns also have the only public facilities in this part of the state. Inquire about road conditions at Plush or Frenchglen before continuing on to the refuge.

Hart Mountain is a huge fault block that rises to an elevation of 8065' (Warner Peak). Excellent views of the rugged west face are found along the entrance road between Plush and headquarters. This winding, climbing stretch of road is good for Golden Eagle, Prairie Falcon, migrating raptors, and Canyon and Rock Wrens. White-throated Swifts are occasionally found along the west face, and it was here that the Chukar was first introduced in the Pacific Northwest, back in the 1940's. This handsome gamebird is quite common in the Hart

Mountain area, especially around the west face. Refuge headquarters is located about 4 miles east of the cliff area along the same road. Obtain maps, checklists, and general information here.

The east side of Hart Mountain is a much less dramatic sight than the sheer cliffs of the west face. Elevations bottom out at about 5000' on this side of the refuge and the terrain is dominated by extensive sagebrush and greasewood flats. In this habitat look for the typical desert birds: Common Nighthawk, Horned Lark, Black-billed Magpie, Common Raven, Loggerhead (summer) and Northern (winter) Shrikes, Western Meadowlark, Sage Thrasher, and sparrows — Vesper, Brewer's, Lark, Savannah, Sage, and even the occasional Black-throated. Hart Mountain is well-known for its large population of Sage Grouse, a species which, although quite common, is difficult to locate. During the summer months these grouse leave the lower areas of the refuge and head for higher elevations. At any time of year it usually takes some hiking to locate this secretive species. During March, April, and May, check at headquarters for locations of leks in the refuge area; this is usually the easiest and most enjoyable way to observe Sage Grouse.

In recent years Hart Mountain has yielded some remarkable passerine records, mainly from the groves of pine, aspen, juniper, and mountain mahogany found along the various creeks and springs of the eastern slope. The variety of land birds found on Hart Mountain is best observed in two areas. The first is at Hot Springs CG, the only camping area found on the refuge. To reach this enjoyable site, turn south on the gravel road at headquarters. About 1.7 miles south of headquarters, take the right (west) fork to the campground, another 2.5 miles or so. The lush riparian growth found here harbors many passerines, especially during migration. The other area for passerines is reached by heading south from headquarters; at 1.7 miles, take the left (east) fork and continue on to the Guano Creek/Blue Sky area, another 12 miles or so. Guano Creek supports a large grove of ponderosa pines with ample undergrowth; nearby is Blue Sky, a private lodge which a local hunting club maintains. An undeveloped road continues up Guano Creek past Blue Sky, and it is well worth walking. White-crowned Sparrows nest in the higher areas of Hart Mountain, and the wooded draws are home to Downy Woodpecker, Red-naped Sapsucker, White-headed Woodpecker (pines), Willow, Dusky, and Cordillean Flycatchers, Violet-green Swallow, all three nuthatches, House Wren, Cedar Waxwing, Warbling and Solitary Vireos, Yellow, Orange-crowned, Nashville, and MacGillivray's Warblers, and Black-headed Grosbeak.

Recently, ornithology students working out of the Malheur Environmental Field Station have been mist-netting, banding, and studying the local breeding White-crowned Sparrows of Hart Mountain. However, other real surprises have shown up, mainly during the traditional "vagrant period" of late May and June. Oregon's first verified Virginia's Warbler and Summer Tanager were banded and photographed at Blue Sky, and other vagrants found here include Broad-tailed Hummingbird, Williamson's Sapsucker, Least Flycatcher, Brown Thrasher, Gray Catbird, Veery, Red-eyed Vireo, Northern Parula, Black-throated Blue, Chestnut-sided, and Blackpoll Warblers, Ovenbird, American Redstart, Scarlet Tanager, and Rose-breasted Grosbeak! The tiny secretive Flammulated Owl has been netted and banded here so often that is is now considered a regular spring migrant in the pine groves.

Winter at Hart Mountain can be harsh but beautiful. Few birds other than Golden Eagles, Common Ravens, Black-billed Magpies, and Song Sparrows remain, but there have been so few birders here at this time of year that it is hard to predict what will appear; good winter finds in the past have included Mountain Chickadee, Pygmy Nuthatch, Mountain Bluebird, Rosy Finch ("gray-crowned"), Tree Sparrow, and Snow Bunting.

Region G
Northeast Oregon

Great Gray Owl

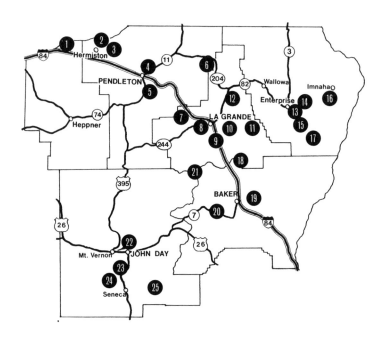

Umatilla
National Wildlife Refuge

Habitats: FW, RA, BR, BF, FA, SS
Elevation: 230-330'
Seasons: Sp ● ● ●   S ● ●   F ● ● ● ●   W ● ● ● ●

About 3 miles east of Boardman, exit I-84 at OR 730; head
northeast toward the town of Irrigon. Turn left (north) on
Paterson Ferry Rd. about 4 miles from the Interstate. Some 2
miles north of OR 730 along this road is the McCormack
Slough area, one of Umatilla NWR's only public access areas,
and the best area of the refuge for birding. A small observation area here has an interpretive sign and brochures, maps,
checklists, etc. Just north of the McCormack Slough area,
gravel roads lead into dry upland parcels of the refuge with
groves of cottonwood, willow, and Russian olive interspersed
with marshy sloughs and ponds. The surrounding open
country is mostly irrigated farmland or dry sagebrush/grass-
land flats. This part of Umatilla County is unique along with
the Alvord Basin in supporting large native populations of
cactus in Oregon (a form of prickly pear).

Umatilla NWR is mainly a migration resting area for geese and
ducks. McCormack Slough is one of the few sites where the
local nesting species can be found in good numbers. Look for
American Bittern, Virginia Rail, Sora, Marsh Wren, Yellow-
headed Blackbird, and Common Yellowthroat in the cattail
marshes here. The dense willows and Russian olives are home
to wintering Barn Owls and Long-eared Owls. Also during the
winter, northern Umatilla Co. is a sparrow haven. Most birds
in the large wintering flocks will be White-crowned Sparrows,
but there are usually a few Golden-crowneds in with them.
Every winter a few Harris' are found — reports have come
from Umatilla, Cold Springs, and McKay Creek NWR's,
Hermiston feeders, and even "downtown" Irrigon! Also look
for wintering Tree Sparrows, another scarce Oregon species.

During spring and fall, thousands of Canada Geese migrate through the Umatilla NWR, and upwards of 80,000 geese and 325,000 ducks winter throughout the refuge. The best places for observing some of these birds is in the McCormack Slough area; the area along I-84 just west of Boardman (visible only from the Interstate); and in the farm fields around Umatilla and Irrigon.

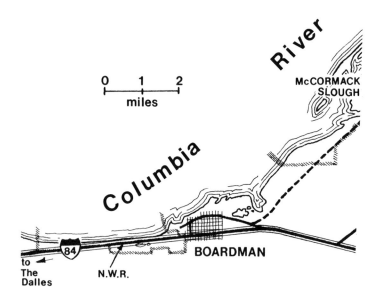

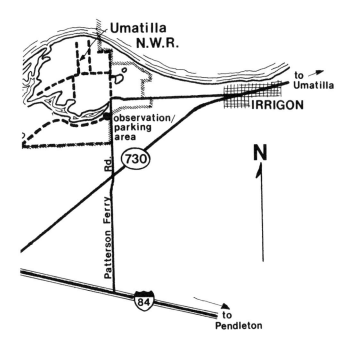

McNary Wildlife Park

Habitats: FW, RA, BR, FA
Elevation: 440'
Seasons: Sp • • • S • • F • • • W • •

Located below McNary Dam, this former gravel pit area has been reconstructed into an excellent birding spot with numerous sloughs, marshes, woodlots, and open fields. To reach the general area, head north on the secondary road at the intersection of OR 730 and US 395. This takes you to McNary Dam, an excellent winter birding area. The wildlife park and its system of trails, picnic facilities, and viewing areas is located just to the west of the dam. Typical summering species here include Great Blue Heron, Black-crowned Night-Heron, nesting Canada Goose, Wood Duck, California Quail, Virgina Rail, Sora, Spotted Sandpiper, Ring-billed and California Gulls, Mourning Dove, and Great Horned Owl. The lush growth of willow, cottonwood, and other riparian plants are a haven for passerines including Yellow Warbler, Common Yellowthroat, Marsh and House Wrens, sparrows, and other species. The conspicuous Bewick's Wren, found almost nowhere else in Eastern Oregon other than the Columbia Basin, is very common here.

The waters around McNary Dam are especially productive during migration and winter. Among the hundreds of wintering ducks and geese — mostly Lesser Scaup, Common Goldeneye, Bufflehead, Canvasback, American Wigeon, Mallard, Pintail, and Common Merganser — small numbers of the rare species such as Common Loon, grebes, Greater Scaup, Redhead, Barrow's Goldeneye, and even Oldsquaw are found every winter. Gull concentrations during late fall and winter have included small numbers of Glaucous-winged and Westerns each year among the more common California, Ring-billed, and Herring. Rarities such as Glaucous, Mew, and Thayer's Gulls, small terns, and even Parasitic Jaeger have been special rewards for patient observers.

Cold Springs
National Wildlife Refuge

Habitats: FW, FA, SS, BR, RA, BF
Elevation: 623'
Seasons: Sp • • • S • • F • • • • W • • •

This refuge consists mainly of a large man-made lake surrounded by extensive stands of willow, cottonwood, Russian
olive, and riparian growth. This is interspersed with upland
desert vegetation and provides a rich island of bird habitat in
the surrounding sea of agricultural land.

To reach the refuge, turn east on East Highland Ave. at the
southernmost traffic light in Hermiston. Follow the road 1.5
miles and bear left onto Stanfield Loop Rd. Another 5.1 miles
turn north (left) onto a gravel road entering the refuge. This
puts you at the southern entrance of the NWR.

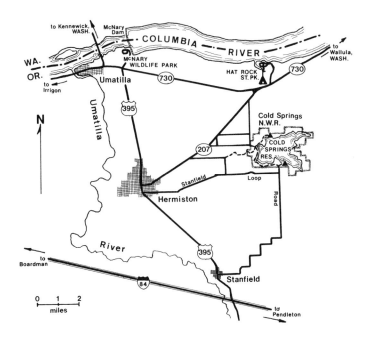

Like many NWR's, much of Cold Springs is closed to entry during hunting season, October through March, but there are still many open roads and viewing areas.

During the dry season beginning in June, Cold Springs Reservoir is gradually drained for irrigation which exposes mudflats that are excellent habitat for shorebirds. The flats at the northeast and southeast corners of the lake are the most productive. Typical migrant species include Western and Least Sandpipers, Long-billed Dowitchers, both yellowlegs, Semipalmated and Black-bellied Plovers, Wilson's Phalarope, and Spotted Sandpiper. The occasional Golden-Plover, Marbled Godwit, Sanderling, Dunlin, and Solitary Sandpiper occur in small numbers each fall. Other migrant waterbirds to watch for include White Pelican, Great Egret, White-fronted and Snow Geese, Eared and Horned Grebes, and Common Loon (deep-water birds are best observed near the dam on the west side of the lake). Gulls that congregate regularly on the flats include Ring-billed and California (the predominant species throughout Eastern Oregon), but check for the occasional migrant Bonaparte's or even Caspian, Common, or Black Terns. Franklin's Gulls have appeared a number of times.

The farm fields surrounding the refuge are an occasional magnet for passing Sandhill Cranes. Migrant landbirds occur in the many groves of trees around Cold Springs Reservoir. Look for the usual chickadees, kinglets, warblers, vireos, wrens, etc. Mountain species often show up here during fall or winter — Williamson's Sapsucker, Hammond's Flycatcher, Steller's Jay, Mountain Chickadee, Mountain Bluebird, Hermit Thrush, and Cassin's Finch have all appeared. Typical nesting species include Northern Oriole, Yellow Warbler, Warbling Vireo, Black-headed Grosbeak, House Wren, American Goldfinch, Marsh Wren, six swallow species, and Western Kingbird. There is a resident local population of Bewick's Wrens on the refuge.

Winter birdlife is much less varied, but surprises still occur. This time of year the lake supports an occasional loon or grebe, flocks of Canada Geese, Pintail, Mallards, and scores of other waterfowl. Raptor numbers increase dramatically. Any of the three accipiters can be encountered, and there are good numbers of Red-tailed and Rough-legged Hawks all over. Bald Eagles patrol the lake, and the Russian olive groves are home to Barn, Great Horned, and Long-eared Owls. Although seldom seen, Screech-Owls are common residents in the cottonwoods, and Saw-whet Owls are rare winter visitors. The open fields support numbers of Northern Harriers, Short-eared Owls, and Northern Shrikes this time of year. Pheasants are abundant in the brushy draws and open country, and California Quail can be found on most trips. Gray Partridge are occasionally seen in the farmland. Winter sparrow flocks may yield such unusual species as Tree, Fox, Lincoln's, Golden-crowned, and Harris' Sparrows.

Wildhorse Creek Area

Habitats: RA, BR, FA
Elevation: 1048'
Seasons: Sp ● ● ●   S ● ●   F ● ● ●   W ● ●

In Pendleton, take OR 11 north towards Walla Walla, WA. About 0.75 miles after crossing the Umatilla River in Pendleton, take a left (northwest) turn onto Mt. Hebron Rd. This road can be followed for about 6.5 miles to the community of Havana where you can return to OR 11 and thus back to Pendleton.

Check this stretch of country road for the rare Northern Bobwhite, a species introduced to the Walla Walla area in the late 1800's. It eventually spread into adjacent parts of Oregon, including the Wildhorse Creek area. It is very elusive compared to the California Quail which also occurs here. Ring-necked Pheasant are abundant and Gray Partridge are also reported, especially during winter.

Many summering birds will be found along this stretch of road including Northern Oriole, Lazuli Bunting, Yellow Warbler, Lewis' Woodpecker, and Black-headed Grosbeak. A year-round resident is the sprightly Bewick's Wren.

During winter and fall check the numerous sparrow flocks as Harris' is possible and Tree Sparrows have occurred. Winter also brings raptors — Cooper's, Sharp-shinned, Red-tailed, and Rough-legged Hawks, Northern Harrier, Prairie Falcon, and even Golden Eagle are regular visitors.

McKay Creek
National Wildlife Refuge

Habitats: BR, FW, FA, SS, BF
Elevation: 1322'
Seasons: Sp ••• sS •• F ••• W •••

McKay Creek Reservoir is located about 6 miles south of
Pendleton, just east of US 395. Established in 1927, McKay
Creek NWR serves primarily as a reserve for wintering waterfowl; an estimated 30,000 ducks (mostly Mallard, Pintail, and
Green-winged Teal) and 10,000 Canada Geese utilize the area
from early September to mid-April. Most waterfowl prefer the
shallower, more marshy south end of the lake. To reach the
best viewing area at this end of the reservoir, take US 395
south from Pendleton about 9 miles to a gravel county road;
turn east here, then north on another gravel road 1.0 mile
from the highway. An observation parking lot with walkable
trail is located about a mile farther north.

In addition to the above species, watch for smaller numbers of
Snow and White-fronted Geese, Sandhill Crane, White
Pelican, and Double-crested Cormorant during migration. The
swans occasionally remain through the winter. Nesting
waterfowl (mostly at the lake's south end) include Canada
Goose, Blue-winged and Cinnamon Teal (and small numbers
of Green-winged), Mallard, Pintail, Gadwall, Shoveler, and
Redhead. In additon, another 11 duck species may be encountered during migration. Almost as impressive as the waterfowl
are the large numbers of Ring-necked Pheasants around in the
upland areas, especially during fall and winter.

Be sure to check the dam area at the north end of the lake for
deep-water birds. Loons, grebes, diving ducks, gulls, and terns
are expected here during migration (especially fall).

Passerines are mostly restricted to the riparian growth and
brushy areas at the south end of the refuge. Bewick's Wrens
can be found here all year, and summer nesters include
Northern Oriole, Yellow-breasted Chat, Lazuli Bunting, Black-
headed Grosbeak, Yellow Warbler, and House Wren. Winter-

ing species also enjoy the shelter found at this end of the lake. Large numbers of sparrows are common, with a good chance for an unusual species such as Harris, Tree, Golden-crowned, or Lincoln's. Also look for House Finch, American Goldfinch, Common Redpoll (rare), chickadees, kinglets, and Downy Woodpecker during the colder months.

Raptors usually put in a good showing during winter. There are usually a few accipiters around (any of the three species is likely), and Red-tailed and Rough-legged Hawks are common. Occasional visitors include Golden and Bald Eagles, Prairie Falcon, and Merlin. Search the thickets of willow and Russian olive for Long-eared and Barn Owls.

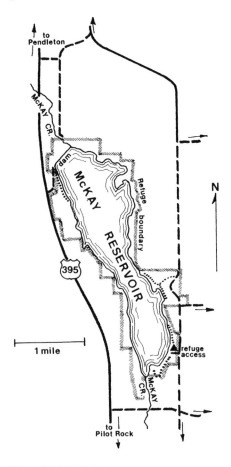

Tollgate

Habitats: WF, DF, FW, BR
Elevation: 5030'
Seasons: Sp • • S • • • • F • • • W •

The small resort community of Tollgate is mostly privately-owned, and the shores of Langdon Lake (visible from the main highway) are not open to public access. Birders can enter the adjacent Woodward CG on the lake's west shore, however, and some good finds have occurred here. Much of the Tollgate area is forested with lodgepole pine, western larch, and grand fir, and this habitat supports some of the highly sought-after mountain birds. Three-toed Woodpeckers have been seen in the camping area (October), and Northern Goshawks are sometimes reported. On the nearby Umatilla N.F. roads, look for Pine Grosbeak, Red and White-winged (rare) Crossbills, Pine Siskin, Cassin's Finch, and Evening Grosbeak during fall and winter. Gray Jays often outnumber Steller's, especially during winter. Mountain and Chestnut-backed Chickadees are resident. During summer check the CG for such species as Vaux's Swift, Calliope Hummingbird, Olive-sided and Hammond's Flycatchers, Hermit Thrush, Yellow-rumped and Townsend's Warblers, Western Tanager, and Chipping Sparrow.

In 1988, birders were surprised by the discovery of Boreal Owls in the higher mountains of this part of Oregon. Although Tollgate is a little too low (the owls were found at 5500-6000'), appropriate habitat may be found to the northeast of this site. Apparently, the Oregon Boreal Owls utilize forests of lodge-pole pine, subalpine fir, and especially Engelmann spruce, usually situated on ridgetops. The closely-related Saw-whet Owl occurs in the Langdon Lake area.

Spring Creek Road

Habitats: WF, DF, BR
Elevation: 3500'
Seasons: Sp • • •   S • • • •   F • • •   W •

About 13.25 miles east of Meacham (about 15 miles west of La Grande) on I-84 is the well-marked Spring Creek Rd. exit. Head south on this excellent gravel road to the first conspicuous fork, 2.75 miles from the Interstate. This fork is at the second crossing of Spring Creek, and there is a small parking area here next to a gravel pile. From the parking area explore the open forest immediately to the west.

Averaging about 3500' in elevation, Spring Creek offers a good sampling of the typical avifauna of the Blue Mountains. Most of the trees will be lodgepole pine, ponderosa pine, and western larch, and there are some cottonwoods found along the small intermittent creek. What really makes this area attractive to birds, however, is the severe damage done to large stands of forest. This is the work of three major insect pests — the spruce budworm, the tussock moth, and the western pine beetle. Because of all the insect life found here, Spring Creek is known as the woodpecker capital of Oregon. Ten species of these birds have been reported here, and only two of those (Downy Woodpecker, Red-breasted Sapsucker) are not regulars. All ten species have been found within a half-mile of the parking area. A particularly good area for Williamson's Sapsucker and Three-toed and Black-backed Woodpeckers is in the burned-off snag area just northwest of the parking pull-out.

Another attraction of Spring Creek is usually seen in this burned-off snag area. This is the secretive Great Gray Owl. A few pairs have nested in this area for about ten years. The birds here use two wooden nesting platforms that ODFW has erected at the southeast end of the burn. They are located in two tall ponderosa pines about 50' off the ground.

At night the owling at Spring Creek can be very exciting. In addition to the Great Gray, look and listen for Great Horned,

Flammulated, Screech, Pygmy, Saw-whet, and even Barred, all which have been recorded from the immediate area. Diurnal raptors frequently encountered include Northern Goshawk and Sharp-shinned, Cooper's, and Red-tailed Hawks.

During May and June, expect such nesting passerines as Hammond's, Dusky, and Olive-sided Flycatchers, Gray and Steller's Jays, Mountain Chickadee, all three nuthatches, Brown Creeper, Hermit and Varied Thrushes, Western Bluebird, Townsend's Solitaire, Solitary Vireo, Yellow-rumped, Townsend's, and MacGillivray's Warblers, Western Tanager, Cassin's Finch, Pine Siskin, Red Crossbill, and loads of Dark-eyed Juncos. Most of the hummingbirds will be either Rufous or Calliope, but Broad-tailed has been seen once and Black-chinned is certainly possible.

Spring Creek Rd. is open from late March through early November, depending on the weather conditions. The best birding is from mid-May to mid-June when most species are in full song. Owling is most profitable from early March through mid-June.

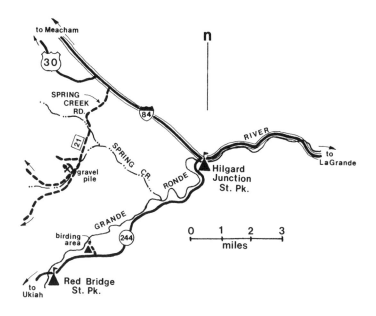

Grande Ronde River Area

Habitats: RA, BF, FW
Elevation: 3030'
Seasons: Sp • • •   S • • • •   F • • •   W • •

About 9 miles west of La Grande on I-84, take the OR 244
turnoff to the south. Hilgard Junction St. Pk. is located on the
scenic Grande Ronde River at this intersection. When not too
crowded, this can be a very enjoyable birding spot. Check the
riverside cottonwoods and willows for such species as Red-
naped Sapsucker, Dusky and Willow Flycatchers, Wood-Pewee,
six species of swallows, House Wren, Veery, Swainson's
Thrush, Warbling Vireo, and Yellow Warbler. Cordilleran
Flycatchers have nested along the river at the west end of the
park. Dippers occasionally occur along this stretch of the
river.

About 6 miles from I-84, look for an unpaved road on the
right side of OR 244 (after passing a ranch house and a stretch
of pine woods that crosses the highway on the left). This dirt
road takes you to a beautiful riparian area interspersed with
large cottonwoods and ponderosa pines. The densely vegetated area is best explored on foot from mid-May to August
(the earlier the better). The boggy willow thickets and groves
of alder, cottonwood, and other deciduous trees in this area
make it the place in Oregon to find Gray Catbird, Veery, Red-
eyed Vireo, and American Redstart. All four of these "eastern"
species are quite common but frequently hard to observe as
they tend to hide deep in the vegetation or high in the tree
tops. The tiny Calliope Hummingbird is almost a guaranteed
species here — look for the territorial males sitting on the
highest available perch atop the willow bushes. Willow
Flycatchers are abundant here, and in recent years the closely
related Alder Flycatcher has been found singing and defending
territory. To make the *Empidonax* game even more challeng-
ing, Dusky, Hammond's, and Cordilleran Flycatchers occur
here during migration, and the rare Least should be looked
for. Although not reported from northeast Oregon as of yet,
this would be an excellent site for Northern Waterthrush and
Ovenbird to occur.

Ladd Marsh
Wildlife Management Area

Habitats: FW, BF, RA
Elevation: 2775'
Seasons: Sp • •   S • • •   F • • •   W • •

Although most of this natural marshland is off-limits to the public, there is a worthwhile viewpoint that offers good birding. At the southeast end of La Grande, take Foothill Rd. south out of town. The Ladd Marsh Overlook is on the left, about 4 miles south of the Foothill Rd.-Geckler Ln. intersection in La Grande. This marsh supports northeast Oregon's only regularly nesting population of Sandhill Cranes (currently 5-10 pairs). Also seen or heard from this overlook during summer are American Bittern, Black-crowned Night-Heron, nesting Canvasback, Northern Harrier, Virginia Rail, Sora, Marsh Wren, and Yellow-headed Blackbird. Of particular interest is the small population of nesting Bobolinks which may be seen in the wetter hay fields anywhere along the 1.5 mile stretch of Foothill Road north of the overlook.

About 0.75 miles south of the overlook are the ODFW horse barns with a small abandoned orchard on the west side of the road. Park here and explore the woodlot anytime of the year (it is open to the public). Western Screech-Owls are resident and it is a good passerine area. Migrant warblers, vireos, flycatchers, thrushes, sparrows, and other birds are quite common. During the winter, ODFW keeps a bird feeder going here (as well as a larger trough for feeding deer). Look for sparrows, thrushes, chickadees, and kinglets. There is usually an attendant Sharp-shinned or Cooper's Hawk present, also.

Grande Ronde Valley

Habitats: FA, FW, SS, RA, BF, UR
Elevation: 2700-2800'
Seasons: Sp • • • •   S • • •   F • • •   W • •

There is a small loop route just south of La Grande off OR 203 that is most productive for the birder with limited time. Take OR 203/US 30 southeast from La Grande toward Union. About 2.75 miles out of La Grande, I-84 passes over OR 203. Just south of this overpass is La Grande's sewage treatment plant. These are some of the largest sewage ponds found in the state, so be sure to bring a scope. The entrance is on the southeast side of the ponds just off OR 203. As with any sewage ponds, ask permission to enter the fenced off areas. During winter, these ponds and nearby Hot Lake are often the only unfrozen bodies of water in the county. Canada Geese and a variety of wintering ducks (dabblers and divers) are found then. During summer there are nesting American Avocets and Wilson's Phalaropes in the smaller, half-dry ponds to the east of the two main lagoons. Blue-winged and Cinnamon Teal are common summer residents here and throughout the Grande Ronde Valley. Ring-billed and California Gulls congregate on the dike between the larger ponds; during August and September they are sometimes joined by Bonaparte's Gulls and Caspian and Black Terns. Twenty-eight species of waterfowl have occurred here during migration, along with Common Loons, five species of grebes, and Double-crested Cormorants. Rarities include Trumpeter Swan, Ross' Goose, Greater Scaup, Oldsquaw, Surf Scoter, Sabine's Gull, and Common Tern. During spring and fall migration look for shorebirds on these ponds. Among the usual yellowlegs (both kinds), Least and Western Sandpipers, Wilson's Phalaropes, and Long-billed Dowitchers, look for uncommon but regular Semipalmated Plover, Solitary, Baird's, and Pectoral Sandpipers, Red-necked Phalarope, and more avocets. In the private farm fields to the east and south of the ponds, look for nesting (or at least summering) Long-billed Curlews and Gray Partridge. The marshy slough between the highway and the northeast edge of the ponds (best observed from the highway) supports nesting Yellow-headed Blackbirds, Virginia Rails, Soras, Marsh Wrens, and American Coots.

Another 1.5 miles south of the I-84 overpass turn left (north) onto Pierce Ln., crossing the railroad tracks. Then make an immediate right (east) turn onto Hot Lake-Airport Rd. This route goes through dry grassland and irrigated farmland. Savannah Sparrows abound here, and Short-eared Owls are a common sight during the late afternoon. To the north is the La Grande Municipal Airport, a good open area for Long-billed Curlews. Common raptors here include Northern Harrier, Red-tailed and Swainson's (summer) Hawks, and Prairie Falcon (mainly during winter).

Another 2.5 miles east of Hot Lake-Airport Rd.'s junction with Pierce Ln. is Peach Ln. to the north. There are some stock-ponds about 0.75 miles north on this road that are attractive to migrating shorebirds and nesting avocets. Also in this area, on the west side of the road, is the only known nesting colony

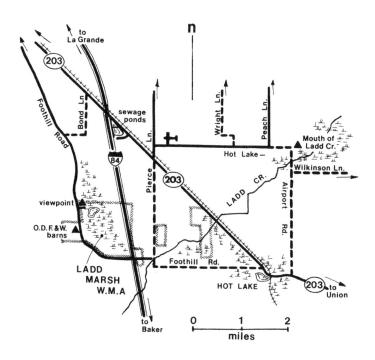

of Burrowing Owls in the Grande Ronde Valley; unfortunately, the sparse native habitat they occupy is being assaulted by grazing cattle and will probably soon disappear. Currently there is only one or two pairs of owls and a few nesting pairs of Long-billed Curlews in these fields.

A half-mile east of the Peach Ln. junction, Airport Rd. takes a 90-degree turn due south. There is a large sand pit at this corner which currently hosts one of the state's largest Bank Swallow colonies. Barn Owls occasionally roost in the larger holes here. This corner is also a good vantage point for scoping the marshy mouth of Ladd Creek immediately to the east. Canada Geese nest here, and the large willow-cotton-wood grove a mile east of the road hosts a Great Blue Heron rookery and wintering Bald Eagles. Between this corner and Wilkinson Ln. to the south (see map), there is excellent country for migrant shorebirds, and Ospreys are regular visitors during spring. Rare migrants found here include Sandhill Crane, White Pelican, Great Egret, Green-backed Heron, Ross' Goose, Black-necked Stilt, and White-faced Ibis. The amount of water in this area is much reduced and frequently frozen during most winters, but check the willow thickets for sparrow flocks during that time of year. Most will be White-crowned and Song, but good numbers of Tree Sparrows are found here every year, usually from November through March. Winter raptors are common — mostly Red-tailed and Rough-legged Hawks and Northern Harriers, but all three accipiters, Great Horned Owls, Prairie Falcons, and even "Harlan's" Red-tailed Hawks are regular.

Continue south from the sand pit 2.75 miles back to OR 203. At this intersection is Hot Lake, whose sulphuric waters support little birdlife. It should be checked during winter, though, for it may be the only unfrozen water in the valley. From Hot Lake return to La Grande or continue on to Union via OR 203.

Moss Springs Guard Station

Habitats: WF, DF, FA
Elevation: 2900-6900'
Seasons: Sp • • S • • • • F • • • W •

This region borders the Eagle Cap Wilderness Area and has been considered for inclusion in the past. The Moss Springs area averages around 6000' in elevation and is characterized by rocky terrain and dense coniferous forests composed of high-elevation tree species such as white fir, larch, lodgepole pine, and Engelmann spruce. The understory can be very dense, especially along creeks and streams. Due to weather and road conditions, the area is accessible only from June through October, and the road north of Moss Springs Guard Station can be impassable some years. Check at the Forest Service headquarters in La Grande for maps and current road conditions.

To reach the area, take Mill Creek Rd. east from the town of Cove (follow signs in town to Moss Springs GS). This becomes N.F. Rd. 6220 upon entering the Wallowa-Whitman N.F., some four miles or so out of Cove. There are numerous spur roads off Mill Creek Rd., but the main road is easily discerned. Some of these more undeveloped side roads may be worth checking out on foot. Moss Springs GS is some 7 miles from Cove; elevation gain along this stretch of road is quite astounding. A camping area and the entrance to the Eagle Cap Wilderness Area are also located here at the guard station.

The main avian attraction of the Moss Springs area is the elusive Spruce Grouse. Restricted in Oregon to the Wallowa Mountain system, this beautiful grouse is highly sought after by both local and visiting birders. Moss Springs GS has been the most consistent site for the species in recent years. Late in the summer (August-September), Spruce Grouse may be seen by driving the more heavily forested roads in the area; if this doesn't work, try hiking one of the many trails branching off the roads. Note that both Blue (common) and Ruffed Grouse also occur here, but they are seldom as tame as the Spruce. Other birds to look for include Gray Jay (very common),

Mountain and Chestnut-backed Chiakadees, Goshawk, Flammulated Owl (lower areas of ponderosa pine), and finches such as Pine Siskin, Cassin's Finch, Red Crossbill, and Evening Grosbeak. White-winged Crossbill and Pine Grosbeak have also been found. Interesting nesting passerines include Olive-sided and Hammond's Flycatchers, Swainson's, Hermit, and Varied Thrushes, Townsend's Solitaire, Solitary Vireo, Yellow-rumped and Townsend's Warblers, Western Tanager, and Chipping, White-crowned, and Lincoln's Sparrows. Open grassy areas support many beautiful wildflowers; Calliope and Rufous Hummingbirds thrive here, and the rare Broad-tailed and uncommon Black-chinned Hummingbirds have also been found.

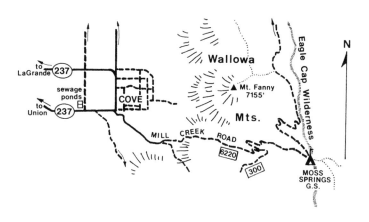

Rhinehart Bridge

Habitats: RA, BF, RR
Elevation: 2711'
Seasons: Sp • • • S • • • F • • W •

Take OR 82 north from La Grande. North of Imbler, the highway crosses the Grande Ronde River (before reaching the town of Elgin). Make the first right turn north of the river onto the old highway; this is just past milepost 18. Follow this deteriorating road southward to its end at the Old Rhinehart Bridge. This structure is closed to cars, and it is best to walk the last 0.5 miles or so to the bridge.

The Grande Ronde River flows through the scenic Rhinehart Canyon at this point and is lined with dense riparian growth. There is a very interesting cottonwood stand at the south end of the bridge that deserves some time. North of the bridge there are some small stands of ponderosa pine which have had Pygmy Nuthatch and Green-tailed Towhee a number of times. The canyon along the river has nesting Rock Wren and occasionally Prairie Falcon. Lazuli Bunting, House Wren, Black-headed Grosbeak, American Goldfinch, Yellow and MacGillivray's Warblers, Northern Oriole, Willow Flycatcher, and House Finch are among the more common summer residents and nesters. American Redstarts are found here infrequently, usually in the cottonwood grove. Specialties to look for from late May through August include Veery, Gray Catbird, and Yellow-breasted Chat, three species more often heard than seen.

From mid-April to early June, and again from late August to early October, check Rhinehart Canyon for migrant passerines. Many of the mountain species occur then, especially during the spring. Hammond's and Dusky Flycatchers, Townsend's, Orange-crowned, Nashville, and Wilson's Warblers, Olive-sided Flycatcher, Cassin's Finch, Chipping Sparrow, and Western Tanager have all occurred. Virtually anything can occur in this small canyon during migration as recent records of Ash-throated Flycatcher, Tennessee Warbler, and Rose-breasted Grosbeak will attest.

Upper Wallowa Valley

Habitats: RA, BF, FA, BR, FW, WF, JW, UR
Elevation: 3500-4190'
Seasons: Sp • • •   S • • •   F • • •   W • •

Enterprise, the county seat and largest city of Wallowa County, is the center of any birding expedition into this isolated area. Not only are gas, food, and lodging available here, but it is the best place to inquire about local road conditions and to obtain information about the nearby Eagle Cap Wilderness Area. And to top it all off, the Enterprise-Joseph area offers some of the best birding in Eastern Oregon any time of year.

Two miles west of Enterprise on OR 82, turn south on Alder Slope Rd. There is a parking pull-out on the east side of the road immediately after crossing the Wallowa River. This is the public access area for the combined Enterprise WMA and Wallowa Fish Hatchery. Bordering the road on the east there is a large wooded pond and marsh which offer excellent birding; an undeveloped trail heads east along the railroad tracks, then south along a dike on the east side of the pond. Look for nesting Virginia Rail, Sora, Marsh Wren, Yellowthroat, and tons of Yellow Warblers here. Although much more unusual, summering American Redstarts and Gray Catbirds have also been found here. During migration and winter (as long as the water remains unfrozen), an amazing variety of waterfowl occurs here including both goldeneyes, Bufflehead, Gadwall, Green-winged Teal, Wood Duck, and Hooded Merganser. This is probably the most productive birding site in Wallowa County during the winter when many passerines are restricted to the sparse riparian river bottoms. Along the dike on the east side of the pond are numerous large cottonwoods — check the nesting boxes here for resident Screech-Owls. Winter sparrow flocks here have included Harris', Tree, and Golden-crowned. Large flocks of California Quail and Ring-necked Pheasants winter in the brushy juniper woodland here. When these conifers have an ample berry crop, Townsend's Solitaires, American Robins, and Mountain Bluebirds are frequent visitors to the fish hatchery area.

During winter, spend a few hours birding in the towns of Enterprise and Joseph. Much of the birdlife this time of year is restricted to these residential areas. Although not recorded every year, this is one of the best areas in Oregon to find the unpredictable Pine Grosbeak, White-winged Crossbill, and Common Redpoll. Among the best locations to check for these birds are the ornamental spruces at the county courthouse in Enterprise, and at the numerous bird feeders scattered throughout both towns.

An amazing site for studying and photographing waterfowl is at Pete's Pond in Enterprise. Located in the southwest corner of town near the railroad grain towers, the pond is best

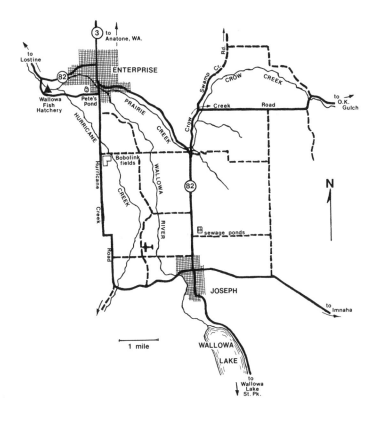

observed from the roadside along Montclaire St. This former mill pond has been converted into a waterfowl display pond by the local owners. During migration and winter, Pete's Pond attracts wild waterfowl, and it is a remarkable place to get close looks at such species as Ring-necked and Wood Ducks, Barrow's and Common Goldeneyes, Bufflehead, Common Merganser, and Lesser Scaup. Migrant geese occasionally drop in for a rest, as is the case with the two resident Ross' Geese which have remained at the pond for at least 7 years!

The rural farmland between Enterprise and Joseph also offers good birding. In addition to the main highway (OR 82), there is a less-travelled backroad of equal mileage that connects the two towns. In Enterprise, head due south on Hurricane Creek Rd. Almost 2 miles south of the Hurricane Creek Rd. - OR 82 junction in Enterprise is a four-way intersection. The field to the southeast of the intersection has been a traditional nesting site for a small colony of Bobolinks, late May to August. South of this intersection, Hurricane Creek Rd. climbs somewhat in elevation and enters the Enterprise Watershed, a heavily forested area good for winter finches, Townsend's Solitaire, Pygmy-Owl, and sparrow flocks.

Crow Creek Area

Habitats: BR, FA, NG, RA
Elevation: 4090-4120'
Seasons: Sp • • S • • F • • W • •

About 2.5 miles east of Enterprise on OR 82 is a five-point intersection; be sure to do some birding at the cattle feedlot and marshy creek bottom here before continuing on. During winter and fall the feed lot attracts large numbers of black-birds, Starlings, Magpies, and sparrows. Also watch for quail, Ring-necked Pheasant, and Gray Partridge in the dense brush. The marshy bottoms are good for winter sparrows and finches; Tree and Harris' Sparrows have occurred here and flocks of Common Redpolls are a definite possibility. Continue on the north-bound paved road — Crow Creek Rd.; about a mile from the five-point intersection it veers due east across the open farm country. Continue north on unpaved Swamp Creek Rd. when Crow Creek Rd. heads off to the east (see map). About 2 miles from the pavement's end (the junction of Swamp Creek and Crow Creek Roads), turn east on another gravel road. This farm road follows the edge of a brushy hillside for 2.5 miles before joining Crow Creek Rd. About a mile farther east on Crow Creek Rd. is the marked turnoff to Zumwalt Rd. and OK Gulch on the right. This is a gravel road which is frequently impassable during the winter; check in Enterprise regarding road conditions before exploring these back roads during this time of year.

This area is mainly open brushy farmland with isolated groves of trees around the farm buildings. Winter birding here can be very exciting despite the harsh weather conditions. The brushy creek bottoms and farm yards are great for sparrows and other seed-eaters. This is one of the most consistent sites in all Oregon for the local Tree Sparrow, a species which usually flocks by itself. Also look for juncos and White-crowned, Harris' (rare), and Song Sparrows where ever there is adequate cover. Winter goldfinch flocks are usually present; check them for Pine Siskins and, if you're fortunate, Common Redpolls. Evergreens in the farm yards often harbor Robins, Bohemian Waxwings, Townsend's Solitaires, Evening Gros-beaks, and House Finches.

The steep hillsides with rocky outcroppings along OK Gulch are frequented by Golden Eagle, Prairie Falcon, Common Raven, and other diurnal raptors. Large flocks of Rosy Finches frequently winter in this area, and the extremely rare "Black" Rosy Finch has been reported a few times. Horned Larks often join the flocks, especially in the more open grassland at the top of OK Gulch. These vast sprawling grasslands also attract large flocks of Snow Buntings most winters, apparently the largest concentrations regularly found in Oregon. Unfortunately, these birds wander great distances and the location of a flock is seldom predictable.

The gravel road continuing north from OK Gulch is seldom passable during winter, even for 4-wheel drive vehicles. During summer, however, this drive is quite scenic with spectacular views of the Wallowas to the south and the Seven Devils Mountains of Idaho to the east. The vast grasslands between OK Gulch and the ghost town of Zumwalt (about 18 miles to the north) are good for Western Kingbird, Savannah Sparrow, Vesper Sparrow, Horned Lark, Long-billed Curlew, Short-eared Owl, and Common Nighthawk. Swainson's and Red-tailed Hawks are sure to be encountered, and these plains support one of Oregon's densest populations of Ferruginous Hawks.

Wallowa Lake State Park

Habitats: FW, WF, BR, RA, AL
Elevation: 4383'
Seasons: Sp • • •   S • • •   F • • •   W • •

Located at the terminus of OR 82 some 6 miles south of
Joseph, Wallowa Lake is one of Oregon's most beautiful state
parks. Nearly 4 miles long and a mile across, Wallowa Lake is
situated in a textbook-perfect glacial morraine which has to be
seen to be believed. The habitat at the north end of the lake is
mainly dry brushy upland area with small scattered conifer
stands. The south end, however, is densely forested with pine,
fir, larch, and, along the Wallowa River, riparian growth and
cottonwoods. The state park and campground are located at
the south end of the lake.

Typical summer species to expect here include Red-naped
Sapsucker, Pileated Woodpecker, Mountain and Chestnut-
backed (dense, wet forest) Chickadees, Golden-crowned
Kinglet, Swainson's and Varied Thrush, Veery, Yellow-rumped
Warbler, Pine Siskin, Cassin's Finch, and Red Crossbill.
Hummingbirds are common; most will be Rufous and Calliope, but both Black-chinned and the much rarer Broad-tailed
have been found at the Wallowa Lake Lodge feeders. Spotted
Sandpipers nest along the rocky Wallowa River just south of
the lake, and Dippers are a common sight throughout the
year. Due to the large human population at the state park
during the summer, these are often the only types of birds to
be found at that time of year.

Wintertime is much quieter at Wallowa Lake, both in terms of
birds and people. Frequently the entire lake freezes except for
the southernmost quarter. Thousands of Mallards and Canada
Geese winter here, and with a scope other less common
species can be seen. The boat basin in the state park often has
Barrow's Goldeneyes when the water is open. The huge dead
cottonwood snags at the mouth of the Wallowa River are
traditional perching sites for wintering Bald Eagles that feed
on the waterfowl concentrations, and other species of raptors
(including the uncommon Northern Goshawk) may occur in
the forested areas.

During fall, when water levels on the lake drop low enough to expose mudflats, check the mouth of the Wallowa River for migrant shorebirds, gulls, and terns. Perhaps you'll be lucky enough to find a Sanderling, Parasitic Jaeger, or Sabine's Gull, as has happened in the past!

It should be noted that Wallowa Lake St. Pk. is the most popular entry point for backpackers, cross-country skiiers, and horse packers headed for the immense Eagle Cap Wilderness Area. Although this part of the Wilderness is unbelievably scenic, it is of only marginal interest to the birder, and should be passed up by those interested in a true "wilderness experience".

Imnaha Area

Habitats: RA, BF, RR, FA, BR, UR
Elevation: 1965-4000'
Seasons: Sp ● ● ●   S ● ● ●   F ● ● ●   W ● ●

To reach the rustic tiny town of Imnaha, head east from Joseph on the well-marked Imnaha Rd. (OR 350). The first 8 miles or so of this highway traverses unexciting open farmland — but do watch for wintering flocks of Rosy Finch, Snow Bunting, or even Common Redpoll here. Gray Partridge are also common (but usually elusive) along the roadsides here and throughout the farmland of the Wallowa Valley. After about 8 miles, the road drops down into Little Sheep Creek Canyon and follows it all the way to Imnaha (another 20 miles or so).

The habitat along Little Sheep Creek consists of dry canyonlands with thick riparian growth along the creek itself. Be alert for rattlesnakes during the warmer months if you choose to explore on foot. Nesting species to look for include California Quail, Western Kingbird, Lazuli Bunting, Black-headed Grosbeak, Rock and Canyon Wrens, and American Goldfinch. Chukar roam these rimrock areas, and common raptors include Golden Eagle, Prairie Falcon, and Turkey Vulture. White-throated Swifts have been seen in the steeper canyons near Imnaha, and Gray Catbird and American Redstart are occasionally reported from the denser riparian areas. Little Sheep Creek apparently is home to one of the state's densest populations of Yellow-breasted Chat.

In the town of Imnaha be sure to check local flower gardens and feeders for summer hummingbirds — Rufous and sometimes Black-chinned are regular breeders, and Calliope and Broad-tailed have been reported. The town's ornamental plantings and gardens attract a wide variety of passerines, especially during migration. Imnaha has potential as a vagrant trap, but so far the only unusual species reported has been a Yellow-billed Cuckoo. As with any small rural community, be sure to inform the residents of your intentions when peering around the town with binoculars; it is recommended that you ask before watching a feeder in someone's yard!

Bonny Lakes/
Eagle Cap Wilderness Area

Habitats: WF, DF, AL, FW, RA, RR
Elevation: 7000-9700'
Seasons: Sp • S • • • • F • • • • W •

Located in the southeastern part of the Eagle Cap Wilderness
Area, Bonny Lakes is the most easily reached alpine area of the
Wallowa Mountains that also offers good birding. Due to the
high elevations, this area is usually snowed in from October to
late June, but during the short summer season, few places in
Oregon can offer such exciting birding opportunities.

This site guide is aimed at the more adventurous birders who
are willing to do some backpacking. The Bonny Lakes trail is
typical of the numerous hiking trails in the Eagle Cap Wilderness — often strenuous (but less so than most), sometimes
difficult to find, but always spectacular and well worth the
effort for birding. For those not up to the 5.5 - 6.0 mile hike
(one-way) from the trail head to the lakes, a more leisurely
walk along N.F. Rd. 100 often yields all but the most alpine-
oriented bird species seen along the trail.

To reach the Bonny Lakes trailhead, head east from Joseph on
the Imnaha Highway. About 8 miles east of that town, the
road drops down into Little Sheep Creek Canyon; turn south
onto Wallowa-Whitman N.F. Rd. 39 (Little Sheep Creek Rd.) at
this point. Continue south on this gravel road for about 13
miles to N.F. Rd. 100 to the west. This is the very rough and
undeveloped Sheep Creek Rd.; due to the rocky terrain and the
bridgeless creek crossings, this road may not be passable for all
vehicles. The best time of year to negotiate this road is during
August and September, when the creeks are most easily
forded. The official trailhead is about 3 miles from N.F. Rd. 39
on this road, but if your car can't make it that far, simply pull
over somewhere to park, ford the main Sheep Creek on the
north side of the road, and continue upslope to the trail on
the north bank of the creek. As with any wilderness area
hikes, it is always best to consult a National Forest map and a
U.S.G.S. topographical map.

Typical habitats of the lower two-thirds of the Bonny Lakes trail include high-elevation forests of lodgepole pine, sub-alpine fir, grand fir, mountain hemlock, and Engelmann spruce. Summer birds to expect along this part of the trail include Gray Jay, Hammond's and Olive-sided Flycatchers, Common Raven, Mountain Chickadee, Hermit and Varied Thrushes, Solitary Vireo, Townsend's Warbler, Western Tanager, and Evening Grosbeak. The high Wallowa Mountains — and this trail in particular — have been the most consistent site in Oregon to find the elusive Pine Grosbeak, a species usually seen feeding on cone-laden trees during late summer. They frequently appear in small family flocks (2-10 birds), and a sighting of a bright rosy male is a special treat. Another highly sought-after bird seen with some regularity in this area is the handsome Spruce Grouse. A drive along N.F. Rd. 100 combined with a hike along the lower Bonny Lakes Trail during August or September is one of the most successful methods for finding this species in Oregon.

Bonny Lakes lie at the border of timberline. The larger of the two lakes is a scenic body of water surrounded by grassy meadows and bogs. This lake is a regular site for the migrant Solitary Sandpiper during August. Nesting passerines around the boggy areas include Nashville Warbler, Fox and Lincoln's Sparrows, Cassin's Finch, and the bouncy Dipper. Spotted Sandpipers can be seen anywhere along the trail where there is ample water.

Just upslope from the lakes, the backpacker enters the true alpine habitat. This is the realm of the conspicuous Clark's Nutcracker, a species easily found on the ridges above Bonny Lakes. In the wet meadows, listen for the tinkling call of the American Pipit — this is one of the few readily accessible nesting sites of the species in Oregon. Another specialty of this region of the Wallowas is the Rosy Finch. Although all sightings from the Bonny Lakes Area to date have been of the "Hepburn's" form, the extremely rare "Black" Rosy Finch has been noted on nearby ridges and should be looked for here.

Averaging well above 8000' in elevation, this area was under-standably one of only three release sites in Oregon for the

White-tailed Ptarmigan. ODFW introduced a small population of this handsome grouse into the Wallowa Mountains in the 1960's and 70's. Although the population remains very small and almost never reported by active birders, sightings have continued right up to 1987. Most recent reports have come from the Imnaha Divide between Dollar Lake and Mt. Nebo.

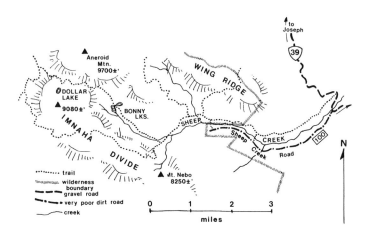

Thief Valley Reservoir

Habitats: SS, FW, RA, RR
Elevation: 3137'
Seasons: Sp • • •   S • •   F • • •   W •

From the town of Union, take OR 237 south for about 7.5
miles to the Telocaset turnoff on the left (east). This stretch of
OR 237 is particularly attractive to wintering Rosy Finches;
flocks numbering in the thousands have occurred more than
once. The steep canyon that the highway passes through here
is also good for wintering raptors such as Golden Eagle, Prairie
Falcon, and accipiters. Continue on the above-mentioned side
road (passing the community of Telocaset) to the Thief Valley
Reservoir turnoff; this marked road is about 2 miles from OR
237. The side road leading down to the lake is another 5 miles
or so from this junction, and the lake is visible from this last
intersection.

Straddling the Union/Baker County line, Thief Valley Reservoir lies in a hollow of the Powder River's course. It is completely surrounded by treeless sagebrush steppe and grassland
and offers good studies of the birds associated with those
habitats. The access road reaches the lake at the mouth of
Cusick Creek. This site is a densely vegetated riparian area
which offers some remarkable birding. Summering species
here include Northern Oriole, Willow Flycatcher, Lazuli
Bunting, Black-headed Grosbeak, House Wren, Orange-
crowned, Yellow, and Wilson's Warblers, and Rufous-sided
Towhee. Yellow-breasted Chats are regular here, late May to
August. Long-eared Owls have nested in this dense vegetation
at least twice, and the closely related Short-eared Owls can be
seen in the surrounding open fields.

Waterfowl and other aquatic birds are best observed from the
fishing jetties in the parking area by the mouth of Cusick
Creek. During April, Common Loons are regular visitors to
the reservoir, and Western, Horned, and Eared Grebes,
Double-crested Cormorant, Great Blue Heron, Pintail, Gadwall, Lesser Scaup, both goldeneyes, and Common Merganser
are all likely to be found. Gulls tend to congregate on the flats

during low water periods; most are Ring-billed and California, but Bonaparte's, Herring, and Franklin's have also shown up. Caspian, Black, Forster's, and even Common Terns occasionally appear. These flats at the mouth of Cusick Creek are also excellent for migrant shorebirds.

Wintertime at Thief Valley is harsh, snowy, and generally not too much fun. Golden Eagles, Rough-legged Hawks, and Common Ravens are frequent visitors, though. The surrounding open country usually yields flocks of Horned Larks or Rosy Finches, and such uncommon species as Lapland Longspur and Snow Bunting have also appeared during these bleak months.

There are undeveloped camping sites located at the mouth of Cusick Creek (BLM maintained), but the nearest gas, food, and lodging are found in Union or Medical Springs.

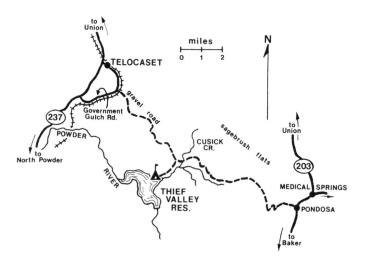

Virtue Flats

Habitats: SS, NG, RR, FA
Elevation: 3337'
Seasons: Sp • • •   S • • •   F • •   W •

From the junction of I-84 and OR 86 in Baker, head east on OR 86. About 6.5 miles from the intersection is a tall Oregon Trail monument on the left (north) side of the highway; another 0.5 miles or so is Ruckles Creek Rd. on the right (south). Follow this gravel road down a gully to the first side road on the right (south), a distance of about another 2.5 miles. This puts you in the general vicinity of Virtue Flats, a broad open expanse of grassland surrounded by sagebrush flats. This is a spring and summer birding site; from November through early March the roads are generally passable but birdlife is very scarce (Horned Larks, Common Ravens, and a few hawks are about all).

Beginning in early March and ending in late April, the main attraction of Virtue Flats is the large Sage Grouse lek occupied by as many as 80 birds at the peak of their display season. The main lek is located on the above-mentioned spur road (unnamed) off Ruckles Creek Rd. About 0.5 miles south of

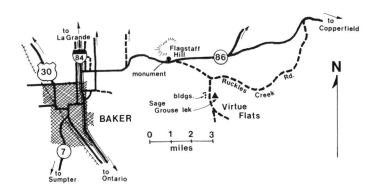

Ruckles Creek Rd. there is an old homestead on the right
(west) side of the spur road. The lek is located in the grassy
field across from the buildings. *Please note that the booming
grounds are located on private property (fenced) and are best
observed from the road.*

Other spring and summer birds found here include Ferruginous Hawk, Golden Eagle, Prairie Falcon, nesting Long-billed
Curlew, Short-eared Owl (seen evenings), Common Nighthawk, Western Kingbird, Say's Phoebe, Sage Thrasher, Loggerhead Shrike (Northern in winter), and sparrows — Savannah,
Vesper, Lark, Sage, Brewer's, and Song. Poorwill have been
heard calling from the small rock outcroppings farther south
on the spur road. Grasshopper Sparrows have been reported
from grassland areas in this part of Baker County and should
be looked for at Virtue Flats.

Phillips Reservoir/Sumpter Area

Habitats: DF, FW, RA, FA
Elevation: 3530-4170'
Seasons: Sp • • •   S • • • •   F • •   W •

Just south of Baker on OR 7 is the narrow Bowen Valley. This wet farmland has hosted nesting Bobolinks a number of times, and it is a good area for American Bittern, Virginia Rail, Sora, Marsh Wren, and other marsh species. The quiet Beaver Creek Loop is a good road for exploring.

About 8 miles south of Baker, watch for the gravel road to the ghost town of Auburn, once the major community in the Baker County area until the gold rush ended and all was abandoned. ODFW owns a plot of land five miles up this road from OR 7 where they regularly feed elk during winter. The road up to the feeding area passes through excellent open ponderosa pine country. Summer species include White-headed Woodpecker, Williamson's Sapsucker, Calliope Hummingbird, Dusky Flycatcher, Pygmy Nuthatch, Mountain and Western Bluebirds, and Cassin's Finch. Watch for Horned Lark, Rosy Finch, Pine Siskin, and Red Crossbill during winter. Rarities have included Common Redpoll and Snow Bunting.

From Baker head south on OR 7 for 9 miles to Salisbury Junction (this is the junction of OR 7 and OR 245). Continue to the right, staying on OR 7, and follow the Powder River. This stretch of the Powder is particularly rough and scenic in some spots; watch for Dipper and Common Merganser. The turnoff to the dam of Phillips Reservoir is about 7.5 miles from Salisbury Junction. This is the best place on the lake to scope for migrant deep-water species such as Common Loon, grebes, Double-crested Cormorant, and diving ducks. During severe winters this part of the reservoir can be the only unfrozen section.

Continuing on from the dam turnoff on OR 7, go another 2.75 miles to Union Creek CG on the lake side of the road. This is another good vantage point to scope out the lake as well as check out the local summering land birds. Great Blue Herons abound, and nesting waterfowl include Canada Goose,

---

Mallard, and Cinnamon Teal. Summer passerines to watch for include House Wren, Yellow Warbler, Black-capped and Mountain Chickadees, all three nuthatches, Chipping Sparrow, MacGillivray's Warbler, and Rufous-sided Towhee. Rufous and Calliope Hummingbirds are common. About 0.5 miles past the campground the highway crosses Bridge Creek. In the brushy tangles here American Redstarts have been found on territory. Also check any of the wet open meadows in the valley for Bobolinks. About 1.5 miles west of Bridge Creek look for an active Osprey nest in a snag on the lake's north shore.

West of Phillips Reservoir the Powder River has been extensively surface dredged for gold mining, and although the resulting landscape may not be very attractive, it is rich wildlife habitat. There are numerous willow-lined sloughs and ponds throughout this area, and it is good habitat for Gray Catbird, Veery, American Redstart, and Yellow-breasted Chat. Sandhill Cranes nest here, and the area is thick with Yellow Warblers. Also watch for deer, beaver, and, if you're lucky, mink or otter. This dredged area (the Sumpter Valley WMA) is best viewed from the roadsides of OR 7.

The town of Sumpter itself sits at the western end of the Powder River Valley. This is a unique town that deserves a visit simply for its rich gold-mining history. But don't ignore the birding possibilities; the undeveloped and forested northeast corner of town has produced White-headed Woodpecker, Goshawk, and Blue Grouse. And hummingbird feeders in the main part of Sumpter have hosted not only Rufous and Calliope, but also the more uncommon Black-chinned and Broad-tailed Hummingbirds.

Anthony Lakes Ski Area

Habitats: WF, RA, FW
Elevation: 7100-7950'
Seasons: Sp • • S • • • F • • • W •

Nestled at the base of the Elkhorn Mountains, Anthony Lakes offer both scenic beauty and good birding. To reach the area, exit off I-84 in North Powder and follow the signs west to the ski area (a distance of about 20 miles from the interstate). Although the road is open and maintained all year, chains or other traction devices are required most winters. When birding this recreation area, keep in mind that it straddles the Union and Baker County lines — two county lists can be worked on at once!

Anthony Lakes Basin averages around 7200' in elevation and supports forests of Engelmann spruce, lodgepole pine, sub-alpine fir, and other high elevation conifers. A specialty of the area are the "boreal" finches which are quite unpredictable in most parts of Oregon. Common residents include Red Crossbill, Pine Siskin, and Cassin's Finch. Pine Grosbeaks are sometimes reported, mainly from June to March, and the extremely rare White-winged Crossbill has occurred here more than once, both in winter and summer.

The six main lakes in the area are shallow and surrounded with marshy wet meadows. Nesting species here include Spotted Sandpiper, Dipper (creeks), Violet-green Swallow, Winter Wren, Nashville and Townsend's Warblers, and Lincoln's, Song, Fox, and White-crowned Sparrows. The surrounding forests are inhabited by various woodpeckers, Mountain Chickadees, Red-breasted Nuthatch, Hermit and Varied Thrushes, Solitary Vireos, numerous warblers, and flycatchers.

A gravel road leads around Anthony Lake (the largest of the six) and offers good birding opportunities. The best birding, however, is off the main roads along the numerous hiking trails. Northern Goshawks are frequently encountered by hiking, and the rare Great Gray Owl is best looked for well-

away from roads and campgrounds. This elusive species has
been reported from Floodwater Flats Meadows (just north of
Anthony Lake) and at the picnic area at Grande Ronde Lake,
about 1 mile farther west along the main road from the ski
area. An exceptionally productive hike leads from the south
end of Anthony Lake to Hoffer Lakes, a round trip of about 1
mile. Species of note that have been seen around Hoffer Lakes
include Three-toed Woodpecker, Blue Grouse, Pine Grosbeak,
Townsend's Warbler (nesting), and White-winged Crossbill.

About the only attraction of Anthony Lakes for the winter
birder is the tameness of what few species remain. The ski
lodge parking area is frequented by Gray Jays and Clark's
Nutcrackers, and a walk into the forest on skis or snowshoes
may yield Mountain Chickadee, Red-breasted Nuthatch, and
the occasional finch flock.

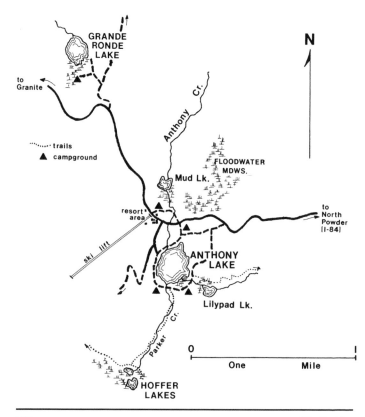

Clyde Holliday State Wayside

Habitats: BF, RA, FW
Elevation: 2899'
Seasons: Sp ••• S ••• F •• W ••

Located on US 26 about 5 miles west of Mt. Vernon, Clyde Holliday Wayside is a good example of the John Day Valley's riparian community. In recent years it has been known for its small "colony" of Least Flycatchers — up to three pairs have summered in the boggy cottonwood grove between the camping and picnicking areas. Other riparian species to be found here include House Wren, Cedar Waxwing, Black-capped Chickadee, Northern Oriole, Black-headed Grosbeak, Downy Woodpecker, Lazuli Bunting, Willow Flycatcher, Yellow Warbler, and Red-naped Sapsucker. Look for Dipper, Spotted Sandpiper, Belted Kingfisher, and Common Merganser along the John Day River which flows through the park.

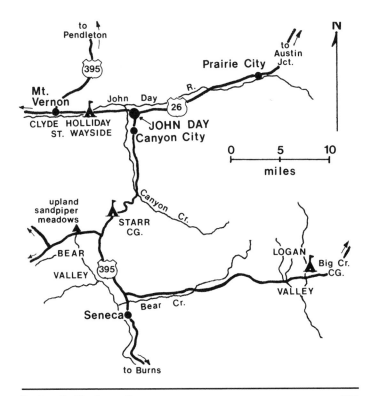

Starr Campground

Habitats: DF, WF, RA, FW
Elevation: 5120'
Seasons: Sp • • S • • • • F • • • W •

Located on OR 397 about 14 miles south of John Day, Starr
CG is an excellent stop to sample the birdlife of the southern
Blue Mountains. In the campground itself look for nesting
White-headed, Hairy, and Pileated Woodpeckers and
Williamson's Sapsuckers. The brushy growth along the spring
in the middle of the camping area itself supports numerous
warblers, wrens, and sparrows, including nesting Lincoln's
Sparrows. Typical summering birds here include Rufous and
Calliope Hummingbirds, Dusky and Hammond's Flycatchers,
Winter Wren, Mountain Chickadee, Gray Jay, Hermit Thrush,
Solitary Vireo, Townsend's Warbler, Western Tanager, and
Chipping Sparrow. Both Black-backed and Three-toed
Woodpeckers have nested in the surrounding lodgepole pine
forests, and Northern Goshawks are occasionally encountered.

One specialty of the area is the secretive Flammulated Owl.
Most common in the extensive ponderosa pine forests, this
diminutive species is frequently heard at night in Starr CG,
but seeing one is another story. The best strategy is to locate
one on territory at night, listening for the quiet, low-pitched,
monotonous call. After roughly determining the extent of a
particular bird's territory, return during daylight and look for
snags that have potential roosting or nesting holes. Flammulated Owls are present from late May to (probably) early
August.

Bear Valley

Habitats: DF, FA, FW, SS
Elevation: 4800'
Seasons: Sp • • S • • • F • • • W •

Bear Valley is best known for its small population of nesting Upland Sandpipers, a very difficult species to find in Oregon. These birds are best looked for during late May, June, and July. To reach the area, turn west on the well-marked Izee Rd., about 15.5 miles south of Canyon City on US 395. In the first 2.5 miles of this side road, you pass through two forest openings; the second and larger of these two wet meadows has been the most consistent for Upland Sandpipers. Look for the birds early in the morning (before 9:00 AM) on fence posts or mounds where they give their territorial calls.   The birds are usually seen in the larger meadows on the south side of the road.

Also during the summer months, watch for Wilson's Phalarope, Common Snipe, Sandhill Crane, Black Tern, Long-billed Curlew, and even Bobolink in these meadowlands. The bordering pine forests support White-headed Woodpecker, Williamson's Sapsucker, Pygmy Nuthatch, and other interesting species. At night, Flammulated Owls may be heard calling from the more mature, extensive stands of pine.

Logan Valley

Habitats: DF, WF, FA, SS
Elevation: 5080'
Seasons: Sp • •   S • • •   F • •   W •

This high country meadowland is one of the most beautiful areas found anywhere in Oregon. In recent years Logan Valley has become famous for its local nesting population of Upland Sandpipers, one of only three or four known sites in Oregon. To reach the valley, take Logan Valley Rd. east from the town of Seneca on US 395. About 17.5 miles east of Seneca, the road enters Logan Valley. Another 2.5 miles or so is the turnoff to Big Creek Forest Camp, the only campground in the area. Although a public camping area, please note that you may have to share your tent site with cattle. The Upland Sandpipers are most frequently found in the large open meadows on the north side of Logan Valley Rd., just west of the campground. Fortunately these lush meadows are fenced off, keeping the cattle out — but this means that people are also excluded. The sandpipers are present from mid-May to mid-August (probably); arrival and departure dates are not firmly established yet. The best time to see them is during the first morning light in May and early June; during this time of day the males proclaim their territories from fence posts (often on the roadside!), low snags, and also on the wing. Listen for their haunting, drawn-out "wolf whistle" calls.

Other summering birds to look for in Logan Valley include Mountain Bluebird, Pygmy Nuthatch, Mountain Chickadee, Cassin's Finch, Chipping and Brewer's Sparrows, Hammond's and Dusky Flycatchers, House Wren, and Hermit Thrush. The surrounding forest (mostly ponderosa pine and aspen) may yield Northern Goshawk, Flammulated, Great Horned, and Pygmy Owls, Calliope and Black-chinned Hummingbirds, Williamson's and Red-naped Sapsuckers, and Pileated, Hairy, White-headed, Black-backed, and Three-toed Woodpeckers. Sandhill Cranes have been known to nest in Logan Valley.

Region H
Southeast Oregon

Black-necked Stilt

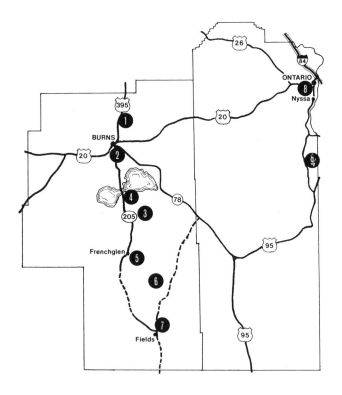

Idlewild Campground

Habitats: DF, BR, RR, FA
Elevation: 4200'
Seasons: Sp • • •   S • • •   F.• •   W •

Easily found alongside US 395 about 17.5 miles north of
Burns, Idlewild CG is an excellent site to sample the birds of
the ponderosa pine forest and its surrounding brushy habitats.
A summer visit to the area is likely to produce White-headed
Woodpecker, Williamson's Sapsucker, Pymgy Nuthatch,
Mountain Chickadee, and Townsend's Solitaire in the open
stands of pine. At night, this campground is a good place to
listen for Pygmy and Flammulated Owls. The brushy open
areas near the main entrance support Green-tailed Towhees
and Fox Sparrows, and the nearby aspen stands often have
Red-naped Sapsuckers or warblers. Also found near the
entrance at the west side of the campground is a small out-
cropping of rimrock — look for Rock Wrens here, and Poorwills have been heard calling at night.

Burns-Hines Area

Habitats: FA, FW, BR
Elevation: 4140'
Seasons: Sp ● ● ●   S ● ● ●   F ● ● ●   W ● ●

Some of the best birding to be had on a "Malheur" expedition is actually in this area, some 35 miles or so north of Malheur NWR. When approaching Burns and Hines from the west on US 20, turn right (east) on the paved road at the north end of Hines — this is Pierce St. After crossing the railroad tracks, turn south onto Hotchkiss/Egan St. About 0.5 miles south of the Pierce St. junction are the Harney County fairgrounds on the west side of the road. From here south along Hotchkiss Ln., check the fields on the east for American Avocet, Black-necked Stilt, Wilson's Phalarope, and other shorebirds; these fields are often as good as Malheur for observing such birds. 1.5 miles south of the Pierce St. junction, Hotchkiss Ln. continues due east with a 90-degree turn. At this T-intersection, turn west (right) to explore a seldom-used road that dead-ends at the Hines Lumber Company. This is a good place to check for migrant shorebirds during fall and spring. Just south of the road are some secondary sewage ponds which often have Eared and Horned (rare) Grebes, hundreds of Wilson's Phalaropes, and Franklin's Gulls. Also look for Redhead, Lesser Scaup, Canvasback, and other diving ducks, especially during migration. North on Hotchkiss Ln. from this area are the main sewage ponds, but these are fenced off and hard to observe. Backtracking to the T-intersection and continuing east on Hotchkiss, watch the wet grassy fields for White-faced Ibis flocks — this species can be quite spotty in distribution, but it's usually easy to find here if the meadows are sufficiently wet. Black and Forster's Terns and Franklin's Gulls are common sights hawking insects over the fields, and Long-billed Curlews and Sandhill Cranes may also been seen. Common Snipe perch on fence posts, and nervous Wilson's Phalaropes frequently escort a car until it leaves their territories. Watch for Short-eared Owls toward evening.

During winter these fields are often devoid of birds, but that's when the raptors move in — Red-tailed and Rough-legged Hawks, Northern Harrier, Golden Eagle, Prairie Falcon, and even Bald Eagle and Peregrine Falcon have been seen.

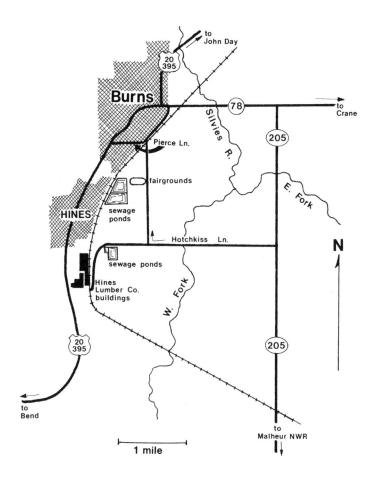

Diamond Area

Habitats: RR, SS, FA, JW
Elevation: 4695'
Seasons: Sp • • •   S • • •   F • • •   W • •

This side trip from Malheur NWR leads to a most remarkable
geological area that is worthy of attention with or without
birds. About 17 miles south of the Malheur Refuge Headquarters turnoff, OR 205 intersects Diamond Lane; turn east here
and drive 7 miles to the Diamond Junction and turn left
(north). If you continue east on Diamond Lane, you will
reach the small town of Diamond, another 5 miles or so from
Diamond Junction. The wet fields just north of Diamond
Junction are excellent for wetland birds — American Bittern,
Sandhill Crane, Black Tern, Franklin's Gull, blackbirds, Marsh
Wrens, etc. There is even a small colony of Bobolinks which
are usually seen in the wet sedge fields east of the main road.
Keeping to the left as you head north, the entrance to Diamond Craters is another 3.5 miles or so from Diamond
Junction. This area is riddled with craters, lava tubes, cinder
cones, and caves. The terrain is high and dry, attracting true
desert species. Great Horned Owls and Common Ravens nest
in the larger craters, Canyon and Rock Wrens are hard to miss,
and Cliff Swallows are common nesters. The mixture of sage,
rimrock, and junipers is excellent habitat for Poorwills and the
occasional Ferruginous Hawk. The edges of main lava flows
are fantastic areas to study the desert sparrows during the
summer — Lark, Sage, Savannah, Vesper, and especially
Brewer's are quite common. Black-throated Sparrows have
occurred with some regularity here. Other species to look for
include Loggerhead Shrike, Sage Thrasher, Chukar, Common
Nighthawk, Say's Phoebe, Western Kingbird, and Horned Lark.
Diamond Craters is also a good site for studying reptiles,
including rattlesnakes.

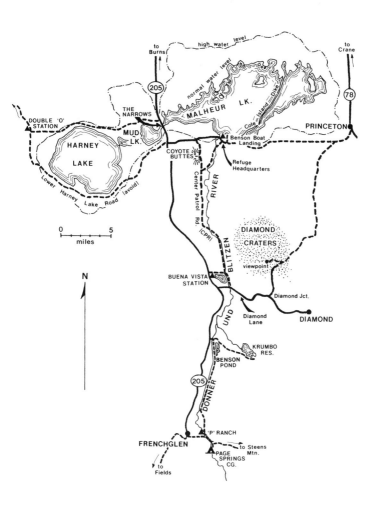

Malheur National Wildlife Refuge

Habitats: FW, SS, RA, RR, FA, BF, JW
Elevation: 4080-4230'
Seasons: Sp • • • • S • • • F • • • • W • •

Established in 1908, Malheur NWR has long been known as Oregon's most popular birding spot, both locally and across the country. Located about 30 miles south of Burns off OR 205, the refuge stretches some 30 miles north to south. The main physical features to the T-shaped refuge include Malheur and Harney Lakes (the former a vast fresh-water marsh, the latter a large alkali lake which, until recently, has had little water in it) and the extensively diked and channeled Donner Und Blitzen River. Habitats include open sagebrush flats, willow-lined river courses, bare volcanic lava flows, extensive cattail and tule marshes, and local "islands" of ornamental plantings.

Malheur is most famous for its tremendous numbers of migrant geese and ducks. Flocks of Canada, White-fronted, Snow, and even Ross' Geese numbering in the tens of thousands are a common sight during spring and fall. The refuge is a major nursery for many species, especially Cinnamon and Blue-winged Teal, Gadwall, Mallard, Pintail, Redhead, and Canada Goose. From 1939 to 1958, the rare Trumpeter Swan was introduced to Malheur NWR; the species has established a nesting population currently numbering about 80-100 birds. Many of the swans can be seen on larger ponds from the main roads.

Another major attraction of Malheur is its large population of migrant Sandhill Cranes. Smaller numbers nest on the refuge during the summer, but during spring and fall the breeding birds are joined by thousands of migrant cranes heading to or from their wintering grounds in California. This is when their spectacular display dances can be observed. A third attraction of this part of Oregon is the early spring mating ritual of the Sage Grouse. Check at refuge headquarters for the most recent locations of active leks, many which are found in out-of-the-way areas far from refuge roads.

There are a number of bird species which are seldom found elsewhere in such numbers or with such regularity as they are at Malheur. The refuge is *the* place in Oregon to see a White Pelican, Snowy Egret, White-faced Ibis, Swainson's or Ferruginous Hawk, Prairie Falcon, Chukar, Black-necked Stilt, American Avocet, Franklin's Gull, Burrowing Owl, Poorwill, Black-throated Sparrow, or Sage Sparrow, among other species.

The main access to the refuge is either by OR 205 or, better yet, the gravel Center Patrol Rd. (hereafter CPR) which parallels the highway to the east. Both roads run the length of the refuge. The only gas and food is found either at Burns, Frenchglen, or Princeton. Camping is permitted only at Page Springs near Frenchglen (see next entry).

When visiting Malheur NWR, an entire week can be spent exploring this fascinating and unique country. The best birding, however, is usually found at the following sites:

Refuge Headquarters. Any trip to Malheur NWR should begin at the headquarters complex. Check with refuge personnel for recent birding news and be sure to visit the excellent museum of mounted birds, including all nesting species. Also pick up maps, checklists, and other information at the museum. The lush brushy growth and large trees of the headquarters grounds attract an incredible number and variety of migrants, mainly from early April to late May, and again during September and October. Most prevalent are flycatchers, warblers, vireos, and thrushes, but virtually anything can (and has) shown up. Over the past twenty years, Malheur headquarters has had records of Yellow-billed Cuckoo, Least Flycatcher, Blue Jay, Northern Mockingbird, Gray Catbird, Brown Thrasher, Veery, Red-eyed Vireo, Black-and-White Warbler, Golden-winged Warbler, Tennessee Warbler, Northern Parula, Magnolia Warbler, Cape May Warbler, American Redstart, Great-tailed Grackle, Scarlet Tanager, Rose-breasted Grosbeak, Indigo Bunting, and Painted Bunting — and even more amazing, most of these species have been reported more than once!

Memorial Day Weekend is one of the refuge's busiest times; it seems that two or three of these eastern vagrants are always present at headquarters during this weekend, and up to fifty birders can be seen at one time as they eagerly search the grounds! Also check the flowers at headquarters for migrant hummingbirds — Calliope, Black-chinned, and Broad-tailed have all appeared more than once. There are resident Great Horned Owls to be seen any time of year, and Common Nighthawks are a common sight roosting in the trees. Franklin's Gulls frequently fly overhead between their nesting areas and feeding grounds.

Coyote Buttes Study Area. Located in the desert west of headquarters, North and South Coyote Buttes are managed by the Malheur Environmental Field Station, an educational facility utilized by a consortium of Pacific Northwest colleges and universities. The Field Station is the complex nestled between the Coyote Buttes; they also rent trailers and dorms to visiting birders. Coyote Buttes are covered with sagebrush and offer good birding opportunities for the desert species. The larger South Coyote Butte has a short interpretive hiking trail leading to the top. Look for Lark, Savannah, Brewer's, and, rarely, Sage Sparrows on the slopes. Some years the handsome Black-throated Sparrow nests on the east slope of the South Butte. There is usually a nesting nighthawk on the summit, and Poorwills have been heard calling from the North Butte.

Buena Vista Station. The large ponds here attract grebes (check all *Aechmophorus* grebes for the uncommon Clark's), diving ducks, gulls, terns, Double-crested Cormorants, and White Pelicans. The fields north of the ponds are a good place to observe large flocks of migrating Sandhill Cranes. The vegetation around the buildings has attracted some of the vagrant "eastern" passerines such as Chestnut-sided Warbler and "Baltimore" Oriole.

P Ranch. Located at the far south end of Malheur NWR, the historic P-Ranch (named for Pete French, an early cattle baron in the Blitzen Valley) has some of the densest vegetation found on the refuge. It is excellent for the local nesting passerines (Yellow Warbler, Black-headed Grosbeak, Northern Oriole, Eastern and Western Kingbirds, Willow Flycatcher, Cedar Waxwing, etc.). Small nesting colonies of Bobolink reside in the wet meadows at this end of the refuge. Check the first open meadows on the west side of the CPR just north of the P-Ranch for the main nesting area. The large observation tower at the P-Ranch often serves as a night roost for up to a hundred Turkey Vultures; they are best observed early in the morning. The P-Ranch is also known for its "eastern" vagrants during spring and fall.

The Narrows. During periods of flooding, overflow from Malheur Lake passes under the bridge here, into Mud Lake, and thereafter into Harney Lake, the lowest point in the basin. The flooded sagebrush flats on either side of OR 205 are excellent habitat for Black-necked Stilt, American Avocet, Willet, Snowy Egret, Black-crowned Night-Heron, and, during fall and spring, migrant shorebirds. Gulls (typically Ring-billed and California) and Caspian Terns frequently loaf on the roadsides where the water is highest. Also watch for Clark's Grebes among the much more common Westerns. The Narrows is also an excellent place to watch the graceful, ballet-like feeding style of White Pelicans.

Page Springs Campground

Habitats: RA, JW, RR
Elevation: 4237'
Seasons: Sp • • • • S • • • F • • • W • •

Operated and maintained by the BLM, Page Springs CG offers the only camping facilities in the Malheur NWR area. Whether or not you camp here, a visit to this beautiful site is not to be passed up. Page Springs marks the south end of the extensive Blitzen Valley, and here the Blitzen changes from a scenic rushing canyon river to the muddy willow-lined slough familiar on the refuge. The campground, situated at the mouth of a canyon, has unique bird species which are hard to find on the adjacent refuge lands. A nature trail leads to the overgrown spring for which the site was named, and from there up a narrow juniper-lined canyon. Local species to look for here include Ash-throated Flycatcher, Bushtit, Canyon and Rock Wrens, Black-throated Gray Warbler, and Lesser Goldfinch. Blue-gray Gnatcatchers have attempted to nest here, but don't expect them. The campground and its junipers attract Northern Orioles, House and (rare) Cassin's Finches, Lazuli Bunting, Black-headed Grosbeak, and House Wren.

The brush-lined road between the P-Ranch and Page Springs is one of the best areas in Oregon for Yellow-breasted Chat, and the river itself may yield Spotted Sandpiper and, during winter, Dipper.

From Page Springs you may continue on to the Steens Mountain Loop Rd. (see site H-6).

Steens Mountain Recreation Area

Habitats: RR, AL, SS, NG, JW, RA, BF, FW
Elevation: 4300-9715'
Seasons: Sp • •   S • • •   F • •   W •

Although worth the visit for its unbelievable scenic beauty alone, Steens Mountain offers only a few items of interest to the birder. The Steens Mountain Loop Rd. begins at Page Springs Campground (see site H-5) where you take the gravel road to the left instead of entering the campground. The road is a 68 mile loop that comes out on OR 205, about 10 miles south of Frenchglen. Steens Mountain Loop Rd. is open only from about July 4 to late September, depending on the weather and snow conditions. Inquire about road conditions in Frenchglen before attempting the drive. Even when the road is passable, the average car should negotiate the summit area's rocky terrain with care.

Lily Lake, about 12.5 miles from the Page Springs start of the Loop Road, is one of two Steens Mountain lakes that offer good birding. This is mostly a passerine area, and the groves of aspen and riparian growth are home to hummingbirds, Tree and Violet-green Swallows, flycatchers, House Wren, Mountain Bluebird (rare), Warbling Vireo, Cassin's Finch, White-crowned Sparrow, and the ever-present Yellow Warbler. Another 1.5 miles from Lily Lake is one of the only campgrounds (BLM-maintained) on Steens Mountain at Fish Lake. Fish Lake is even more productive than Lily Lake for birdlife. In addition to the typical species mentioned above, there are a number of Broad-tailed Hummingbird records from this beautiful site, and Black-chinned Hummingbirds are occasionally reported. Although of minor importance to birding, be sure to check the breathtaking view at Kiger Gorge; the viewpoint road is located about 6 miles past Fish Lake. It can be said with little disagreement that this spectacular vista is one of the top ten in the Pacific Northwest.

The East Rim Viewpoint offers another unsurpassed panarama looking down on the Alvord Basin and Steens Mountain's sheer east face. The viewpoint road is located some 9.5 miles from Fish Lake; it is a .4 mile walk to the rim itself from the Loop Road (the East Rim Viewpoint Road is usually far too rugged to drive). Golden Eagles, Prairie Falcons, Kestrels, White-throated Swifts, and Violet-green Swallows may be seen among the cliffs, and bighorn sheep favor the numerous cirques visible below the rim. Steens Mountain is the only place in Oregon (if not the entire Pacific Northwest) that has a somewhat reliable population of the "black" Rosy Finch. They are usually seen cavorting and feeding among the snow fields just over the rim. At the East Rim Viewpoint and the nearby summit (9715') look for Rock and Canyon Wrens, Horned Lark, American Pipit, and White-crowned Sparrow, the latter three species which are much rarer in the surrounding low-lands during the summer.

Steens Mountain is without a doubt the most unique and spectacular natural area in Oregon. It cannot be stressed heavily enough that the area is extremely fragile and will not tolerate extensive human disturbance. Remain on the existing roads and walk the spur roads whenever possible. Do not camp at any site other than the designated campgrounds at Fish Lake, Jackman Park, and the Little Blitzen Crossing. And, above all, do not even touch the vegetation; there are numer-ous plant species which are endemic to Steens Mountain and are considered endangered.

A nearby site of interest for birders is the oasis-like Roaring Springs Ranch, located along OR 205 about 5 miles south of the highway's junction with Steens Mountain Loop Rd. Although the ranch is privately-owned, there is a good birding area along the roadside just north of the buildings. Where the spring comes cascading down from Catlow Rim, check the cliffs above for White-throated Swifts among the common Violet-green Swallows; also watch for Common Ravens and Prairie Falcons. On the west side of the road search (listen) for nesting Bobolinks in the wet fields. Chukars are a common species along the cliffs of Catlow Rim. The brushy growth along the spring may yield Lazuli Bunting, Yellow-breasted Chat, House Wren, Black-headed Grosbeak, and Northern

Oriole. Roaring Springs is another famous Southeast Oregon "vagrant trap"; recent finds at the spring and the ranch include Broad-winged and Red-shouldered Hawks, Yellow-billed Cuckoo, Least Flycatcher, Brown Thrasher, and Tennessee Warbler!

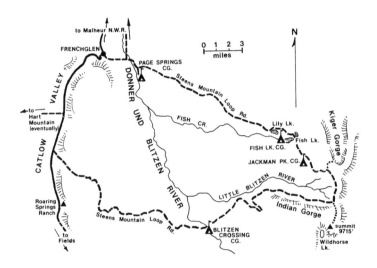

Alvord Basin

Habitats: SS, RR, NG, RA, JW, FW
Elevations: 4090-4250'
Seasons: Sp ••• S •• F ••• W •

This large basin at the foot of Steens Mountain is truly one of the most unique and memorable sites in all the Pacific Northwest. Such bizarre and impressive attractions as the Alvord Desert, the east face of Steens Mountain, numerous hot springs, and historic relics like the Borax Works offer the visitor more than just excellent birding — bring a camera. The only community here which caters to the public (i.e., gas, food, lodging) is the tiny town of Fields, located about 52 miles south of Frenchglen. Be sure to fill your gas tank at every opportunity when exploring this corner of Oregon!

Across the main road from the buildings in Fields is a small U-shaped woodlot with a spring centered in it — this is the Fields Oasis. There is always a family of Great Horned Owls here, but the site is best known among Oregon birding circles for its spring vagrants. In addition to most of the species mentioned at Malheur headquarters (see site H-4), Fields has come up with Oregon's only Gray-cheeked Thrush, LeConte's Sparrow, and other surprises including Summer Tanager, Alder Flycatcher, Wood Thrush, and Broad-winged Hawk. The hummingbird feeders at the Fields Cafe and Hotel often host Black-chinned Hummingbirds during migration, and Broad-tailed and Calliope have occurred a number of times. There is also a conventional bird feeder at the cafe that should be checked. For the usual spring and fall migrants, this oasis town is an excellent spot to spend a few hours.

About 4.5 miles north of Fields is the entrance road to the Borax Works and Borax Lake, marked by a small cluster of locust trees. This side road is extremely rough in places and you may wish to walk as much of the 2.5 miles to the lake as possible. During late fall and winter this hot springs-fed lake is the only open body of water in the basin — this is where the water birds will be found. Also, in the larger bodies of water

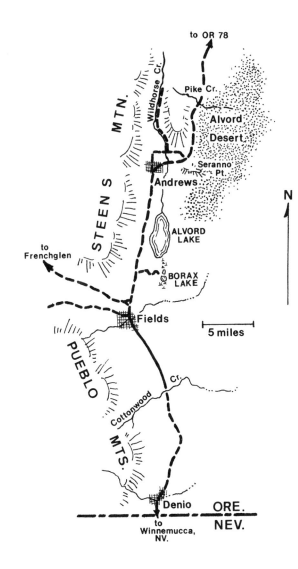

look for the unimpressive Alvord chub, an endangered species of minnow found only in the Alvord Basin.

Where the road passes the community of Andrews and heads east, you get your first view of the Alvord Desert. Explore the desert later because this is the site where the local and rare Black-throated Sparrow is most easily found in Oregon. Simply walk up the slopes covered with large sage west of the road. This hot-desert species and the closely related Sage Sparrow prefer pure older stands of Great Basin sagebrush with open ground between the plants. Further more, the Black-throated Sparrow seems partial to boulder-strewn hillsides covered with this habitat, whereas the Sage Sparrow favors flat open stretches of it.

A series of willow- and cottonwood-lined creeks drain the eastern slopes of Steens Mountain and, south of Fields, the Pueblo Mountains. Many of these have trails or jeep roads following the watercourses. Of particular interest is Cotton-wood Creek, located 8 miles south of Fields on the road to Denio. Black-throated Sparrows have been found here, and it appears to be the most frequent site in Oregon for the very rare Rose-breasted Grosbeak, a late May and June migrant. Other creeks that have turned up rare vagrants include Wildhorse Creek near Andrews and Pike Creek, about 10 miles north of that.

During late fall and winter the Alvord Basin is virtually an avian mystery due to the severe climate that deters most birders. What birdlife that does remain seems to cluster around the shelter and food offered at Fields. Snow Buntings have been found a number of times, as have Tree Sparrows. A Scrub Jay appeared at the cafe feeder one winter, and "Gray-headed" Juncos have been reported twice.

Ontario Area

Habitats: FA, SS, RA, UR
Elevation: 2140-2660'
Seasons: Sp ••• S •• F ••• W ••

This small town located on the Snake River is virtually unexplored when it comes to birds. Of particular interest, however, are the numerous farm country roads south and west of town. A good route for birding begins at the south exit off I-84 (there are two Ontario exits). Head west from this junction to OR 201 (4th St.) which leads to the farmland west of town. The Ontario Municipal Airport and the nearby Treasure Valley Gun Club areas have yielded Northern Bobwhite in recent years. The species was introduced in the Boise, ID. area during the late 1800's and has subsequently spread to this part of Oregon. The species is very local and more often heard than seen. Gray Partridge are also found in this area, but they are even more difficult to locate. Just west of the gun club and airport, turn north onto Clark Blvd. which crosses the Malheur River. Brushy riparian habitat here supports such species as Lazuli Bunting, Yellow Warbler, Yellow-breasted Chat, Black-headed Grosbeak, and Willow Flycatcher. Gray Catbird has been seen here once. Just south of the Malheur River bridge turn east on Malheur Rd. which takes you back into Ontario.

About 4.5 miles or so south of Ontario on OR 201, turn west onto US 20. Four miles west of this junction turn north on Butte Dr. to reach Malheur Butte. Rock and Canyon Wrens have been found here and Prairie Falcons occasionally show up. This is good habitat for Poorwill.

About 9 miles south of Ontario on OR 201 (2.5 miles north of Nyssa), turn west on Gem Ave. This road is good for sagebrush species such as Brewer's, Sage, and Lark Sparrows, Sage Thrasher, Horned Lark, and even Gray Flycatcher.

Succor Creek State Park

Habitats: RR, SS, FW
Elevation: 4060'
Seasons: Sp • • S • • • F • • W •

About 33 miles south of Ontario on OR 201, turn right
(southwest) onto the gravel road to Succor Creek St. Pk. — the
park itself is another 13 miles or so south of that junction.
This isolated dry canyon area is best known for its rock-
hounding opportunities, the main attractions being thunder-
eggs (Oregon's state rock), agates, and petrified wood. Of
interest to the birder is the nesting colony of White-throated
Swifts present most years. These birds are found along the
creek (and main road) in the steepest, narrowest canyons.
Other species found here include Rock and Canyon Wrens,
Prairie Falcon, Chukar, Golden Eagle, and lots of Rock Doves.
In the sparse riparian growth along Succor Creek look for
Yellow-breasted Chat, Lazuli Bunting, Black-headed Grosbeak,
Yellow Warbler, Western Kingbird, and House Wren. Poor-
wills have been heard at night in the park.

Bird-Finding Guide

This part of the book is an aid in locating a specific species of bird in Oregon. It is geared for both the visiting out-of-state birder looking for the Pacific Northwest "specialties" (i.e., Trumpeter Swan, Tufted Puffin), as well as the Oregon birder interested in finding the more local species that may be much more common elsewhere in the country (i.e., White-faced Ibis, Red-eyed Vireo). To use this guide, first consult the Checklist of Oregon Birds located on page 279 to be sure the desired species occurs in the state. Those species listed as "accidental" are not covered in this bird-finding guide because their occurrence is too sporadic to be predicted. If the species is listed in the main list, but not here in the bird-finding guide, then it is relatively common and easy to find in virtually any site (in the appropriate habitat and season, of course). Although this section is not designed to serve as an identification column, some notes are included on the more obscure species and those species which are likely to be split in the near future. The sites marked with an asterisk (*) are the best bets for finding that particular species. Also note that the terms "Eastern Oregon" and "east of the Cascades" are interchangeable, referring to that part of the state east of the Cascades Mountains' crest; this definition likewise applies to the terms "Western Oregon" and "west of the Cascades."

Loons

All three of the common Oregon loons — Red-throated, Pacific, and Common — can be found in virtually any coastal bay or estuary waters during migration and winter (September to mid-April is best). Most abundant is generally the Common Loon, and it is the only species that occurs frequently inland. Red-throated is the second most common in coastal waters, followed by the Pacific Loon. Frequently, the Pacific Loon outnumbers the other species during migration when flocks numbering in the hundreds are observed off major headlands, April to May, and again during September and October.

Yellow-billed Loon

Mainly a winter visitor, November to March. Prefers quiet bay waters in company of Common Loons. Most Oregon records are from *A-11, where the species occurs roughly every other winter.

Red-necked Grebe

October to April, this species is regular along the coast. Prefers bay waters, frequently near the mouth. Good sites include *A-5, *A-8, *A-11, B-1, *B-4. As a nesting species, the Red-necked Grebe is found only in Eastern Oregon, preferring cattail and tule marshes. The only reliable nesting sites are *F-3, *F-5, and occasionally F-7, F-9.

Western and Clark's Grebes

These two sibling species are easily identified during the summer, especially on their nesting grounds. Throughout most of Oregon, the Western Grebe is the predominant species; major nesting areas of the Clark's Grebe are found at *F-5, F-7, F-9, F-12, and at *Goose Lake in southern Lake County. Smaller numbers nest at H-4 each year. During migration, Clark's Grebe may occur anywhere in Oregon, but in very small numbers.

Black-footed Albatross

Strictly pelagic, almost never seen from land. Most sightings are at least 10 miles offshore; most abundant from June through late October, but may be encountered any time of year.

Laysan Albatross

Very rare in Oregon, usually seen well offshore (+10 miles out). Most records are from winter (November to April).

Northern Fulmar

A common pelagic species, most abundant from October to March. Sometimes seen from prominant coastal viewpoints (see next account) during late fall and winter storms.

Shearwaters

Five shearwater species occur regularly in Oregon's offshore waters — Pink-footed, Flesh-footed, Sooty, Short-tailed, and Buller's. The Sooty is by far the most abundant species, most migrating past Oregon from July to November; small numbers are present all year. Good coastal viewpoints for observing hundreds of thousands of migrating Sooties (August, early September) include *A-1, A-5, *A-7, *A-9, *A-10, B-4. The second most common species, the Pink-footed Shearwater, occurs mainly from August to October; rarely seen from land. The Short-tailed and Buller's are about equally common, occurring in small groups well offshore. The Short-tailed Shearwater is best seen late in the fall and early winter when most Sooties have left Oregon waters. Buller's occurs during August to early November. The fifth species, the Flesh-footed Shearwater, is virtually a rarity in Oregon; it is seldom reported every year, and most records occur during the main shearwater migration, August to October.

To see these species and others (albatrosses, fulmar, storm-petrels, jaegers, skua, and alcids), it is best to join a pelagic birdwatching trip. Most excursions are organized by local Audubon groups or bird clubs — for information, especially contact the Audubon Societies of Portland, Corvallis, Salem, or Eugene, or Oregon Field Ornithologists (see Appendix II for addresses). A good pelagic trip during late August or early September can be a truly memorable birding experience.

Storm-Petrels

These birds are seldom seen from land; two species occur regularly in Oregon. The Fork-tailed Storm-Petrel is not as numerous as the Leach's, but it is seen far more frequently due to the latter species' nocturnal habits. Both nest on offshore rocks (Haystack Rock near A-3, A-7, B-5, B-6, Goat Island at B-8), but almost all sightings occur during the July to October offshore trips. Adverse fall weather occasionally brings small groups of storm-petrels into bay mouths and to major head-lands — most will be Fork-tails.

Brown Pelican

After nesting in extreme southern California and Mexico, large numbers of Brown Pelicans disperse northward into Oregon's coastal waters. May be seen at any bay or estuary. Most common from July to early November.

American White Pelican

Occurs regularly only east of the Cascades. Nesting colonies found at F-5, F-7, F-9, *F-12, and *H-4; may also occur during summer at F-3, F-4, F-6, and F-10, but not known to nest at these sites. Migrants (April to May, August to October) can occur anywhere in Eastern Oregon. Extremely rare west of the Cascades.

Cormorants

One species, the Double-crested, may be found throughout Oregon, both East and West. Occurs in Eastern Oregon strictly as a migrant and summering species, March to September. Inland nesting colonies are found at *F-5, *F-7, *F-9, F-12, *H-4; post-breeding wanders from these sites may occur anywhere in Eastern Oregon.

Two other cormorants, the Pelagic and Brandt's, are strictly coastal (marine) species in Oregon. Both are very common along the entire coast (as is the Double-crested), and all three may be seen side-by-side in any bay. Pelagic Cormorants are usually more prevalent along headlands and offshore rocks and shoals; Brandt's are usually most common around their large nesting colonies at choice sites (A-3, A-7, B-4, B-5, B-6, B-8), and in sheltered bays where the Double-crested is also most common. Particularly good sites for cormorant watching include *A-5, A-6, *A-11, B-1, *B-3, *B-5.

Green-backed Heron

Quiet sheltered backwaters, almost strictly west of Cascades; most common along coast. Good sites include *A-3 (Cannon Beach sewage ponds), A-4, *A-5, *A-11, B-1, *B-4, *C-3, C-5, C-13, C-15, *C-17, D-1. Resident, but most common during summer.

Least Bittern

Very rare and local, April to September (?). Found only in Regions F and H, preferring dense cattail and tule marshes. F-3, F-4, *F-5, F-6, *F-7, F-9, *H-4 have produced the most reports.

Black-crowned Night-Heron
Most common east of Cascades; summers (and is common) at F-3, F-4, *F-5, F-6, *F-7, *F-9, F-12, G-2, *G-9, G-10, H-2, *H-4 (April to September). Post-breeding wanderer throughout Eastern Oregon in small numbers. Occurs very locally in Western Oregon; recent winter roosts located at A-5, A-8, A-11, B-4, C-5, C-17. Not present at these sites every year.

Snowy Egret
Local summer visitor only, strictly Eastern Oregon (see exception below). Best sites (April to August) are F-6, *F-7, F-9, F-12, H-2, *H-4. Only regular wintering site is at *B-4 (Pony Slough; also the only regular site for the species in Western Oregon).

Cattle Egret
Local winter visitor to Western Oregon, mainly in coastal meadowlands. Most frequent from November to February at *A-4, A-5, *A-6 (Tillamook Airport area), B-3, B-4, and along the *Coquille River Valley southeast of the Coos Bay area.

White-faced Ibis
Very local summer visitor (April to August) with traditional nesting/summering sites in Eastern Oregon at F-7, F-9, F-12, *H-2, *H-4.

Trumpeter Swan
Resident population introduced at *H-4 where easy to find. Small numbers winter regularly in Tundra Swan flocks at *C-1, *C-3, C-4, *C-9 (farm fields south of Forest Grove), C-11, C-12, C-15, C-17.

Tundra Swan
Migrant and winter visitor throughout Western Oregon, especially at B-1, *C-1, *C-3, C-4, *C-9, C-12, C-13, C-15. Major migration stops in Eastern Oregon include F-5, *F-6, *F-7, *F-9, *F-12, G-1, G-3, G-5, G-10, H-2, *H-4, H-7. Winters at F-6, *F-7, F-9, F-12, *H-4. Occurs during spring and fall migration throughout the state.

Greater White-fronted Goose
A local migrant throughout the state. Winters at traditional sites in Western Oregon (A-4, A-11, B-4, *C-3, *C-11, *C-12, *C-15, C-17). Choice migration stops in Eastern Oregon (February to April; September to October) include F-5, *F-6, *F-

7, *F-9, F-12, G-1, *G-3, G-5, H-2, *H-4.   May occur anywhere in state during migration.

Snow Goose
Much the same general status as White-fronted Goose, but even more local in occurrence in most areas. Main wintering areas at *C-3, C-11, C-12, C-13, C-15. In Eastern Oregon, major migration stops at *F-6, *F-7, F-9, *H-4.

Ross' Goose
Local and rare migrant in Eastern Oregon during spring (February to April) and fall (October to November) migration. Most likely to be found at *F-6, F-7, F-9, *H-4.

Brant
Strictly coastal, found on backwaters of bays and estuaries, October to April. Try A-4 (Nehalem Bay), *A-5, *A-6, A-8, *A-11, B-1, B-3, *B-4. Very rare in Willamette Valley during winter among flocks of other geese.

Emperor Goose
Very rare winter visitor, strictly Western Oregon. As likely to occur in Willamette Valley goose flocks (*C-3, *C-11, *C-12, C-15, C-17) as along the coast (A-4, A-11, B-1, B-4). One or two reports each year.

Cinnamon and Blue-winged Teals
Mostly summering and migrant species in Oregon, both more common east of Cascades. Throughout most of Oregon, the Cinnamon Teal is the more common species — it arrives earlier (February or March as opposed to May for the Blue-wing) and is more likely to winter (especially west of Cascades). Both species are especially common during summer in Regions F, G, and H. In Western Oregon, look for them especially at *C-3, C-4, *C-9, C-11, C-12, C-15, *C-17, D-2, D-7.

Lesser and Greater Scaups
One of the major field identification problems for Oregon birders, the scaups are best separated by head and bill shape, not head color. See identification tips in National Geographic, 1983 and Madge, 1987 (see Recommended Reading List, Appendix I). Lesser Scaup nests very locally in Eastern and Southwest Oregon; it is by far the most abundant scaup in Eastern Oregon (probably 49 out of 50 scaups east of the Cascades will be this species). Greater Scaups are mainly coastal birds, preferring salt water where it usually outnumbers

Lesser. In interior Western Oregon (Regions C and D), flocks may be mixed, but Lesser generally outnumbers Greater, probably 3 to 1.

Redhead
Most common in Eastern Oregon wetlands, April to August. Some winter, mainly along Columbia River and in Klamath Basin. Very common at E-4, E-12, F-4, *F-5, F-6, *F-7, *F-9, F-10, *F-12, G-1, G-3, G-5, *G-9, G-10, *H-2, *H-4.

Canvasback
A common migrant throughout Oregon. Nests in small numbers in Eastern Oregon, especially in regions F and H. Most common in Oregon along coast during winter — prefers bay and estuary backwaters.

Ring-necked Duck
Most common as a wintering species on fresh water throughout Western Oregon. Winters only locally in Eastern Oregon (especially Klamath Basin). Nests both east and west of Cascades in forested areas; good summer sites include *C-10, *C-14, *C-16, C-17, D-2, *D-6, D-9, *F-3, F-4, *F-5, G-9, G-15, *G-20.

Barrow's Goldeneye
Nests in high mountain lakes of Cascades; moves to lower elevation lakes and ponds in those mountains and the Blue Mountains. Summer sites: C-14, C-19, D-9, *E-5 (sure bet at Lost Lake), *E-13 (northern lakes), F-2. Winter sites: C-14, C-16, D-9, *E-4, *E-9, *E-10, E-11, *E-12, *F-5, F-6, F-9, G-2, G-3, G-5, *G-10, *G-13 (Pete's Pond in Enterprise), *G-15, G-20.

Harlequin Duck
Most frequently encountered as a wintering species along the coast. Prefers rocky headlands, jetties, and offshore rocks. Best coastal sites (August to May) are A-3, *A-5 (rocks by Garibaldi, Barview Jetty), *A-11 (South Jetty Road), A-12, *B-4, *B-6, B-8. Nests on rough rivers on west slope of Cascades; look for them during late spring and summer at C-6, C-10 (Clackamas River), *C-14 (Santiam River above lake), C-16, C-19.

Scoters
All three scoters occur along the Oregon coast during migration and winter (September to April). Surf Scoter is the most common, followed by White-winged, then Black. The first

two species are easily found in any bay along the coast; they are most frequent near the mouth. The Black Scoter prefers rocky headlands and waters with gravelly bottoms; good sites include *A-3, A-5, A-8, A-9, A-10, *A-11 (South Jetty Road), A-12, *B-4, B-5, *B-6.

Oldsquaw
A local, almost rare winter visitor along coast. Best sites are A-1, A-3, A-5, A-9, *A-11, B-4, B-6. Occurs regularly only at mouth of Yaquina Bay. Prefers same habitat as Black Scoter (see above).

Red-breasted Merganser
Almost exclusively a salt-water species, seen in bays and estuaries from September to May.

Hooded Merganser
Prefers fresh-water ponds and forested lakes; much more common west of Cascades. Usually seen during migration and winter, especially at *A-1 (Coffenbury Lake), A-3, A-4, A-8, A-11, B-1, C-3, C-5, *C-8 (nests), *C-13, *C-16 (nests), *C-17, D-1, D-6, D-9.

Black-shouldered Kite
Strictly west of Cascades, especially during winter. Increasing and probably nests regularly in small numbers. Most often found at *A-4 (best site in state), A-6 (Tillamook Airport area), B-1, B-3, *B-4, *B-5, B-7 (meadows), C-15, *C-17, D-1, D-2. Prefers coastal meadows and ungrazed grasslands.

Bald Eagle
Nests very locally along coast (A-4, A-6, A-8, B-4) and in high Cascades (C-14, C-16, C-19, E-5, E-13, F-2, F-3, F-4). More frequently encountered during winter, especially at coastal bays and meadowlands, at Willamette Valley waterfowl concentrations, along entire length of Columbia River, and at Klamath Basin (a winter roost of up to 500 birds is located on the Bear Valley NWR, west of F-7). Winters locally throughout Eastern Oregon, especially Regions E, F, and G.

Northern Goshawk
Resident in forested mountains of Oregon; most often seen during summer in Cascades (C-7, C-10, C-14, C-19, D-9, *E-5, E-6, *E-13, *F-2, F-4) and Blue Mountains (E-9, *G-7, *G-11, G-13, *G-17, *G-21, G-23, G-25). Often reported from more open areas at lower elevations during winter.

Red-shouldered Hawk

Resident species in coastal Southwest Oregon (Region B), as far north as Cape Arago. Prefers woodland on edges of meadows; especially try B-7, *B-8. Occasionally reported farther north along coast and in Umpqua, Rogue, and Willamette Valleys during winter. Occurs somewhat regularly (one or two birds per year) at C-17.

Ferruginous Hawk

Strictly an Eastern Oregon species, occurring from March to September (rarely winters). Found in open desert country or grassland; best sites include E-10, E-14, *F-8, F-9, *F-10, F-12, F-13, *G-5 (near Pilot Rock), *G-19, H-2, *H-3, *H-4, H-7, H-9.

Swainson's Hawk

Another hawk restricted to Eastern Oregon, April to August (even less likely in winter than Ferruginous). Local and decreasing, due to habitat loss (open grassland) and competition with increasing numbers of Red-tailed Hawks. Look for summer Swainson's Hawks at E-4, E-10, F-7, F-8, F-9, *F-10, *F-12, *G-10, G-13, *G-14, *G-18, *G-19, H-2, *H-3, *H-4, H-8, H-9.

Golden Eagle

Most common east of Cascades; resident in mountains, deserts, grassland, open farmland. Much less common (mainly during winter) in Southwestern Oregon (Region D). Good sites include E-2, E-8, E-9, *E-10, E-13, *E-14, F-7, *F-8, F-9, *F-10, F-12, *F-13, G-11, G-13, *G-14, *G-16, *G-18, *G-19, G-25, *H-3, *H-4, H-8, H-9.

Osprey

Occurs throughout state, near ample water supply, from April to August. Easily found along lower Columbia River, lakes in Cascades and Blue Mountains, and on many coastal lakes. Reliable sites include A-1 (Coffenbury Lake), *B-3, C-3, *C-6 (nests at Oxbow Park), C-14, C-16, *D-5 (nests), *D-6 (nests), D-9, E-2, *E-9, *E-13, *F-5, G-8, G-10, *G-20. The densest nesting population of Osprey in the country is reportedly at Crane Prairie Reservoir (E-13); ODFW has interpretive trails and special viewing areas at this site.

Gyrfalcon

Very rare winter visitor, usually one or two reports per year, mostly from coast. Most records are from *A-1, *A-4, A-5, A-6, A-7. May occur virtually anywhere in state.

Prairie Falcon

Resident east of Cascades, mostly open farmland, desert, grassland, rimrock areas. Most common from April to October; occurs as a rare wintering species in Willamette Valley.

Peregrine Falcon

Mainly a winter visitor, most regular along coast and northern Willamette Valley. Try *A-1, A-3, *A-4 (probably the best site in Oregon), A-5, *A-6, A-7, B-4, *C-5. Nests very locally only in high Cascades (less than 10 active nests) and seldom seen during summer. May occur anywhere throughout Oregon during winter and especially during migration.

Sage Grouse

Almost entirely restricted to areas of extensive sagebrush steppe. Resident, but some move to lower elevations during winter. Usually seen on mating leks, February to April. For locations of these, contact local birders, BLM or ODFW offices, or NWR personnel. Best sites include *F-13, G-19, *G-19, G-24, *H-4, H-6, H-7.

Sharp-tailed Grouse

Probably extirpated in Oregon — last reported in the 1950's. Formerly found in open grassland areas; last reports came from eastern Baker County (near G-19).

Ruffed Grouse

Resident in forested areas throughout Oregon. Like most grouse, the observer must usually do some walking to see this retiring but handsome species.

Blue Grouse

Resident in most forested areas throughout the state. Seldom reported during winter due to inaccessibility of habitat. More often heard than seen. Most often reported from Coast Range (A-2 good site), western slope of Cascades, and Blue and Wallowa Mountains.

Spruce Goose

Entirely restricted to high elevation coniferous forests of Wallowa Mountains in extreme Northeast Oregon. Best sites (accessible from June to October) include *G-11, G-15, *G-17. Very tame, but quiet and easily overlooked — do some hiking to find this species.

White-tailed Ptarmigan
Introduced to the high Wallowa Mountains in the mid-and late 1960's; currently the species is extremely local and seldom reported. All recent reports (1981, '86, and '87) have been from the Bonny Lakes area (G-17); this is the one species that will probably never be seen from a road in Oregon!

Mountain Quail
Resident in Coast Range (where California Quail is often absent), western slope of Cascades, and in Southwest Oregon (Region D). Much shier and harder to locate than other quails; more often heard than seen. Look for Mountain Quail in brushy foothill areas — forest openings, clear-cuts, etc. Particularly good areas include *A-2, C-2 (hilly areas), C-7, *C-8, C-15, C-16, D-1, D-2, *D-6, D-7, *D-8. Occurs locally and is very rarely reported in mountain areas of Northeast Oregon and along the east slope of Cascades.

Northern Bobwhite
Locally introduced throughout many areas of the state, but the prudent birder recognizes only two "countable" popula-tions in Oregon — one in the farmland of northern Umatilla County (G-1, G-2, G-3, *G-4), the other along the lower Malheur River Valley of northeastern Malheur County (*H-8).

Gray Partridge
An introduced resident of Eastern Oregon, usually reported in open farmland and brushy areas of Region G. Best sites include G-3, *G-9, *G-10, *G-13, *G-14, G-16, G-18, G-19.

Chukar
Introduced to numerous regions of Eastern Oregon. Resident in rugged rimrock areas and desert. Look for the species at *E-2, E-8, E-10, E-14, F-8, *F-10, *F-13, *G-16, G-18, G-19, *H-3, H-4, H-5.

Wild Turkey
Another game bird introduced to Oregon with varying levels of success. The oldest population in the state (released 1960's) is found in the northern Cascades — especially at *E-1. Other "countable" populations are found in Blue Mountains of Union and Wallowa Counties; southern Morrow County; and near Medford. Those turkeys found in Douglas County near Glide and along the Umpqua River are of questionable origin and should not be counted.

Sandhill Crane

Occurs locally both east and west of the Cascades. Nesting birds occur only in Eastern Oregon — best known sites include F-3, F-12, *G-9, G-20, *G-24, G-25, *H-2, *H-4. Migrants stop in huge flocks at traditional sites — *C-3, F-7, *F-9, *F-12, G-3, *H-2, *H-4. Only regular wintering site in Oregon is at *C-3.

Rails

Only three rails occur regularly in Oregon — the Yellow, Virginia, and Sora. The latter two species are distributed throughout the state in appropriate habitat (marshes, wet meadows, swamps). The Sora is more common in Eastern Oregon, especially in Region H's extensive marshlands. Virginia Rails regularly winter in unfrozen wetlands through-out Western Oregon and at choice sites east of the Cascades. Soras are very local winterers only in Western Oregon.

Yellow Rail

In 1978, Yellow Rails were discovered summering in Klamath County — they are highly suspected of breeding although only one actual nest has been found. Most records fall between May and August; these very elusive and secretive birds are often heard (at night) but almost never seen. See the account under Site *F-4, the only known area for the species.

American Avocet

Strictly an Eastern Oregon species, present during summer (April to August). Best sites include F-5, F-6, *F-7, *F-9, *F-10, *F-12, G-10, *H-2, *H-4. Prefers alkali ponds and flats, wet meadows, lake margins.

Black-necked Stilt

Same as American Avocet, but somewhat more local. Try the same sites.

Black Oystercatcher

Resident along the entire Oregon Coast, salt water only. Look for them anywhere there are rocky shores, tidepools, jetties, or offshore rocks. Almost guaranteed at A-3, A-5, A-9, A-11, A-12, B-4, B-6.

Migrant Shorebirds

Approximately 25-30 species of plovers, sandpipers, and other shorebirds regularly pass through Oregon during spring and fall migrations. The best sites to observe these species (and to look for the rarities) are, of course, along the immediate coast.

Major staging areas are found at *A-1, A-4, A-5, *A-6, *A-8, *A-11, *B-1, B-3, *B-4, and *B-5. These sites can be farther broken down based on the major shorebird groups that use them — for peeps, try A-6 and B-1; for godwits and the larger species, try B-5; and for fresh-water species and *Tringas*, try A-1 and A-4. Peak coastal migration periods occur from April 15 to May 10 (spring, northward-bound), and again from August 15 to October 10 (fall, southward-bound). The best time of observe migrant shorebirds along the coast is during a high or a near-high tide when most birds are pushed up on the higher flats by rising water.

In Eastern Oregon, migrant shorebirds are restricted to areas of ample water. Good sites include wet farm fields, lake margins, and especially sewage ponds. When water levels are appropriate, the best sites include E-4, *E-12, F-6, *F-7, *F-9, *F-10, F-12, *G-3, G-5, G-10, *G-18, H-2, *H-4. Spring migrations fall roughly between April 20 and May 15; fall movements occur between July 10 and September 15.

Lesser Golden-Plover
Almost entirely a Western Oregon species, occurring regularly only during fall migration (August through October). Most common on salt water shores. Especially try *A-1, *A-4, *A-6, A-8, *A-11, B-1, *B-5. Although much rarer inland, Golden-Plovers have occurred a number of times at C-3, C-17, E-12, F-7, and G-3.

Two races of Lesser Golden-Plover are distinguishable in the field; currently (1990), these two forms are considered races, but they will most likely be elevated to full specific status in the near future. Throughout most of Oregon the prevalent form is *Pluvialis dominica dominica,* known as the American Golden-Plover. This is the only form reported east of the Cascades, and the predominant form in interior Western Oregon. The more golden-colored *P. d. fulva,* the Pacific Golden-Plover, is found almost strictly along the immediate coast, often outnumbering the other form there. *P. d. fulva* is also believed to be the more likely form that winters rarely in Oregon. For a thorough identification discussion on these birds, consult Marchant, Prater, et.al., 1983, or the National Geographic field guide, 1983.

Snowy Plover

A resident species along the coast, but numbers increase during winter when inland nesters join these birds. Very local and diminishing; restricted to undisturbed open beaches at A-1, *A-6, *B-1 (South Spit), B-2, *B-3 (Oregon Dunes National Recreation Area), *B-4 (North Spit), B-5. Occurs in Eastern Oregon as a summer breeder, May through August. Prefers alkali lake beds with some standing water present. Best recent sites include F-7 (White Lake), *F-9, *F-10, F-12, H-4, and *H-7. The recent high water levels of Harney Lake at H-4 have all but obliterated nesting birds from that site, but these birds may yet return when water levels drop.

Long-billed Curlew

Summer resident east of Cascades in open grassland and meadows, March to September. Good sites include E-4, E-10, F-4, *F-7, *F-9, *F-10, *F-12, G-1, G-9, G-10, G-18, *G-19, *G-24, *G-25, *H-2, *H-4, H-7, *H-8. Occasional as a spring or fall migrant along coast, especially at A-11, B-4, B-5.

Upland Sandpiper

A very local nesting species in wet highland meadows of Eastern Oregon, May to September (?). Known from only five recent sites including *G-24 and *G-25. Rare and sensitive, these birds should not be disturbed with voice recordings or by trampling through the nesting areas.

Wandering Tattler

Mainly a migrant, strictly coastal. Prefers rocky shorelines, jetties, or gravelly beaches. Try *A-1, *A-5, A-8, A-11, *A-12, B-1, *B-4, B-8.

Yellowlegs

Both species occur throughout the state during migration, both spring and fall. The Greater occurs more widely and has lengthier migration periods; Lessers may be more numerous during its shorter migration period. The Greater is the only species that regularly winters, almost exclusively west of the Cascades. Both yellowlegs species prefer shallow fresh-water ponds, flooded fields, and lake margins.

Marbled Godwit

A migrant (spring and especially fall) in Oregon, mainly along the coast. Prefers the larger estuaries and open beaches. Try *A-1, A-6, *A-8, *A-11, B-4, and especially *B-5. Occurs during fall infrequently in Eastern Oregon, especially at E-4, E-12, F-7, F-9, F-10, F-12, G-3, H-4. Winters locally along the coast, somewhat regularly at A-11, B-4.

Surfbird, Turnstones

These are birds of the rocky shores, jetties, offshore rocks, and tidepools; they are limited to the immediate coast and are most common during the winter months. Best sites include *A-1, A-3, *A-5 (Barview Jetty), *A-9, A-10, *A-11, *A-12, B-1, B-3, B-4, *B-5.

"Peep" Sandpipers

Flocks of "peeps" (Western, Least, Baird's, and other small sandpipers) can be found throughout the state during the traditional migration periods, but all are by far most common along the immediate coast. Major migrational staging sites include A-1, *A-6, A-8, B-1, and *B-4. It is at these sites that the highly sought-after, rarer "peeps" have been recorded — species such as Semipalmated Sandpiper, Rufous-necked Stint, Little Stint, and Long-toed Stint. The Siberian strays are most regularly reported from *A-1 and *A-6. Check the local birding news weekly during spring and especially fall for information on rare shorebird sightings.

Semipalmated Sandpiper

Recorded annually along the Oregon coast, locally elsewhere in the state. By far most frequent as a fall migrant, peaking July 20 to September 10. Very rare in spring, mainly in early May. The most reliable site for the species is *A-6, where up to 10 may be reported at once. Other frequent locations include A-1, *A-4, A-11, *B-4, B-5, *C-3 (almost annual at Coon Point), C-9.

Sharp-tailed Sandpiper

Now recorded annually along the Oregon Coast. All records to date are of juvenile birds, most appearing from September 20 to October 20, later than most other sandpipers. Check large concentrations of Pectoral Sandpipers; the closely-related Sharp-tailed prefers this species' company. The most reliable site in Oregon for the species is *A-1, in the tidal ponds at Parking Lot C. Other good sites include *A-4, A-6, A-11. The species is very rare inland, but there are multiple records for *C-3 (actually, one of the better sites anywhere in Oregon), C-9, C-15, C-17, C-18.

Rock Sandpiper

Strictly a coastal species, local and uncommon during winter (October to March). Prefers rocky areas, tide pools, and jetties, usually in mixed flocks of Surfbirds and turnstones. The most reliable site remains *A-12, a good location for any rock-loving shorebirds. Also frequently found at A-1, A-3, *A-5 (Barview Jetty), *A-9, A-11, B-1.

Stilt Sandpiper

Now reported annually in the state, the Stilt Sandpiper is a rare migrant through Western Oregon, July 20 to September 15. Most records are coastal; the species prefers fresh-water ponds and brackish backwaters. The best bet in Oregon is *A-4, at the sewage ponds. Other frequent sites include A-1, A-6, A-11, B-4, B-5. Inland, the Stilt Sandpiper is much rarer, but records have come from C-3, C-9, C-11, C-17, D-1, E-12, F-6, F-9, G-3.

Buff-breasted Sandpiper

Another "Great Plains" species being reported yearly in Oregon — rare and in small numbers from August 15 to September 10. Almost entirely coastal. Prefers grassy margins to bay mudflats as well as coastal meadows (especially check recently plowed farm fields). Best sites have been at *A-1, A-4, A-5, *A-6, A-11, B-4. Very rare in interior Western Oregon.

Ruff

Reported roughly every other year somewhere along the Oregon Coast. Most records fall between August 20 and September 20; almost all Oregon reports are coastal. Very rare, but most reports are from *A-1, *A-4, A-6, A-11, *B-1, B-4, B-5.

Dowitchers

Another frequent identification problem in Oregon. In general, Short-billed Dowitchers prefer coastal areas where they frequently outnumber the Long-billed species during migration (July to September, and early April to mid-May). The Long-billed is a common fall and spring migrant through-out the state; it greatly outnumbers the Short-billed in Western Oregon away from the coast. The Short-billed Dowitcher is virtually accidental in Eastern Oregon, and any suspect birds found there should be carefully scrutinized. Long-billed Dowitchers winter in small numbers throughout

Western Oregon (especially along the coast) and occasionally in milder regions of Eastern Oregon. The Short-billed Dowitcher is virtually unheard of in Oregon during winter.

Wilson's Phalarope

Most common as a migrant and summering bird in Eastern Oregon. Hard to miss at F-5, F-6, *F-7, *F-9, *F-10, *F-12, G-3, G-5, G-10, G-20, *H-2, *H-4, H-7. An occasional spring and fall migrant west of Cascades, especially in Region D.

Red-necked Phalarope

Spring and fall migrant throughout state, almost no reliable winter records. Most common west of Cascades, especially along coast. Best bet is to check coastal ponds such as at *A-1, *A-4, *A-5 (Bay City Sewage Ponds), A-6, A-8, *A-11, *B-1, *B-3, *B-4, B-5. Prefers sewage ponds, sloughs, and similar bodies of water inland. Main migration periods are April 15 to May 10; and again during August and September.

Red Phalarope

The least-common phalarope in Oregon, almost entirely a coastal species. Most often seen during fall, late September to mid-November; occasionally encountered during winter. The most pelagic phalarope, Reds are usually seen during adverse weather when they may appear in "wrecks" all along the coast. Much less common in Western Oregon away from the coast — here they prefer sewage ponds, reservoirs, and lakes. The beautiful breeding plumage is rarely noted in Oregon.

South Polar Skua

Recorded occasionally on offshore pelagic trips, seldom every year. Not apt to be seen from land. Most records occur during September and October; skuas are most likely to be encountered at offshore shearwater or gull concentrations.

Jaegers

All three species are most frequently seen on offshore boat trips, July to October. The most common species, the Parasitic, is also the most frequently seen jaeger on-shore or inland (all three are rare away from the ocean). Pomarine is the second most common, followed by the rarely-seen Long-tailed which is almost never seen from the land. Good on-shore sites for jaegers include *A-1 (the open beach at the Columbia River mouth), *A-5, A-6, *A-7, A-9, *A-11, B-1, *B-4. Look for jaegers wherever there are concentrations of shearwaters, gulls, or terns.

Franklin's Gull

Local nesting species in wetlands of Southeast Oregon (Region H), April to August. Best sites are at *H-2 and *H-4. Rare fall migrant elsewhere in Oregon.

Heermann's Gull

A post-breeding wanderer that drifts north to Oregon from nesting grounds in California and Mexico. Most common from mid-July to early October; found along the immediate coast only — prefers bay mouths, open beach, warfs, docks, etc. Frequently associates with Brown Pelicans. Hard to miss in any coastal bay during late summer and fall.

"Typical" Gulls

Eight species of "typical" gulls occur in Oregon, mainly during winter from September to April. These are the Mew Gull, Ring-billed Gull, California Gull, Herring Gull, Thayer's Gull, Western Gull, Glaucous-winged Gull, and the Glaucous Gull. As a general rule of thumb, all these birds are most common along the immediate coast and at choice inland sites including C-3, C-13 (McGilchrist Pond), C-17, and locally in cities and towns. Identification of adults is well-covered in standard field guides, but juveniles and immature plumages are a completely different story — for best reading, consult Grant, 1982, or Harrison, 1983.

A recent identification problem that has appeared is the increasing number of hybrid gulls seen along the coast and in interior Western Oregon. The major culprits are cross-breeding Western and Glaucous-winged Gulls; these birds can be nearly as dark as pure Westerns, as light as Glaucous-wings, or any shade between the two species. The pure Western Gull is relatively rare inland, but nearly identical hybrids are common at C-3, C-5, C-13, and other Willamette Valley sites. For identification tips on these difficult birds, consult the above references or the National Geographic Guide (1983).

Fortunately, identification of "typical" gulls east of the Cascades is much simpler. Only two species, the Ring-billed and California, occur regularly throughout most of Eastern Oregon. Beware of other species occasionally appearing in the Klamath Basin (Mew, Glaucous-winged) or along the Columbia River (Mew, Herring, Thayer's, Glaucous-winged, Glaucous).

Glaucous Gull

A very uncommon winter visitor to the northern half of Oregon, most frequent west of Cascades. Most reliable sites include A-1, *A-4, A-5, *A-11, *C-3, C-5, *C-13 (McGilchrist Pond). In Eastern Oregon, check G-2 (below McNary Dam).

Black-legged Kittiwake

Another offshore species, most often reported from land during spring and fall migration (March to early May; September to early November). Best bet is on open beach of *A-1 during fall when individuals join major gull and tern flocks at the Columbia River mouth. Also try A-5 (Barview Jetty), A-6, *A-7, A-9, *A-10, *A-11, B-1, B-3, *B-4.

Sabine's Gull

A highly pelagic gull, seldom seen from land. Most often reported on offshore boat trips, August to October. Occasionally seen from shore at A-1, A-7, A-9, B-1, B-6. Vagrant birds, usually juveniles, can occur virtually anywhere in Oregon during fall migration.

Caspian Tern

Nests or summers in Eastern Oregon, April to August, at E-3 (islands in Columbia), *F-5, F-7, *F-9, *F-10, *F-12, G-1, G-18, H-2, and *H-4. May occur during migration anywhere in Eastern Oregon. Also a common migrant and post-breeding wanderer to Oregon's coast; appears in late April, numbers thin out during June to early August, reaches dramatic numbers in late August and September. Best sites are at *A-1 (open beach at Columbia River mouth), A-5, *A-6, A-8, *A-11, B-1, B-3, *B-4.

Common Tern

Usually seen as a spring or fall migrant along coast, April 20 to May 10, and again during Ausust to early October. Encountered just offshore or seen from jetties, headlands, or resting on beach. Try *A-1, A-5, *A-6, A-7, *A-11, *B-1, B-3, B-4 (North Spit). A rare migrant throughout the rest of Oregon.

Arctic Tern

Almost strictly a coastal species, recorded as a migrant during the same time period as Common Tern; indeed, the two species are sometimes seen side by side on open beaches, making identification much easier! Generally less common and more pelagic than Common. Best sites are *A-1, A-5, A-11, B-1. Most often reported on offshore boat trips.

Forster's Tern

A common summer nester in fresh-water marshes of Southeast and Southcentral Oregon, April to August. Look for it at E-13 (Davis Lake), F-3, F-5, *F-7, *F-9, F-10, F-12, H-2, and especially *H-4. Rare to uncommon migrant throughout the rest of Oregon.

Black Tern

Much the same as Forster's Tern, but occurs even more widely in marshes, wet meadows, ponds, etc. More likely to be encountered elsewhere in Eastern Oregon during migration than Forster's Tern.

Common Murre

Nests on large inshore rocks, winters offshore. Major nesting sites include *A-3, *A-7, *A-10, *B-4, B-6, B-8. Frequently seen in bay mouths, especially when adults are feeding the accompanying young.

Pigeon Guillemot

Very common nesting species all along coast at rocky headlands, cliffs, offshore rocks, even under bridges. Hard to miss from May to early August. Seldom seen during winter when most head for offshore waters.

Marbled Murrelet

Summer nester in dense coastal coniferous forests (never seen on nesting grounds), usually encountered during spring and fall off major headlands and jetties. Best sites include A-1 (South Jetty of Columbia River), A-3, *A-5, *A-7, *A-9 (probably best site in Oregon), A-10, A-11 (South Jetty), B-1, B-3, B-4.

Ancient Murrelet

Very uncommon winter visitor along coast, usually seen from November to March from headlands and jetties. Most reliable sites are *A-5 (Barview Jetty) and especially *A-9. Also try A-1, A-7, A-10.

Cassin's Auklet

Very common offshore during spring, fall, and winter, but seldom seen from land. Reported most often from jetties and headlands at A-1, A-5, A-7, *A-9, and capes at B-4, B-8. Guaranteed on a September or early October pelagic boat trip.

Rhinoceros Auklet
Nests locally on inshore rocks, winters offshore. Common on fall pelagic trips. Occasionally seen from land at A-1, A-5, *A-7, A-9, *A-10, A-11, B-1, B-4, B-8.

Tufted Puffin
Nests locally at *A-3 (Haystack Rock), A-7 (not every year), A-10, B-5 (Coquille Point), B-6, and B-8 (Goat Island). A-3 remains the most reliable site in Oregon, late April to August. Occasionally encountered on fall pelagic trips.

Band-tailed Pigeon
Common summer visitor in Western Oregon, most abundant in coastal forests and mixed coniferous-broadleaf woodland. Also widespread in similar habitat along western slope of Cascades, and in mixed oak-coniferous woodland of Southwest Oregon. Rare and local wintering species in Western Oregon.

Flammulated Owl
Summer resident, late May to August, in mountains of Eastern Oregon. Prefers ponderosa pine forests of Cascades and Blue Mountains. Best sites include E-9, G-7, G-11, *G-20, *G-23 (best site in state), *G-24, *G-25, H-1. More often heard than seen.

Snowy Owl
Irregularly reported during winter in northern half of state. Most reliable site by far is *A-1 (near the jetty). Also likely to appear at A-6, C-3, C-17, *G-1 (farmland west and south of Boardman), G-3, G-10, G-14.

Northern Pygmy-Owl
Resident in forested areas throughout state. Frequently heard in Western Oregon, but seldom seen. East of the Cascades it is much easier to see one. During winter, Pygmy-Owls are frequent roadside sights (during day!) at G-8, G-9, *G-10, *G-13 (best site in state), G-14, *G-15, *G-16, G-20, H-1. Also try various sites along the east slope of the Cascades (especially *E-6, E-7, E-13) during summer.

Burrowing Owl
Summer visitor to open country of Eastern Oregon, present from March to August. Regular sites include E-10, F-9, F-11, F-12, *F-13, G-1, G-10, G-19, *H-2, H-3, *H-4, H-9.

Barred Owl

A recent invader species to Oregon; resident, but seldom encountered during winter. Until recently, most records were from the Blue and Wallowa Mountains, but the species has never been easy to locate here. Has appeared at G-6, G-7, G-10, G-11, G-13, G-20, but no where with regularity.

Since the late 1970's, Barred Owls have been reported from the southern Cascades (west slope only), especially in eastern Douglas and Lane Counties. A regular area has been along the Umpqua River east of the town of Glide. Check with local birders or ODFW personnel for recent sightings.

Spotted Owl

A rare and declining species, resident and restricted to old-growth forests of southern Coast Range and west slope of Cascades. To locate one, it is best to contact local birders or ODFW personnel in Portland, Salem, or Eugene. In recent years, reports have come from A-7, near C-7, C-10, C-14, C-16, C-19, and in the previously-mentioned area east of Glide in Douglas County.

Great Gray Owl

Resident in open forests of the Blue and Wallowa Mountains and along the east slope of the Cascades. Best sites include E-9, E-13, F-2, *F-4, *G-7, G-11, G-20, *G-21, G-25.

Northern Saw-Whet Owl

Resident throughout Oregon in coniferous or mixed forest. More frequently reported (seen) in Eastern Oregon. Commonly heard at A-2, A-7, C-7, C-10, C-14, D-6, E-5, E-13, F-2, F-4, G-6, G-7, G-11, G-15, G-17, G-20.

Boreal Owl

Discovered summering in the Blue Mountains of Northeast Oregon in 1988; probably resident, but preferred habitat is inaccessible during winter. Found in spruce-subalpine fir-lodgepole pine forest about 12 miles northeast of site G-6 at about 6000' elevation. This habitat zone also exists at sites G-11, G-17, above G-20, and G-21. Boreal Owls should be looked for at all these sites.

Common Poorwill

Summer resident in Southwest and Eastern Oregon, preferring open or lightly wooded, arid country with rocky outcroppings. Try D-7, *D-8, E-8, E-9, *E-10, E-14, *F-4, *F-7, *F-8, F-9, *F-10,

F-11, F-12, *F-13, G-16, G-18, *G-19, H-1, *H-3, *H-4, H-5, *H-6, *H-7, *H-9. Much more often heard than seen.

Black Swift
Usually encountered as a spring or fall migrant along coast, less commonly in interior Western Oregon. Extremely rare migrant in mountainous areas of Eastern Oregon. Only reliable site known in Oregon is at Salt Creek Falls (Site *C-19), where the species is suspected to nest. It is seen here from May to July. During August and September, watch for migrants at A-1, A-7, B-4, B-6, C-3, C-7.

White-throated Swift
Migrant and summer resident in rocky canyonlands of Eastern Oregon, April to August. Known nesting sites include E-8, E-10, E-14 (Picture Gorge), *F-8 (best site in state), F-10, *F-12 (face of Hart Mountain), G-16, *H-6 (Roaring Springs Ranch and summit of Steens Mountain), H-7, *H-9.

Black-chinned Hummingbird
A locally uncommon summer visitor east of Cascades, early May to August. May occur anywhere in Eastern Oregon, but appears partial to lower mountains and foothills (especially in Blue Mountains) and arid canyons. Try E-9, F-9, G-7, G-10, *G-11 (feeders in Cove), *G-13 (feeders), *G-16, *G-20, G-24. During migration (May), appears infrequently at H-2, *H-4 (headquarters), H-5, *H-7 (feeders in Fields).

Anna's Hummingbird
Resident throughout Western Oregon, local and in smaller numbers during winter. Most common in Regions D and B. Also locally common summer visitor to east slope of Cascades near Bend.

Costa's Hummingbird
Since about 1975, one to three adult males have summered annually in the Bend area, May through August. Check with local birders for recent sightings. Also appears accidentally each year in Western Oregon, especially in Region D.

Calliope Hummingbird
A common summer visitor to mountainous and foothill areas in Eastern Oregon. Especially try *E-6, E-7, E-9, E-13, F-1, F-4, G-7, *G-8 (best site in Oregon), G-11, G-13, G-15 (feeders), *G-16, G-17, *G-20, G-23, G-24, G-25. Accidental west of Cascades.

Broad-tailed Hummingbird

Much the same as Black-chinned Hummingbird, but much more local. Most records are from mountains of Northeast Oregon during summer or from Region H during migration (May). Best bet is to locate active feeders in Regions G or H, from May to August. Check with local birders for latest sightings.

Allen's Hummingbird

In Oregon, restricted to the extreme southern coastal strip, from the California border north to Cape Arago. Present from March to August. Best sites include B-6, B-7, *B-8 (Azalea St. Pk.). Also check local feeders.

Lewis' Woodpecker

Summer resident (local) through most of Eastern Oregon, April to August. Prefers riparian areas, burns, oak-pine woodlands. Good sites include *E-1, E-2, E-9, E-11, F-8 (Cabin Lake CG), F-11, G-4, G-8, G-13, G-16, G-20, G-22. A common resident, especially during winter, in similar habitats in Region D.

Acorn Woodpecker

Resident in Western Oregon, closely associated with oak woodlands. Very common throughout Region D; local farther north. Look for them at *C-9 (Pacific University), C-11, C-12, C-13, *C-15 (near headquarters), C-17, C-18.

Red-naped Sapsucker

Locally common summer resident east of Cascades, April through September. Prefers aspen or cottonwood woodlands (often mixed with pine), riparian areas, or residential woodlots. Good sites include *E-6, *E-7, E-9, *E-13 (lower lakes), F-1, F-2, F-4, F-13 (aspen groves), G-7 (cottonwoods), *G-8, *G-13, *G-20, G-22, *G-23, G-24, G-25, H-1. The very similar Yellow-bellied Sapsucker has occurred accidentally in Oregon; see National Geographic Guide for identification tips.

Red-breasted Sapsucker

A local, often hard to locate species resident in Western Oregon. Prefers hardwood or mixed woodlands, riparian areas, residential areas, and orchards. Most common in Regions C and D, especially in wooded hilly areas. Overlaps with above species along east slope of Cascades, especially in vicinity of E-6, E-7, E-11, and F-4; hybrids may occur in this zone.

Williamson's Sapsucker
Summer resident, April to September, in pine or pine-aspen forest of Eastern Oregon. Best sites are *E-6, E-7, *E-9, E-13 (lower lakes), F-2, *F-3, *F-4, G-6, *G-7, *G-20, *G-23, G-24, G-25, H-1.

White-headed Woodpecker
Resident in Eastern Oregon, preferring ponderosa pine forests. The sites listed for Williamson's Sapsucker should also produce this handsome species.

Three-toed and Black-backed Woodpeckers
Both are locally uncommon residents in lodgepole pine forests of the Blue and Wallowa Mountains and the east slope of Cascades. Partial to burned or insect-infested timber. Most often reported from *E-5 (Big Lake), E-13, F-2, G-6, *G-7, G-11, G-17, G-20, *G-21, G-23. The Black-backed appears to be somewhat more common, at least in the Cascades.

Alder Flycatcher
Territorial calling birds believed to be this species have been found annually in Northeast Oregon since about 1983, generally during May and June when they are most vocal. The most reliable site has been the wet riparian areas of *G-9 where nesting has been verified. See the standard field guides, especially the National Geographic, regarding the difficulty in distinguishing Alder from Willow Flycatcher. It is best to differentiate the two species only by voice. Migrant calling Alder Flycatchers have been reported a number of times at *H-4 (headquarters and P-Ranch) and H-7 (Fields). The Willow Flycatcher is very common at all these sites as well as through-out the rest of Oregon.

Least Flycatcher
In 1977, territorial Least Flycatchers were discovered at G-22, and they returned to that site for the next nine years, May to September. The species should be looked for there and at other riparian areas of Region G (records exist for G-9 and G-11). Least Flycatchers are recorded during migration (May) almost annually at *H-4 and *H-7.

Hammond's and Dusky Flycatchers
These two species are present in forested regions of Eastern Oregon from April to September. Both prefer coniferous forest, the Dusky also being found in mixed coniferous-

hardwood-riparian areas. See the standard guides, especially the National Geographic, for identification tips.

During migration, habitat does *not* provide a good clue to *Empidonax* identification. Both species can occur side by side during April and May virtually anywhere in Eastern Oregon. Hammond's seems to be the predominant *nesting* species at E-13, F-2, *G-6 *G-11, *G-17, G-21. This species also ranges throughout higher forested areas of Western Oregon such as A-2, C-7, C-8, C-10, C-14, C-16, C-19. Dusky Flycatcher is extremely rare west of the Cascades crest; when present here, they usually are found in clear cuts and open brushy forest edges.

"Western" Flycatchers

Originally considered one species until 1989, the very similar Pacific-slope Flycatcher (*Empidonax difficilis*) and Cordilleran Flycatcher (*E. occidentalis*) were formerly known as the Western Flycatcher. Both occur in Oregon, roughly from late April (Western Oregon) or May (Eastern Oregon) to August. The former species occurs west of the Cascades and is identified by its upslurred, one-syllabled *"sueeeet!"* call. The Cordilleran occurs mostly east of the Cascades crest; it differs by its distinctly two-syllabled loud *"see-WHEET!"* call, accented on the second syllable. Both species are virtually identical in physical appearance. The Pacific -slope Flycatcher is found in moist deciduous or mixed forests in foothills and valleys; it is widespread and easily found throughout Regions A, B, C, and D. The Cordilleran is a bird of riparian areas and hardwood forests; it is most common in the Blue and Wallowa Mountain system where it is still a hard-to-locate species. Good sites include *G-9, G-11, G-13, G-20, and, during migration (May), at *H-4, H-5, H-7. These species are believed to overlap in range along the upper Rogue Valley and possibly elsewhere in Southwest and Southcentral Oregon.

Black Phoebe

Locally uncommon resident on the South Coast north to Cape Blanco; best sites include *B-8 and *B-7. Check coastal meadows at river mouths (under bridges, overpasses, buildings). Also a local resident, more common during summer, in Rogue Valley at D-5 (rare), *D-7 (Kirtland Road sewage ponds), and in Ashland.

Say's Phoebe

Widespread and local throughout open farmland and foothills of Eastern Oregon, early March to September. Check around barns, farm buildings, ranches, and bridges.

Ash-throated Flycatcher

Summer visitor, April to September, mainly in Regions D, E, F, and H. In Southwest Oregon, found in dry open woodland; good sites include *D-4, *D-7, D-8. Eastern Oregon birds prefer dry juniper-sage regions with rimrock outcroppings. Try E-8, E-9, *E-11, F-7, F-13, H-1, *H-3, *H-5 (one of the best sites in Oregon), H-7.

Tropical Kingbird

Very rare late fall visitor from Mexico, most records during late September and October. Strictly coastal, more likely to be seen on South Coast.

Purple Martin

A locally common summer breeder mainly west of Cascades; most frequent along coast and in Willamette Valley (April to August). Good sites include *A-4, A-5 (Bay City sewage ponds), B-1, B-4, C-3, *C-5 (Marine Drive), *C-17, *C-18, D-1, D-3.

Bank Swallow

The least common of Oregon's swallows; restricted to Eastern Oregon, May to August. Locally common at sand bank nesting colonies at *E-11 (near Tumalo St. Pk.), E-12, F-4, F-9, G-3, *G-10, *G-18, G-20, H-2, *H-4.

Gray Jay

Prefers higher hills and mountains where it is resident. Occurs regularly in coniferous forests of the Coast Range, Cascades, Southwest Oregon ranges, and in the Blue-Wallowa-Ochoco System. Very tame, easiest to find in campgrounds and towns at A-2, C-7, C-10, *C-19, D-9, *E-5, *E-13, *F-2 (probably the easiest site in Oregon), *G-6, G-7, G-11, G-15, *G-17, *G-21, G-23. Also try Timberline Lodge on Mt. Hood.

Pinyon Jay

A resident of the extensive juniper woodland of Central Oregon (Regions E and F). Very local, hard to locate as the birds travel in nomadic flocks most of the year. Best sites are at E-4, E-8, *E-10 (south end of reservoir), *E-11 (near airport),

E-12, *F-8 (at Cabin Lake during August and September —
probably the best bet in the state), *F-9, F-10.

Clark's Nutcracker

A relatively common resident of higher mountains, especially
near or above timberline. Entirely restricted to Eastern Oregon
and the highest parts of the Cascades. Try C-19, *E-5 (Big
Lake), *E-13 (the northern lakes and Davis Lake), *F-2 (one of
best sites), G-6, G-11, G-15 (top of gondola lift), *G-17, *G-21.

Northwestern Crow

Resident only on North Coast, probably only in Clatsop
County. Identification is *very* difficult; see account under Site
*A-1 for tips and locations.

Mountain Chickadee

Occurs in higher hills and mountains of Eastern Oregon only;
resident. Try C-19, D-9, E-5, *E-6, *E-7, E-9, E-11 (mainly
winter), *E-13, *F-2, *F-4, G-3 (winter), *G-6, *G-11, *G-15, *G-
17 (guaranteed), G-20, *G-21.

Chestnut-backed Chickadee

Most common in Western Oregon, but also occurs in wetter
parts of Blue and Wallowa Mountains. Resident throughout
range. Most common along coast and in Coast Range; also
common and easy to find in dense forests of the Cascades'
western slopes.

Plain Titmouse

Resident in extreme Southwest and Southcentral Oregon only.
Prefers oak woodlands in Region D, juniper and riparian areas
in Region F. Best sites are *D-4, *D-7, *D-8; less likely but
possible at F-7, F-11, F-12.

Pygmy Nuthatch

A resident species of pine (mainly ponderosa) forests throughout Eastern Oregon. E-1, *E-6, *E-7, E-9, *E-11, E-13, F-2, F-3,
*F-4, *F-8 (Cabin Lake), F-12, F-13, G-7, G-15, G-20, G-23, G-
24, G-25, H-1 are all good sites.

Bewick's Wren

Very common resident in brushy riparian areas throughout
Western Oregon. In Eastern Oregon, occurs only along
Columbia River Basin areas (G-1, G-2, G-3, G-4, G-5) and
along lower Deschutes river system.

Rock Wren

Most common as a summer resident throughout Eastern Oregon, mainly in open, dry, rocky regions and canyons. Especially common in Regions E, F, and H. A very few remain to winter in Eastern Oregon.

Canyon Wren

Similar status as Rock Wren, but more restricted to larger canyons and ravines. More likely to winter than Rock Wren. Both species are particularly common at *E-8, E-10, F-7, F-9, F-10, *F-12, *F-13 (west face of Hart Mountain), *H-3, *H-4, *H-5, *H-6, *H-7, *H-9.

Blue-gray Gnatcatcher

Restricted to extreme Southwest Oregon (Rogue Valley and tributaries), most common from April to August. Found in dry, brushy, chaparral areas, especially fond of ceanothus shrubbery. Most reliable at D-4, *D-7, *D-8. Has occurred a number of times in the brushy juniper woodland at H-5 and should be looked for there again.

Western Bluebird

Local and declining in most of Western Oregon where it is resident in foothill areas. Especially try *C-2 (clearcuts outside Vernonia), C-7, *C-8, C-15, C-16, C-17, *D-1, D-2, D-4, *D-7, *D-8, *D-9. In Eastern Oregon, a bird of lightly forested foothills — look for them at *E-1, E-9, *E-13, *F-4, F-11, *G-7, G-10, *G-13, G-14, *G-20, *G-24, *G-25.

Mountain Bluebird

Restricted to Eastern Oregon, generally found at higher elevations during summer — try *F-2, F-4, F-13, *E-1, *E-5, E-9, *E-13, G-6, *G-7, *G-11, *G-16, *G-17, *G-21, G-24, G-25. During winter and migration, prefers lower, more open terrain along east slope of Cascades and foothills of the Blue-Wallowa-Ochoco System; best sites then include E-1, E-4, *E-8, *E-9, *E-10, *E-11, E-14, F-4, F-7, *F-8, *F-9, F-10, F-11, F-12, G-2, G-3, G-5, *G-10, *G-13, *G-14, G-15, G-19, G-20.

Townsend's Solitaire

Much the same status as Mountain Bluebird; see the sites listed above. Also occurs very locally during summer in higher areas of the Coast Range and west slope of Cascades.

Catharus Thrushes

Three species of these brown-backed, spot-breasted thrushes occur in Oregon. Two, the Hermit and Swainson's, are widespread summer residents in forested regions throughout the state. The third, the Veery, is locally distributed in the Blue, Wallowa, and Ochoco Mountain Systems. The Veery prefers dense riverside riparian growth, usually at lower elevations; it is present from late May to August. Good sites include E-9, *G-8 (best site in state), G-10, *G-12, *G-13, G-14, G-16, *G-20.

During summer, the Hermit Thrush generally prefers much higher elevations than the Swainson's Thrush or Veery; look for it above 4000' in wet coniferous forests. Swainson's Thrush breeds at intermediate elevations between the other two species — higher than the Veery, but lower than the Hermit. The Swainson's is present in Oregon from late April to August, and it prefers mixed or coniferous forests and woods.

The Hermit is the only *Catharus* thrush found in Oregon during winter (October to early April); at this time of year it is very rare in most of Eastern Oregon, but uncommon in the lowlands west of the Cascades.

Varied Thrush

Resident in wet forests throughout Western Oregon; often moves to more open country during winter. In Eastern Oregon, found in higher wet forests of Cascade, Blue, and Wallowa Mountains with some down-slope movement during winter.

Wrentit

Resident in Western Oregon, most abundant along coast. Found in interior valleys (Rogue, Willamette, etc.) north to about Corvallis; north of that it is strictly a coastal species. Prefers dense brush and chaparral; easy to find at *A-1 (Coffenbury Lake), A-3, *A-6, A-7, *A-11, B-1, B-3, *B-4 (Cape Arago and Shore Acres Parks), B-5, B-8, D-1, D-5, *D-7, D-8. Interestingly, the Wrentit is very common as far north as Clatsop Spit, but the species is unreported in Washington state as of this writing!

Gray Catbird

Restricted to valleys of the Wallowa and eastern Blue Mountains of Region G. Prefers dense riparian growth and broadleaf forest; present from latest May to late July. Best sites are *G-8, G-10, *G-12 (best site in Oregon), G-13, *G-14, G-18, G-20. Occurs as a rare spring (May, June) migrant at H-4 and H-7.

Northern Mockingbird

A rare species throughout Oregon; occurs most frequently as a rare spring migrant and summer resident in Region D (Rogue Valley) and Region B. A regular spring migrant almost annually at H-4 and H-7. Winters rarely in Western Oregon, most frequently along coast. There is no reliable Oregon location for this species; the best way to find one is to listen to Portland Audubon's weekly Rare Bird Alert.

Sage Thrasher

Summer visitor, April to August, in sagebrush areas east of the Cascades. Best locations are at E-10, F-7, *F-8, *F-9, *F-10, F-12, *F-13, G-18, *G-19, *H-3, *H-4 (best area in state), *H-7, H-9.

Bohemian Waxwing

A winter visitor to Eastern Oregon, rarely occurring in Western Oregon some winters. Most easily found in valleys and residential areas of Region G, November to March. Try G-4 (Pendleton), *G-8, *G-9, G-10, *G-13, G-14, G-16, G-20.

Shrikes

The two Oregon shrikes — Loggerhead and Northern — seldom overlap in seasonal occurrence. The smaller Loggerhead is mainly a summer species, April to August; it is most common east of the Cascades and in Region D in open dry country. Good sites for this species include F-7, *F-9, F-12, *F-13, G-1, G-3, G-19, H-2, *H-3, *H-4, *H-7, H-8. The Northern Shrike is a winter bird, appearing in mid-October and departing by late March. It is locally common in Eastern Oregon, less so west of the Cascades. This is also a bird of open or lightly wooded areas. In Western Oregon, look for it at *A-1, A-6, B-1, *B-4 (North Spit), *C-3, C-11, C-12, *C-15, *C-17.

Hutton's Vireo

Resident, found only west of the Cascades. More common and easier to locate during summer. Prefers deciduous or mixed forest, especially in Coast Range and along west slope of the Cascades. Try *A-1 (Coffenbury Lake, especially in winter), A-2, B-4, B-6, *C-1, C-2, *C-5 (Forest Park, winter), *C-7, *C-8, C-15, *C-16, *C-18, D-1, *D-4, D-5, *D-6, *D-7, D-8.

Red-eyed Vireo

A very local summering species, late May to late July. Prefers mature (tall) deciduous woodlands, especially cottonwood, willow, and alder. Very local and rare west of the Cascades — recent reliable sites have included *C-3, *C-6, C-16. Much more regular in Eastern Oregon, especially at *G-8 (best site in state), G-12, G-13, *G-14, G-20. Occasionally found as a spring migrant (May, June) at H-4, H-7.

Townsend's, Black-throated Gray, and Hermit Warblers

These three "throated" warblers are so closely related that their habitat preferences and voices are often the only differences that prevent them from interbreeding. This is especially true of the Townsend's and Hermit, and hybrids between these two species are not rare.

The Townsend's is the most widespread of the three species, occurring in coniferous or mixed forests throughout mountainous regions of the state. This is the only "throated" warbler that winters in Oregon, mainly along the coast and in Region D. In Eastern Oregon, this bird summers in the Blue-Wallowa-Ochoco System, and it is frequently encountered at lower elevations during migration.

The Hermit Warbler is strictly a summer visitor only in Western Oregon. It breeds in coniferous forests, but also occurs in other habitats at lower elevations during migration. When on breeding territory, the Hermit Warbler is generally found below 4500', whereas the nesting Townsend's prefer elevations above 4500'. The Hermit Warbler is easy to locate during summer in the Coast Range and along the west slope of the Cascades.

The Black-throated Gray is the "throated" warbler of the Western Oregon lowland deciduous forests. The other two species occur in these broadleaf woodlands only during migration. In Eastern Oregon, the Black-throated Gray Warbler is also found in dry juniper woodlands; especially look for it at *E-1, *E-11, and *H-5.

"Eastern" Warblers

Each spring and fall, hundreds of birders flock to choice "vagrant traps" in Southeast Oregon. These sites are usually islands of trees and brushy growth situated in arid desert lands. The most famous include the headquarters complex at Malheur NWR (H-4); the oasis-like spring across the main road from the buildings in Fields (H-7); the P-Ranch and Benson and Buena Vista Ponds also at Malheur NWR; and Page Springs Campground (H-5). Typical "Eastern" vagrants reported each year from these sites may include Tennessee, Chestnut-sided, Magnolia, Black-and-White, Black-throated Blue, and Cape May Warblers, Northern Parula, Ovenbird, or American Redstart, as well as other more unusual species. Prime timing for viewing these birds is early in the morning or following a spring thunder shower. May 20 to June 10 is best for the spring vagrants; September 15 to October 10 for the fall rarities.

Palm Warbler

Regularly found along the coast each year, October to March. Prefers brushy areas where it remains low to the ground. Best site by far is at *A-11 near the Marine Science Center. Other good sites include A-1, A-4, *A-5, A-6, B-1, *B-4, B-8.

American Redstart

Occurs as a summer resident in Region G and locally at E-13 (Odell Creek at Davis Lake), mid-May to late July. Prefers brushy riparian growth and broadleaf woodlands, usually near water. Best Oregon site is at *G-8. Also try G-10, *G-12, *G-13, G-15, G-16, G-20. A rare migrant during spring and fall at H-4, H-7.

Northern Waterthrush

A rare but regular summer resident, late May to July, at wet brushy areas in vicinity of *F-1. To be looked for in nearby regions of the Cascades. A rare spring and fall migrant elsewhere in Oregon, but most frequently at H-4, H-7.

Yellow-breasted Chat

A local summer visitor throughout the state, late May to August; much more common in Eastern Oregon. Prefers lower elevation water courses with brushy growth. Best sites in state are *G-8, *G-12, *G-18, H-4, *H-5 (main road between Frenchglen and the campground).

California Towhee

Formerly known as the Brown Towhee, this southern species was split from the similar Canyon Towhee of the Southwestern U.S. in 1989. The California Towhee is a resident species in Oregon only in brushy chaparral areas of Region D, especially in the Rogue, Applegate, and Bear Creek Valleys. The species is easy to find at D-4, *D-7, and *D-8.

Green-tailed Towhee

A local summer visitor, late April to July, almost strictly east of Cascades. Prefers open juniper-pine-sage areas and dry brushy hillsides. Especially try *E-6, *E-7, E-11, F-2, *F-8, F-9, F-11, F-13, G-20, *H-1.

American Tree Sparrow

An uncommon and local winter visitor mainly to Region G, November to March. Less common during winter in Region H, virtually accidental elsewhere in Oregon. Found in brushy hedgerows, gardens, farm fields, usually away from towns. Best sites are G-1, G-3, G-4, *G-5, G-9, *G-10, *G-14, H-7.

Brewer's Sparrow

A summer visitor, March to August, in Eastern Oregon sagebrush areas. Very common at E-10, E-11, E-14, F-7, *F-8, *F-9, F-10, F-11, *F-12, *F-13, G-18, *G-19, G-24, *H-3, *H-4, *H-7, H-8.

Clay-colored Sparrow

A rare but regular winter visitor in brushy lowland areas of Western Oregon. Recent records come from A-3 (Cannon Beach sewage ponds), A-4, A-11, B-4, B-8, C-3, C-15, C-18, D-3, but the species is not to be expected anywhere — check with local bird alert circuits.

Lark Sparrow

Locally common summer visitor to Eastern Oregon grasslands and sagebrush areas, April to September. Most common in Regions F, G, H. Especially try *F-12, *F-13, G-18, *G-19, *H-3, *H-4, H-7.

Sage Sparrow

Locally uncommon summer species closely associated with extensive areas of sagebrush. By far most common in Region H, March to August. Good sites include *H-3, *H-4, *H-7 (best area in Oregon), H-8. See notes under Site H-7 for finding this species and the closely related Black-throated Sparrow.

Black-throated Sparrow

Entirely restricted to desert areas in extreme Southeast Oregon; prefers sagebrush habitats, late April to August. Regularly reported only at H-3, *H-4 (near Coyote Buttes, Wright's Point), *H-7 (best site in Oregon).

Grasshopper Sparrow

This very inconspicuous summer visitor (May to August) is most frequently encountered in the extensive foothill areas of the Blue Mountains and the eastern Columbia Basin. Most reports come from the dry, ungrazed, native grass areas of Morrow, Umatilla, and Gilliam Counties. Good recent sites have been along OR 74 just west of Nye Junction in central Umatilla County; and in the Blackhorse Canyon area near Heppner, Morrow County. Consult local maps for backroads in these areas.

White-throated Sparrow

A local and uncommon species in Western Oregon, much more common during winter (October to March). Most records are from coastal areas and interior valleys (Willamette, Rogue, etc.). Often closely associated with city environments, preferring brushy hedgerows, feeders, and woodland edges. Usually found in wintering flocks of Golden-crowned or White-crowned Sparrows. Best sites include B-4, *C-3, *C-5, C-9, C-13, C-15, *C-17, *C-18, D-1, *D-3, D-5, D-7.

Golden-crowned Sparrow

A winter visitor throughout Western Oregon, October to April. Easy to find in open areas bordered by brush and hedgerows. A rare migrant (fall) and winter visitor in Eastern Oregon, usually in Regions E, G.

Harris' Sparrow

This species occurs mainly as a winter visitor throughout the state — there are numerous records for all 8 Regions covered in this book. Most regular from October to April, especially in Columbia Basin counties, along the North Coast, and in Willamette Valley winter sparrow flocks. Numerous winter reports for A-3, *C-3, C-5, *C-9, C-13, *C-18, D-3, F-12, *G-1, *G-2, *G-3, *G-4, *G-5, G-10, G-13.

Lapland Longspur

A locally uncommon winter visitor, October to early March. May occur virtually anywhere in Oregon, but by far most regular along North Coast. The best site is easily *A-1, especially during October and November. Also try A-4, *A-6, *B-4 (North Spit), B-5, F-6, *F-7. Prefers open grassy areas, farmland, dunes, or beaches.

Snow Bunting

A rare and local winter visitor to the northern third of Oregon, usually from November to March. Found in open country, farmland, dunes, beaches, etc. Flocks of hundreds of Snow Buntings are found in Northeast Oregon most winters, especially at Site *G-14 (OK Gulch area — the best bet in Oregon). Also found in small numbers at *A-1, A-6, B-4 (North Spit).

Bobolink

A locally-distributed summer visitor to traditional nesting sites in Eastern Oregon, mid-May to August. Found in wet meadows, fields of alfalfa, and occasionally in grasslands. Good sites are at *G-9, *G-13, G-20, G-24, G-25, H-2, *H-4 (fields just north of P-Ranch), H-6 (across the road from Roaring Springs Ranch).

Tricolored Blackbird

A summer breeder mainly in the Klamath Basin, especially at *F-6, *F-7. Usually occurs in compact, isolated nesting colonies away from Red-winged and Yellow-headed Blackbirds, almost strictly in marshes of cattail or tule. Also a local summer resident in Rogue Valley near Medford. A small isolated population has existed in North Portland (C-5) since about 1986, but this is sporadic and difficult to locate from year to year — contact local birders for information.

Rosy Finch

Three distinct races of this handsome alpine finch occur in Oregon, including the rare "Black Rosy Finch", a form that may once again be given full species status in the near future. The Black form occurs regularly only at the summit of Steens Mountain (*H-6), where it may be seen from July to September when the area is accessible to birders. This form has also been reported rarely from the Wallowa Mountains.

The other two races that occur in Oregon, the "Hepburn's Rosy Finch" and the "Gray-crowned Rosy Finch" are quite similar in appearance, and will most likely remain as races of one species. The Hepburn's form nests on the absolute highest peaks of the Cascades (Hood, Jefferson, Three Sisters, Washington, McLoughlin, and Crater Lake), and it descends to adjacent lowlands of Eastern Oregon during winter. It is most easily seen at Site *F-2 and near Timberline Lodge on Mt. Hood.

Bird-Finding Guide

The third form, the Gray-crowned, is probably the easiest of the three races to locate. It nests above timberline in the Blue and Wallowa Mountains, and has been found with some regularity at Site *G-18 from July to October. During winter it descends to lower elevations when tremendous flocks may be seen in the open country, especially at such sites as *G-14, G-16, *G-18, G-19.

Pine Grosbeak

A local and hard-to-locate winter visitor mainly to mountainous regions of Northeast Oregon. Small numbers may be found summering (probably nesting) in the Wallowa, Blue, and Cascade Mountains. A bird of the high-elevation coniferous forests, the Pine Grosbeak is most familiar as a nomadic feeder seen in small flocks at tree-top level. Good sites during winter have included G-10, *G-11, *G-13, G-15, G-20, G-21. One of the best places to find this species is along the Bonny Lakes Trail in the Wallowas (*G-17) during the summer (July to September).

Cassin's Finch

Almost strictly an Eastern Oregon species. Prefers mid- to high-elevation coniferous forests of pine, fir, larch, etc. Moves to lower elevation forests during winter (may then visit feeders, especially in Regions E, F, G). Good sites include D-9, E-1 (winter), *E-5, *E-6, E-7, *E-9, *E-11 (especially winter), *E-13, F-1, *F-2, F-3, *F-4, F-5, F-8 (Cabin Lake), *G-6, *G-7, *G-11, G-13, *G-15, *G-17, *G-20, *G-21, *G-23, G-24, G-25.

The similar Purple Finch is seldom found in the same area as the Cassin's; the only areas where the two species' ranges normally overlap is along the extreme northern East Slope of the Cascades (Hood River and Wasco Counties), and in extreme southern Klamath County. In these areas the Purple Finch is usually found in broadleaf or mixed lowland forests, while the Cassin's prefers the coniferous higher elevation areas.

White-winged Crossbill

Usually encountered as a rare winter visitor from the north, October to March, especially in Region G. Winter sightings have come from G-7, G-11, G-15, G-21. In the high Cascades, this species' numbers can erupt virtually any time of year, but this usually occurs in late summer or fall. The most reliable site in the Cascades has been C-19 and nearby lakes.

Common Redpoll

A very irregular winter visitor (November to March) to Region G in open brushy country or residential areas. Seldom occurs every year or in large numbers. Good sites have been G-5, G-9, *G-10, *G-13, *G-14, G-15, G-16, G-20. Virtually accidental elsewhere in Oregon.

Lesser Goldfinch

Uncommon to very common resident in Western Oregon, especially in Region D where it is easy to find in brushy, open country. Try C-12, C-13, C-15, *C-17, D-1, D-2, D-3, *D-4, D-5, *D-7, *D-8. Occurs locally in Eastern Oregon, mainly in the juniper woodland areas of the east slope of the Cascades. Regularly found at H-5.

Checklist of Oregon Birds

The following checklist includes those species of birds known to have occurred in Oregon since approximately 1900. Nomenclature and arrangement of species and families follows that of the Sixth Edition of the American Ornithologists' Union's *Checklist of North American Birds* (1983) and its most recent supplements (up to 1989). Those species which regularly nest in Oregon are indicated by an asterisk (*). Species which are believed to be extirpated in Oregon are indicated by an "E". Introduced species which are successfully established in the state are indicated by an "I".

LOONS (Gaviidae)
__ Red-throated Loon
__ Pacific Loon
__ Common Loon
__ Yellow-billed Loon
GREBES (Podicipedidae)
__ Pied-billed Grebe*
__ Horned Grebe*
__ Red-necked Grebe*
__ Eared Grebe*
__ Western Grebe*
__ Clark's Grebe*
ALBATROSSES (Diomedeidae)
__ Short-tailed Albatross (E)
__ Black-footed Albatross
__ Laysan Albatross
SHEARWATERS, FULMAR, PETRELS, ETC. (Procellariidae)
__ Northern Fulmar
__ Pink-footed Shearwater
__ Flesh-footed Shearwater
__ Buller's Shearwater
__ Sooty Shearwater
__ Short-tailed Shearwater
STORM-PETRELS (Hydrobatidae)
__ Fork-tailed Storm-Petrel*
__ Leach's Storm-Petrel*
PELICANS (Pelecanidae)
__ American White Pelican*
__ Brown Pelican
CORMORANTS (Phalacrocoracidae)
__ Double-crested Cormorant*
__ Brandt's Cormorant*
__ Pelagic Cormorant*
HERONS, BITTERNS, ETC. (Ardeidae)
__ American Bittern*
__ Least Bittern*
__ Great Blue Heron*
__ Great Egret*
__ Snowy Egret*

__ Cattle Egret
__ Green-backed Heron*
__ Black-crowned Night-Heron*
IBISES (Threskiornithidae)
__ White-faced Ibis*
SWANS, GEESE, DUCKS (Anatidae)
__ Tundra Swan
__ Trumpeter Swan (nesting birds introduced)
__ Greater White-fronted Goose
__ Snow Goose
__ Ross' Goose
__ Emperor Goose
__ Brant
__ Canada Goose*
__ Wood Duck*
__ Green-winged Teal*
__ Mallard*
__ Northern Pintail*
__ Blue-winged Teal*
__ Cinnamon Teal*
__ Northern Shoveler*
__ Gadwall*
__ Eurasian Wigeon
__ American Wigeon*
__ Canvasback*
__ Redhead*
__ Ring-necked Duck*
__ Greater Scaup
__ Lesser Scaup*
__ Harlequin Duck*
__ Oldsquaw
__ Black Scoter
__ Surf Scoter
__ White-winged Scoter
__ Common Goldeneye
__ Barrow's Goldeneye*
__ Bufflehead*
__ Hooded Merganser*
__ Common Merganser*
__ Red-breasted Merganser
__ Ruddy Duck*

NEW WORLD VULTURES (Cathartidae)
__ California Condor (E)
__ Turkey Vulture*
HAWKS, EAGLES, ETC. (Accipitridae)
__ Osprey*
__ Black-shouldered Kite* (rare nester)
__ Bald Eagle*
__ Northern Harrier*
__ Sharp-shinned Hawk*
__ Cooper's Hawk*
__ Northern Goshawk*
__ Red-shouldered Hawk (probably nests)
__ Swainson's Hawk*
__ Red-tailed Hawk*
__ Ferruginous Hawk*
__ Rough-legged Hawk
__ Golden Eagle*
FALCONS (Falconidae)
__ American Kestrel*
__ Merlin* (rare nester)
__ Peregrine Falcon* (rare nester)
__ Gyrfalcon
__ Prairie Falcon*
PHEASANTS, PARTRIDGE, GROUSE, QUAIL, ETC. (Phasianidae)
__ Gray Partridge* (I)
__ Chukar* (I)
__ Ring-necked Pheasant* (I)
__ Spruce Grouse*
__ Blue Grouse*
__ White-tailed Ptarmigan* (I)
__ Ruffed Grouse*
__ Sharp-tailed Grouse (E)
__ Sage Grouse*
__ Wild Turkey* (I)
__ Northern Bobwhite* (I)
__ California Quail*
__ Mountain Quail*
RAILS, COOTS (Rallidae)
__ Yellow Rail*
__ Virginia Rail*
__ Sora*
__ American Coot*
CRANES (Gruidae)
__ Sandhill Crane*
PLOVERS (Charadriidae)
__ Black-bellied Plover
__ Lesser Golden-Plover
__ Snowy Plover*
__ Semipalmated Plover
__ Killdeer*
OYSTERCATCHERS (Haematopodidae)
__ Black Oystercatcher*
STILTS, AVOCETS (Recurvirostridae)
__ Black-necked Stilt*
__ American Avocet*

SANDPIPERS, CURLEWS, GODWITS, PHALAROPES, ETC. (Scolopacidae)
__ Greater Yellowlegs
__ Lesser Yellowlegs
__ Solitary Sandpiper
__ Willet*
__ Wandering Tattler
__ Spotted Sandpiper*
__ Upland Sandpiper*
__ Whimbrel
__ Long-billed Curlew*
__ Marbled Godwit
__ Ruddy Turnstone
__ Black Turnstone
__ Surfbird
__ Red Knot
__ Sanderling
__ Semipalmated Sandpiper
__ Western Sandpiper
__ Least Sandpiper
__ Baird's Sandpiper
__ Pectoral Sandpiper
__ Sharp-tailed Sandpiper
__ Rock Sandpiper
__ Dunlin
__ Stilt Sandpiper
__ Buff-breasted Sandpiper
__ Short-billed Dowitcher
__ Long-billed Dowitcher
__ Common Snipe*
__ Wilson's Phalarope*
__ Red-necked Phalarope
__ Red Phalarope
GULLS, JAEGERS, TERNS (Laridae)
__ Pomarine Jaeger
__ Parasitic Jaeger
__ Long-tailed Jaeger
__ South Polar Skua
__ Franklin's Gull*
__ Bonaparte's Gull
__ Heermann's Gull
__ Mew Gull
__ Ring-billed Gull*
__ California Gull*
__ Herring Gull
__ Thayer's Gull
__ Western Gull*
__ Glaucous-winged Gull*
__ Glaucous Gull
__ Black-legged Kittiwake
__ Sabine's Gull
__ Caspian Tern*
__ Common Tern
__ Arctic Tern
__ Forster's Tern*
__ Black Tern*
AUKS, MURRES, ETC. (Alcedidae)
__ Common Murre*
__ Pigeon Guillemot*
__ Marbled Murrelet*
__ Ancient Murrelet
__ Cassin's Auklet*

__ Rhinoceros Auklet*
__ Tufted Puffin*
__ Horned Puffin
PIGEONS, DOVES (Columbidae)
__ Rock Dove* (I)
__ Band-tailed Pigeon*
__ Mourning Dove*
BARN OWLS (Tytonidae)
__ Barn Owl*
TRUE OWLS (Strigidae)
__ Flammulated Owl*
__ Western Screech-Owl*
__ Great Horned Owl*
__ Snowy Owl
__ Northern Pygmy-Owl*
__ Burrowing Owl*
__ Spotted Owl*
__ Barred Owl*
__ Great Gray Owl*
__ Long-eared Owl*
__ Short-eared Owl*
__ Northern Saw-whet Owl*
NIGHTHAWKS, NIGHTJARS, ETC. (Caprimulgidae)
__ Common Nighthawk*
__ Common Poorwill*
SWIFTS (Apodidae)
__ Black Swift*
__ Vaux's Swift*
__ White-throated Swift*
HUMMINGBIRDS (Trochilidae)
__ Black-chinned Hummingbird*
__ Anna's Hummingbird*
__ Calliope Hummingbird*
__ Broad-tailed Hummingbird
   (probably nests)
__ Rufous Hummingbird*
__ Allen's Hummingbird*
KINGFISHERS (Alcedinidae)
__ Belted Kingfisher*
WOODPECKERS (Picidae)
__ Lewis' Woodpecker*
__ Acorn Woodpecker*
__ Red-naped Sapsucker*
__ Red-breasted Sapsucker*
__ Williamson's Sapsucker*
__ Downy Woodpecker*
__ Hairy Woodpecker*
__ White-headed Woodpecker*
__ Three-toed Woodpecker*
__ Black-backed Woodpecker*
__ Northern Flicker*
__ Pileated Woodpecker*
FLYCATCHERS (Tyrannidae)
__ Olive-sided Flycatcher*
__ Western Wood-Pewee*
__ Least Flycatcher (may nest)
__ Willow Flycatcher*
__ Alder Flycatcher (probably nests)
__ Hammond's Flycatcher*
__ Dusky Flycatcher*
__ Gray Flycatcher*

__ Pacific-slope Flycatcher*
__ Cordilleran Flycatcher*
__ Black Phoebe*
__ Say's Phoebe*
__ Ash-throated Flycatcher*
__ Western Kingbird*
__ Eastern Kingbird*
LARKS (Alaudidae)
__ Horned Lark*
SWALLOWS (Hirundinidae)
__ Purple Martin*
__ Tree Swallow*
__ Violet-green Swallow*
__ Northern Rough-winged Swallow*
__ Bank Swallow*
__ Cliff Swallow*
__ Barn Swallow*
CROWS, JAYS, ETC. (Corvidae)
__ Gray Jay*
__ Steller's Jay*
__ Blue Jay
__ Scrub Jay*
__ Pinyon Jay*
__ Clark's Nutcracker*
__ Black-billed Magpie*
__ American Crow*
__ Northwestern Crow (may nest)
__ Common Raven*
TRUE TITMICE (Paridae)
__ Black-capped Chickadee*
__ Mountain Chickadee*
__ Chestnut-backed Chickadee*
__ Plain Titmouse*
BUSHTITS (Aegithalidae)
__ Bushtit*
NUTHATCHES (Sittidae)
__ Red-breasted Nuthatch*
__ White-breasted Nuthatch*
__ Pygmy Nuthatch*
CREEPERS (Certhidae)
__ Brown Creeper*
WRENS (Troglodytidae)
__ Rock Wren*
__ Canyon Wren*
__ Bewick's Wren*
__ House Wren*
__ Winter Wren*
__ Marsh Wren*
DIPPERS (Cinclidae)
__ American Dipper*
THRUSHES, KINGLETS, GNAT-CATCHERS, ETC. (Muscicapidae)
__ Golden-crowned Kinglet*
__ Ruby-crowned Kinglet*
__ Blue-gray Gnatcatcher*
__ Western Bluebird*
__ Mountain Bluebird*
__ Townsend's Solitaire*
__ Veery*
__ Swainson's Thrush*
__ Hermit Thrush*
__ American Robin*

__ Varied Thrush*
__ Wrentit*
THRASHERS, ETC. (Mimidae)
__ Gray Catbird*
__ Northern Mockingbird
__ Sage Thrasher*
PIPITS, WAGTAILS (Motacillidae)
__ American Pipit*
WAXWINGS (Bombycillidae)
__ Bohemian Waxwing
__ Cedar Waxwing*
SHRIKES (Lanidae)
__ Northern Shrike
__ Loggerhead Shrike*
STARLINGS (Sturnidae)
__ European Starling* (I)
VIREOS (Vireonidae)
__ Solitary Vireo*
__ Hutton's Vireo*
__ Warbling Vireo*
__ Red-eyed Vireo*
**WARBLERS, SPARROWS,
BUNTINGS, TANAGERS, ICTERIDS,
ETC. (Emberizidae)**
__ Tennessee Warbler
__ Orange-crowned Warbler*
__ Nashville Warbler*
__ Yellow Warbler*
__ Yellow-rumped Warbler*
__ Black-throated Gray Warbler*
__ Townsend's Warbler*
__ Hermit Warbler*
__ Palm Warbler
__ Black-and-white Warbler
__ American Redstart*
__ Ovenbird
__ Northern Waterthrush (probably
   nests)
__ MacGillivray's Warbler*
__ Common Yellowthroat*
__ Wilson's Warbler*
__ Yellow-breasted Chat*
__ Western Tanager*
__ Black-headed Grosbeak*
__ Lazuli Bunting*
__ Green-tailed Towhee*
__ Rufous-sided Towhee*
__ California Towhee*
__ American Tree Sparrow
__ Chipping Sparrow*
__ Brewer's Sparrow*
__ Vesper Sparrow*
__ Lark Sparrow*
__ Black-throated Sparrow*
__ Sage Sparrow*
__ Savannah Sparrow*
__ Grasshopper Sparrow*
__ Fox Sparrow*
__ Song Sparrow*
__ Lincoln's Sparrow*

__ Swamp Sparrow
__ White-throated Sparrow
__ Golden-crowned Sparrow
__ White-crowned Sparrow*
__ Harris' Sparrow
__ Dark-eyed Junco*
__ Lapland Longspur
__ Snow Bunting
__ Bobolink*
__ Red-winged Blackbird*
__ Tricolored Blackbird*
__ Western Meadowlark*
__ Yellow-headed Blackbird*
__ Brewer's Blackbird*
__ Brown-headed Cowbird*
__ Northern Oriole*
FINCHES (Fringillidae)
__ Rosy Finch*
__ Pine Grosbeak*
__ Purple Finch*
__ Cassin's Finch*
__ House Finch*
__ Red Crossbill*
__ White-winged Crossbill (may nest)
__ Common Redpoll
__ Pine Siskin*
__ Lesser Goldfinch*
__ American Goldfinch*
__ Evening Grosbeak*
WEAVERS (Passeridae)
__ House Sparrow* (I)

The following birds are considered accidental in Oregon; generally, there are fewer than twenty records for each species in the state. Those enclosed in brackets [ ] are considered sight records only — there is no physical evidence to support their occurrence. The others have all been verified by identifiable photographs, specimens, or audio or visual recordings.

[Black-vented Shearwater]
Mottled Petrel
Murphy's Petrel
[Wilson's Storm-Petrel]
Black Storm-Petrel
Magnificent Frigatebird
Tricolored Heron
Little Blue Heron
Fulvous Whistling-Duck
Baikal Teal
Garganey
Tufted Duck
King Eider
Broad-winged Hawk
Common Moorhen
[Piping Plover]
Mongolian Plover
Mountain Plover
Spotted Redshank
Bristle-thighed Curlew
Bar-tailed Godwit
Hudsonian Godwit
Little Stint
Rufous-necked Stint
Long-toed Stint
[White-rumped Sandpiper]
Curlew Sandpiper
Ruff
Laughing Gull
Little Gull
[Common Black-headed Gull]
Red-legged Kittiwake
Ross' Gull
Least Tern
Elegant Tern
Thick-billed Murre
Xantus' Murrelet
Parakeet Auklet
White-winged Dove
Yellow-billed Cuckoo
[Black-billed Cuckoo]
Northern Hawk Owl
Boreal Owl (probably regular)
Costa's Hummingbird
Red-headed Woodpecker
Yellow-bellied Sapsucker
Nuttall's Woodpecker
Scissor-tailed Flycatcher
Cassin's Kingbird
Tropical Kingbird
Northern Wheatear
Wood Thrush

Gray-cheeked Thrush
Brown Thrasher
Black-backed Wagtail
Phainopepla
[Bell's Vireo]
[Philadelphia Vireo]
Virginia's Warbler
Lucy's Warbler
Northern Parula
Yellow-throated Warbler
Black-throated Blue Warbler
Blackburnian Warbler
Chestnut-sided Warbler
Cape May Warbler
Magnolia Warbler
Black-throated Green Warbler
Bay-breasted Warbler
Blackpoll Warbler
[Prairie Warbler]
[Mourning Warbler]
[Connecticut Warbler]
[Kentucky Warbler]
Canada Warbler
Hooded Warbler
Scarlet Tanager
Summer Tanager
Rose-breasted Grosbeak
Blue Grosbeak
Indigo Bunting
Painted Bunting
Dickcissel
Clay-colored Sparrow
Black-chinned Sparrow
Lark Bunting
LeConte's Sparrow
Chestnut-collared Longspur
[McCown's Longspur]
McKay's Bunting
[Rustic Bunting]
Rusty Blackbird
Common Grackle
Great-tailed Grackle
Orchard Oriole
Hooded Oriole
Hoary Redpoll
Brambling

Appendix I:
Recommended Reading List

General Field Guides.
Ferrand, John. (Editor). 1983. *The Audubon Society Master Guide to Birding.* (Three volumes). Alfred A. Knopf, New York.

Grant, Peter J. 1982. *Gulls; A Guide to Identification.* Berkhamstead, England.

Harrison, Peter. 1983. *Seabirds; An Identification Guide.* Houghton Mifflin Co., Boston, MA.

Hayman, Peter, John Merchant, Tony Prater. 1986. *Shorebirds; An Identification Guide.* Houghton Mifflin Co., Boston, MA.

Madge, Steve, Hilary Burn. 1988. *Waterfowl: An Identification Guide to the Ducks, Geese, and Swans of the World.* Houghton Mifflin Co., Boston, MA.

National Geographic Society. 1987. *Field Guide to the Birds of North America.* National Geographic Society, Washington, D.C.

Peterson, Roger Tory. 1961. *A Field Guide to Western Birds.* Houghton Mifflin Co., Boston, MA.

Robbins, Chandler S., Bertel Bruun, Herbers S. Zim. 1983. *A Guide to Field Identification: Birds of North America.* Golden Press, New York.

Birds in Oregon and Nearby Regions.
Gabrielson, Ira N., Stanley Jewett. 1970. *Birds of the Pacific Northwest.* Dover Publications, Inc., New York.

Nehls, Harry B. 1989. *Familiar Birds of the Northwest.* Audubon Society of Portland, Portland, OR.

Pettingill, Olin S. 1981. *A Guide to Bird Finding West of the Mississippi.* Oxford Univ. Press, New York.

Ramsey, Fred L. 1978. *Birding Oregon.* Audubon Society of Corvallis, Corvallis, OR.

Roberson, Don. 1980. *Rare Birds of the West Coast.* Woodcock Publications, Pacific Grove, CA.

General Guides to Oregon's Natural Areas.

Ferguson, Denzel and Nancy. 1978. *Oregon's Great Basin Country.* Maverick Publications, Bend, OR.

Mainwaring, William L. 1979. *Exploring Oregon's Central and Southern Cascades.* Westridge Press, Ltd., Salem, OR.

Perry, John, Jane Greverus Perry. 1983. *The Sierra Club Guide to the Natural Areas of Oregon and Washington,* Sierra Club Books, San Francisco, CA.

Spring, Bob and Ira. 1981. *Oregon Wildlife Areas.* Superior Publishing Co., Seattle, WA.

Periodicals and Journals.

American Birds, published by National Audubon Society. 950 Third Avenue, New York, NY. 10022.

Birding, published by American Birding Association. Box 4335, Austin, TX. 78765.

Oregon Birds, published by Oregon Field Ornithologists. P.O. Box 10373, Eugene, OR. 97405.

Western Birds, published by Western Field Ornithologists. P.O. Box 595, Coronado, CA. 92118.

Appendix II: Oregon Birdwatching Organizations

The following list of organizations is current up to the summer of 1989. It is advisable to write or phone ahead of time when visiting a part of Oregon served by one of these organizations. Local members can often fill in the visitor on the latest birding news, good birding sites, or further contacts for other areas.

Oregon Field Ornithologists (O.F.O.)
P.O. Box 10373
Eugene, OR. 97440
publication: *Oregon Birds*

O.F.O. is the only state-wide birding organization in Oregon. They sponser an annual convention somewhere in the state, featuring workshops, guest speakers, field trips, and other events. O.F.O. also financially supports and maintains the Oregon Bird Records Committee, a nine-member panel responsible for determining the official state list and keeping records of unusual or rare bird occurrences in the state. Their publication, *Oregon Birds*, features articles on bird identification, status of birds in Oregon, local site guides, quarterly field notes, and other items of interest.

Cape Arago Audubon Society.
P.O. Box 381
North Bend, OR. 97459
newsletter: *The Tattler.*

Central Oregon Audubon Society.
P.O. Box 565
Bend, OR. 97709
newsletter: *The Eagle Eye.*

Audubon Society of Corvallis.
P.O. Box 148
Corvallis, OR. 97330
newsletter: *The Chat.*

Grande Ronde Bird Club.
P.O. Box 29
La Grande, OR. 97850
newsletter: *The Rav-on.*

Grant County Bird Club.

P.O. Box 111
Canyon City, OR. 97820
newsletter: *The Upland Sandpiper.*

Klamath Basin Audubon Society.

P.O. Box 354
Klamath Falls, OR. 97601
newsletter: *The Grebe.*

Lane County Audubon Society.

P.O. Box 5086
Eugene, OR. 97405
newsletter: *The Quail.*

Portland Audubon Society.

5151 N.W. Cornell Rd.
Portland, OR. 97210
phone: (503) 292-6855 (Audubon House)
        (503) 292-0661 (Rare Bird Alert recording)
newsletter: *The Warbler.*

Rogue Valley Audubon Society.

189 Meyer Creek Rd.
Ashland, OR. 97520
newsletter: *The Chat.*

Salem Audubon Society.

mailing address: P.O. Box 2013, Salem, OR. 97308.
Salem Audubon Center: 1313 Mill St. S.E., Salem, OR. 97301.
phone: (503) 585-5689
newsletter: *The Oregon Grape Leaf.*

Siskiyou Audubon Society.

P.O. Box 1047
Grants Pass, OR. 97526
newsletter: *The Siskin.*

Umpqua Valley Audubon Society.

P.O. Box 381
Roseburg, OR. 97470
newsletter: *Wing Tips.*

Yaquina Birders and Naturalists.

P.O. Box 1467
Newport, OR. 97365
newsletter: *The Sandpiper.*